The Decline and Fall of the American Empire

Corruption, Decadence, and the American Dream

The Decline and Fall of the American Empire

Corruption, Decadence, and the American Dream

TONY BOUZA

PLENUM PRESS • NEW YORK AND LONDON

Library of Congress Cataloging-in-Publication Data

Bouza, Anthony V.
    The decline and fall of the American empire : corruption,
decadence, and the American dream / Tony Bouza.
        p.   cm.
    Includes bibliographical references (p.   ) and index.
    ISBN 0-306-45407-6
    1. United States--Moral conditions.   2. United States--Social
conditions--1980-   3. United States--Politics and government--1989-
I. Title.
HN90.M6B68   1996
306'.0973--dc20
                                                          96-18615
                                                              CIP

ISBN 0-306-45407-6

© 1996 Tony Bouza
Plenum Press is a Division of Plenum Publishing Corporation
233 Spring Street, New York, N.Y. 10013-1578

10 9 8 7 6 5 4 3 2 1

Printed in the United States of America

For
Dominick, Cynthia, and Tony

Acknowledgments

Acknowledgments always struck me as inane rituals. Didn't, after all, the author write the thing?

Alas, wisened on the hard anvil of experience, I now know better. A book is the flawed effort of one, polished and helped—as much as possible—by many.

My first and foremost debt is to Linda Greenspan Regan—editor, mentor, scold, teacher, and originator of too many ideas to enumerate, including the one for the book and its title. Linda very simply drove me to produce the best work within me, and wouldn't let up until I did it and redid it. Thank you.

Two mentors and consciences who died in recent months, Mae Churchill and Ping Ferry, insisted on serving the cause of simple justice and never failed to demand these concerns from me. I will miss them, and an unknowing world will miss them more.

Others, like George Kateb, Larry Sherman, Pat Murphy, Anne Beller, Gisela Konopka, Constance Caplan—and more—helped me make whatever discoveries they could lead me to.

My wife of 39 years, Erica, has been—in this and everything else—stalwart and friend. Tony and Dominick are now old enough to offer insights and counsel. Our discussions are frequently distilled on these pages.

I know too well that, despite all these efforts, flaws remain—and they are mine.

Contents

The Decline and Fall of the American Empire

Corruption, Decadence, and the American Dream

Introduction

"It tolls for thee."

Thus did John Donne answer the smug skeptic who asked the identity of the corpse. The poet understood the linkages we strive so hard to forget.

Exotic and distant crimes of unknowably powerful and celebrated masters of the universe translate into wins and losses for lowly observers who cluck disapprovingly. The sufferers are blind to their connection to these rarefied transgressions.

It has always been hard to see how the wrongdoings of the mighty lead, as ripples in the water, to swamping the distant and the unsuspecting.

It is equally difficult to observe how the unimaginable depredations of the untouchably lofty influence the actions of the lowly. We will see how actions at the top of the economic, social, political, educational, and even political arenas are mirrored by those committing pettier crimes.

A society is an organism—with a birth, adolescence, maturity, and decline. This analogy, however, is unsatisfying if one considers timing and inevitability. Unlike the individual, a society of citizens—a nation—can prolong or truncate the joys and agonies of its existence through choices. Such choices are expressed as values and are exhibited in the laws, customs, and behaviors adopted to achieve the goals and ideals of the society.

Thoughts of national destiny, the preservation of community or family, and even love of God reflect a commitment to valuing something larger than ourselves. On the other hand, concern for personal gratification and individual aggrandizement leads to hedonism, materialism, and consumerism—and the exaltation of the self over communal values.[1-3] In such cases, the commitment to altruism is threatened by the need to gratify the search for pleasure. This struggle between community and the individual can be described as a battle between the concept of "us" versus "me."

The shaping of a value system is a subtle and dynamic process that defies easy measure. A society declines and regenerates at the same time. The questions are: Which is happening faster, and at what rate of speed? And how can we tell?

There are many ways.

ART

Artists are the antennae of the race, as a disgraced poet once said. They serve to tell us where we are, where we came from, and the direction in which we seem to be heading. They are prophets. Some are wise and accurate, and others are superficial and mistaken. Across the expanse of time we discern the mountains of insight amidst the valleys of hubris and error.

Simply looking at twentieth-century America—rightly called The American Century—is instructive.

The innocence, energy, and optimism of pre-World War I America fetchingly illustrates the vigor with which the nation would embrace the promise of technology and the wealth of a rich land peopled with a polyglot mix of determined newcomers.

After World War I came the horrors of The Great Depression, yet Hollywood—*our* artists—spoke of a belief in the nation's destiny and its dreams. *The Grapes of Wrath* etched the grimness of poverty and dislocation, but this vision was laced with an unshakable faith in social justice. *Mister Smith Goes to Washington* extolled the triumph of decency over the blandishments of cynicism and power. And the ubiquitous *It's A Wonderful Life* celebrated family, community, human decency, the future, and God.

Despite the overwhelming poverty and unemployment of the 1930s—and, incidentally, relatively little crime—there was a sense of a shared fate and a belief in what was to come. Even the thirteen years of Prohibition failed to quench our confidence in our ability to legislate virtue and preordain the future.

As we reach the end of The American Century we need to ask whether there is that same ebullient faith in the future, whether we are as willing to sacrifice—ourselves or our pleasures—for the greater good of country or family, and whether we can rely on our leaders and institutions to pursue the common weal, resisting the lures of those promising celebrity, power, immediate gains, or other temptations.

If we can see the decline of families and cities and remain smugly confident of our inviolability, if we can witness the corruption of high figures and be blind to their connection to our prospects, if we can watch the loss of faith and remain secure in our confidence of salvation, and if we can sense the general moral decline yet think we will survive, then we can assert that we remain happy, dancing, singing, drinking passengers on the Titanic.[4]

CHEATING

A Chicago high school's students score miraculously high on a national test in 1994 and receive widespread adulation. When a conscience-stricken student confesses to having cheated, she is reviled as a turncoat. The others hang tough, but decline a verification test, labeling it an insult.

The offending coach quits. The whistle-blower asserts that the coach had persuaded them to go along because "Everybody cheats: it's how the world works: you'd be fools not to."[5]

Could the coach have taken his lesson from the reports of bankers, accountants, lawyers, famous executives, or enormously paid athletes or entertainers getting theirs?

And what vision conjures up a healthier picture of America than the 4H farm youngster saving for college through the winnings of lovingly attended livestock?

Only it turns out that about 30% of exhibitors used Clenbuterol, a steroidlike drug that has proven fatal to people in Europe who'd eaten the tainted meat.

A series of disclosures of cheating—with rescinded ribbons and withdrawn cash prizes—finally led organizers of the competition, in late 1995, to acknowledge the existence of a widespread problem that was getting worse. The echo resonated ominously through a heartland that was still believed to be rooted in American virtue.[6,7]

YOU MAY ALREADY BE A WINNER

It was a telling commentary on shifting morals that the recipient of one of those junk mail "nonnegotiable" checks, this one for $95,093.35, deposited the check in a bank machine. He then withdrew it in the form of a cashier's check and resisted giving it back. He justified it all on the basis that banks kick you when you're down with their charges.

No one seemed to think that this attempt at theft was anything but a commendable whack at Goliath by a latter-day David.

In the end, after being sued by the bank, he agreed to return the untouched cashier's check.

The sweepstakes operators had shrieked hysterically to "finalists" that they had a real chance of winning, when the truth was that the odds against them were unimaginably high. There would be tens of millions in the "final drawing"—a perversion of the usual expectation that, if you made it that far, you had a real chance. And all in the name of selling magazine subscriptions. Talented writers fashioned tortured versions of the truth that only served to spread more cynicism.

Is the lesson learned from the studied silence of sports figures, whose task of winning easily outdistances any need to correct an official's mistaken call? Or from the betrayals of priests and ministers or the carefully prepared denials of the mighty caught in crimes? Ours has become a nation of boldfaced liars and skillful evaders of responsibility,[8] and we have created industries to put the proper spin on these mendacities.

A nation lay mesmerized by the spectacle of one of the trials of the century—yet the question seemed to be whether celebrity, power, and wealth would enable an accused to get away with murder.

Yes, the O.J. Simpson murder trial has become the leitmotif of the age. An icon from our national religion—sports—brought low. Race, sex, and beauty. Gore. And all on television.

America sat riveted for many months. It was a circus to match anything in Rome's ancient Colosseum. And it capped a daily fare of daytime talk show explorations of incest, sodomy, sexual fantasies, and grotesque depredations and sick relationships on television, which wouldn't have been allowed to exhibit such salacious titillations on what was laughingly called "family-viewing" evening prime time. Othello! Live!

The denouement proved a shock to a white America that thought it had worked out a lot of its racial problems. The verdict seemed more an indictment of racism than an exoneration of O.J.

That the decadent voyeurisms of daytime television can sometimes lead to murder—as in the case of the tormented male lured on stage to meet "a secret admirer"—was conveniently forgotten. This guest on *Jenny Jones* delighted in spying on a female neighbor he'd lusted after, only to be shocked to find that it was a gay man who'd lusted after him from behind the icon. After three days of fuming and tortured musings, the humiliated participant went to the gay admirer's home and shot him dead. The contretemps was self-righteously examined by television hosts who were "shocked, shocked, to discover such awful goings on."

This is life imitating the artistry of Claude Rains in *Casablanca*, pocketing his payoff as he professes outrage that there is actual gambling going on in Rick's cafe.[9]

Radio talk shows reflected, in the angry barks of mad-as-hell callers and the exploitative and mirroring angst of the hosts, the disaffection of a disillusioned public. There was, on the air, a national search for the villain delivering the national malaise. Heaven help the target of this disquiet.

Since the media was both the reflector and transmitter of all these visions, the popular reaction—endorsed and vigorously reinforced by those in public life or who enjoyed a measure of celebrity—was to shoot the messenger. Thus did the media gradually evolve into becoming the monster from which the evils of decadence, violence, and rampant sexuality emerged.[10–12]

It wasn't the content of rap lyrics that was discussed, but the rapacious greed of the companies purveying the ugly message and the evil nature of the rappers. The source of the anger or the meaning of the words were conveniently shelved.[13]

Certainly there were grotesqueries on our screens and airwaves, but which came first, the image or the demand for it? Were we ignoring the substance behind the images? Couldn't it have been said that, in a society with bountiful choices, the O.J. circus would have been ignored or tuned out if there was no market for it?

Yes, the incredibly inventive and artistic 30-second television commercials were creating appetites and urges that had us focusing determinedly on feeling good—and, yes, the images on our screens were prurient, virulent, and sometimes monstrous—but weren't we the best-informed of all peoples, ever? And didn't we have the greatest panoply of choices? And wasn't the media a fiercely competitive industry—across the board—where those who failed to meet the public's demand perished? And wasn't it natural that a frightened and disoriented people—speaking vaguely of "declining values" and other moral afflictions—should search about for a scapegoat on which to wreak vengeance?

It seemed very clear that the last place for the morally ill to look would be within—the first injunction of the Greeks. It seemed equally clear that the media was transmitting profoundly troubling images, but had they created them, simply filmed and reported what they saw, or rushed to meet a perceived—if, perhaps, unarticulated—demand?

BUSINESS

An increasingly complex world engages in activities that challenge the imaginations of the highly educated while sending the less-prepared into stunned silence and helpless inner writhings that lack voice.

Multinational corporations, the global economy, the arcana of politics, and the symbiosis and interchangeability of the movers who shape the rules of unfathomable transactions function in the rarified atmospheres of boardrooms, leathery club warrens, intimidating official chambers, and dauntingly elegant restaurants and hotels.

The grubby realities of ghetto life never intrude into the lives, or consciousness, of our masters.

What have these rulers to do with the rest of America?

How can international deals, involving unimaginable sums and earth-shattering proposals, affect the lives of the humble millions scampering below?

How can the actions of these shadowy figures influence the behavior of millions?

How can the very fate of the nation—and my home—be impacted by such distant events?

It has always been the conceit of the ignorant to exult in the inviolability of distance and the false comfort of indirectness. The easy answers have been to move to the suburbs and escape the city: in the city, to move from the west to the east side; to heave a sigh of relief that we don't own stock in that company or live in that speculating county. "It can't happen either here or to me" becomes the protective shell. Is there anyone left who believes that the fate of the nation is inextricably intertwined with Detroit's?

We can all see how the crooked plumber, electrician, dentist, car repairer, salesperson, or other provider of needed, felt, quotidian, visible services touches us. We bridle in indignation and rail at the injustice.[14] But how can the actions of Savings and Loan (S & L) moguls, international bankers, Japanese auto manufacturers, traders in Cuban sugar, inventors of clever fiscal strategies, corporate heads, philanthropic leaders, revered clerics, respected lawyers and accountants, famous politicos, wonderfully skilled doctors, university leaders, and other denizens of the hallowed halls of the powerful touch me? Where is the relevance? How can there be any connection?

It is the absence of a clearly visible and direct link that enables the unscrupulous among these rulers to pick our pockets, even as we hurl imprecations at the artisan struggling with our more immediate concerns.

It may take only a penny from each of us to create a pot of gold for one of us, but that is precisely what is at stake when a lobbyist corrupts a politician to enrich a corporation at the general expense. Nothing is more amorphous—or, seemingly, less painful—that identifying the pennies. The recipient is there—in the plenitude of identity and gratitude—and the people making up the gift are an invisible, and unfelt, presence. And there is the comforting knowledge that no one ever storms into the office, pounding the desk and demanding that the people's interests be served. Nothing is ever easier for those in power to sacrifice than the people's interests.

A look at Latin America, or Africa, will quickly reveal that a nation's wealth can easily by siphoned into the pockets of the few while the masses hunger, amidst sometimes unimaginable wealth. It isn't the existence of resources that matters nearly as much as how they're managed. The genius of Scandinavia, much of the rest of Europe, North America, and Japan—and others—has lain in how sedulously the cleverness of capitalism was pursued and how intelligently and, yes, equitably its produced wealth was managed and distributed. We often forget that the agency employed to level these playing fields is a government that works for the benefit of the people.

Mismanagement, criminality, or loss of way have repeatedly led to the destruction of many—sometimes even taking the exploiters down with them. This, however, doesn't occur often enough to allow us the comfort of such sights, or the suspicion that their nimble spirits would be deterred by such possibilities.

Our intricate and interlocking lives are predicated on arrangements that are based on truth. This confidence in the integrity of others relies on our faith in the honesty of the individual and in the creation of controls to verify and ensure that faith.

The issue centers on the "tipping factor"—that is, at what point does the number of predators seem such as to panic the rest of us into getting ours while we can? A society may look very calm and orderly from without, but history has seen monoliths crumble because of the unseen rot within.

A perfect example of this rot is the vast, vibrant, but hardly visible underground economy that functions in cash transactions and that robs our treasury of many billions of dollars a year.

In examining the white collar crimes of corporate America, we are not looking at distant and irrelevant acts of wrongdoing, but at our own fate. American taxpayers discovered that it was they who guaranteed the fiscal integrity of failed (that seems altogether too tepid a word for the colossal bill laid at our doorsteps) S & Ls.[15,16]

The challenge to our understanding and any hope for reform will center on how the headlines trumpeting the fall of cabinet officers is seen as impinging on our lives and futures. Our failure to make the connections enables the process to widen and accelerate.

Of course, some defalcations influence us not at all—yet can any comfort be derived from the victimization of others? If we don't protect them, who will protect us? And protections can occur in unknowable ways. Our lives are predicated on trust— that the water we drink won't sicken us and that the food we ingest has been carefully prepared. We entrust ourselves, body and treasure, to custodians whose behavior has been assured by the ethics of the professions and the monitorings and licensings society has imposed.

In the final analysis every fraud imposes both obvious and hidden costs as well as direct and observable results and subtle and invisible penalties.

America is the product of over two hundred years of stable,

reasonably honest, and efficient government that mostly sacrificed personal gain for the public good. Despite robber barons and piratical corporate lootings and despoliations, reformers did come along to impose constraints. The end result has been a product of countless—and largely invisible—negative and positive actions, with the outcome decided by the preponderance of either.

The recent history of the behaviors of corporate America reveals—as we shall see—a tipping toward the unscrupulous enrichments that bid fair to accelerate the flight toward the economic nihilism that characterizes disintegrating societies. When a few get theirs by breaking the rules, the many storm the cashier and fill their pockets.

The blurring of boundaries—legal, moral, and ethical—has created a climate in which only winning matters.

POLITICS

The rulers—rulemakers—of our nation are those voted into office. Nowhere in our national life is winning more crucial. Defeat means extinction—public death. Victory means remaining on center stage, free to indulge professions of altruism, even as the practical realities impose the need for unfortunate compromises. Victory brings wealth, power, celebrity, and sexual gratification—and, sometimes, hubris and humiliation, too.

Yet to win today, the candidate needs to package the product he wants to present. The seeker of office must be marketed, and the one vehicle that can convert a sow's ear into a silk purse is television. And that means money—lots of it.

It seems likely that the American people have not yet cottoned to the central importance of television in political races. It works. The 1994 campaign served as the most recent, and dramatic, example of its power, yet, curiously, this example appears to be a negative one, at least for now.[17] Campaign after campaign—for Congress or state elections—illustrated the gains that could be made through often vicious, and not always accurate, attacks on the enemy. The residue would be the benefit accruing to "the other." It was not so much a game of taking the high road as it was of showing—in graphic detail—the low road taken by opponents. In a milieu where it was impossible personally to define yourself to the voters, it became clear that the opposition could define you negatively—or make the often unseen sponsor of the commercial the less offensive alternative.

Some campaigns were notable for the silence of the candidate on the issues—the avoidance of debate or specific discussion of questions—relying, instead, on the accumulation of funds for a last-minute blitzkrieg of televised messages. Thus did the genius of our 30-second television commercial get enlisted into the packaging of political victories. The devilish cleverness of it all lay more in the unpackaging of the opposition than in packaging the candidate.

In such a game of hammering impressions, the key weapon becomes the money with which to buy the needed air time and to hire the spin doctors. Where are such gargantuan sums to come from?

Despite tepid and tentative efforts at reforms, through the public financing of campaigns, incumbents have made certain that the bulk of the money needed would have to be raised from beholden contributors looking for favors. And favors are not to be sought from outsiders. Thus public office is gained, and perpetuated, from the extension of favors to the candidate in the form of perfectly legal funds that create the indissoluble bond sustaining future encounters.

In this law-abiding scenario, what chance does the public weal stand against the requests of heavy donors? And are any of these politicians ready to exalt the public good over the narrow needs of their patrons—whether these be management or labor?

These dolorous facts apply to the most honorable of the men and women presuming to rule our lives. And they enter the process in the overwhelming majority, determined to do good, and get transformed by the process into doing well instead.

What becomes, then, of the idealists who enter the lists determined to save the nation, or at least to do some useful service?

We will see how storied pillars of national life loaned their reputations to criminal enterprises and how sharp traders were able to call senators off the floor of Congress to scold them into behaving more acceptably. We will see how the American public gradually—through the Chinese water torture drippings of continuing scandals—came to lose faith in the government and began to withdraw into sullen, suicidal, hostility. What better example of imperial decay than the account of a general who was flown from Italy to Colorado with only one aide and his cat as company, in September 1994, at a taxpayer cost of $116,000?[18]

Recent American elections, in which as few as one-fourth of eligible voters decided the identity of presidents, confirm the profound skepticism of a disaffected people.[19]

The secrets and lies of the government during the Vietnam War; the tawdry crimes and unworthy acts of Watergate—and the subsequent and mostly successful public relations efforts at rehabilitating a ruined presidency; the wrongdoings of office holders and the sheer paucity of honor in our high offices; the prevalence of lies and absence of shame and admitted error—all contribute to the panicky flight to "get yours while you can," as well as to the cold indifference with which voters now greet campaigns.[20]

As we examine the actions of our political figures at all levels, the cynicism of the electorate is confirmed. Our process of self-selection for public office (usually involving the expenditure of large amounts of personal wealth) and suspicious subsidizings virtually ensure the steady march of the reckless and feckless to the seats of the mighty. The cost of campaigns reduces the field of candidates to the economic elite seeking new thrills and/or celebrity.

Folksy television ads—featuring Everyman and Every-woman—managed to convince the American people that universal healthcare (a benefit extended to all in every other industrialized society) was bad for them.

While this was going on before our eyes, lobbyists plied the halls to influence votes and speeches, and advertisers monitored the content of publications eager for the ad revenue that would be withdrawn if articles gave offense to corporate interests.

And when academics and professionals can be tempted into writing or including erudite articles that appear to be intended to influence an outcome of litigation—as occurred in pieces distorting the record of breast implants in a respected journal—what real chance does the poor, bombarded shnook really have?[21]

Can we any longer tell whether the words spoken by a presidential aspirant constitute his carefully considered views or are simply the cunning creations of skilled flacks with secret, and profitable, agendas? Or might they simply reflect the regurgitated findings of the latest poll?[22]

Even at its cleanest, the current political system is geared for the profit of the specific at the expense of the general. The lobbyists plying Congress' corridors are, after all, doing something that is—currently—perfectly legal. At its dirtiest it becomes a criminal betrayal that, sooner or later, affects every last one of us.

Good causes tend to be peopled with folks brought to the arena because of some personal tragedy. Gun control groups often have victims of violence on their boards or pursuing the organization's aims. Gamblers and Alcoholics Anonymous members understand the horrors of addictions and can be found in the trenches, battling them. Battered women's groups are strengthened by the presence of so many sufferers in their ranks. Hosts of noble enterprises would be weakened by the absence of those brought to the issue because of their sufferings. But the challenge is to be foresighted enough to attack the problem before it has reached your doorstep.

How to measure prevented events?

A hard question. Involvement in prevention implies having faith in good works and faith that their ripple effects may benefit us or those we love, or even society at large.

Without denigrating the real contributions of victims—to the eradication of the factors that brought the victimizations about—true vision requires participation before victimization. The analogy that fits is the German's comment: "The Nazis came for the gypsies and I said nothing. They came for the Jews and I remained silent. They came for me and there was no one to raise an objection." The need is to understand how the private favor in Washington becomes the public deficit in Peoria. The taxpayer, ultimately, foots the bill.

Since the rules regulating our economy are mainly made by politicians, the symbiosis existing between the office seeker's need for funds and the corporation's need for favors creates a climate in which the amorphous interests of the people become easy sacrifices. The lobbyist is there to bridge the gap between the client and the lawmaker.[23]

What made the S & L crisis understandable to the masses was the need to repay every depositor, up to $100,000, with taxpayer funds. The liability was measurable, direct, and easily grasped. That is a rarity. Most of the costs of most of the transactions are hidden, indirect, or subtle.

In the pages ahead we will examine a few of the political actions that contribute to the "malaise" that has so many of us feeling—in a time of peace and relative prosperity—that we're somehow being flushed down the toilet.

ORGANIZED CRIME

While corporate America attempts legitimate commerce—albeit sometimes taking illegal turns, with politicos at the wheel—organized crime[24] exists mainly to satisfy our cravings for sinful, illicit services.

In providing these services they impose a hidden tax, on all of us, that may increase the cost of a fish we're having for dinner, or the price of a ticket to an event, or the amount it takes to build a house or buy a car. Or it may result in unemployment, as jobs are handed to criminal associates.

As a permanent, continuing, organized, profit-making satisfier of illegal appetites, organized crime impacts our lives and our economy with enormous force. Again, as with corporate or political acts, the activities of organized crime may appear exotic and distant, at least until we learn of specific acts closer to home.

Many years ago, a racketeer was alleged to have boasted, "We're bigger than U.S. Steel." Of that there seems little doubt, but organized crime's costs far exceed the relatively paltry takings of street criminals, on whose depredations the nation's energies seem so tightly focused. Of course, it is the violence of the mugger that we fear, but violence—discreetly aimed and rationally employed—is organized crime's ultimate tool. Visiting misery and destruction on their targets constitute the policies of the clan. When you borrow from a loan shark your collateral is your body.

Street crime—in the forms of rising and enormously high levels of violence and concomitant monetary losses—is rightly the cause of deep concern. It may not be too much to say that this domestic crisis is America's greatest problem—internally or externally.[25]

But the less visible crisis being created by the widening expanse of white collar and organized crime, and the contributions being made by politicians to this decay, threaten us individually and collectively.

The bitter exchanges between Teamster leader James R. Hoffa and Senate Counsel Robert F. Kennedy in the 1950s very likely led to the future attorney general's appreciating the full scope of organized crime's danger to the nation. On ascending to the cabinet in 1961, Kennedy's enduring legacy was to launch an all-out, decades-long assault on organized crime, despite the resistance of the reluctant dragon at the helm, J. Edgar Hoover. It had been Hoover's position that organized crime didn't exist. The obvious reason behind his reluctance was his fear that the lure of narcotics and the activities of organized crime would prove corrupting to an agency he needed for his private agendas.

The results of this attack on the Mafia by the FBI, more than three decades after it was launched, are nothing short of astonishing. The penetration of the tightest-lipped organization has been repeated over and over. Formerly clam-shut mouths spewed betrayals once believed unthinkable. Manicured hands unaccustomedly clutched iron bars. By 1996, the FBI's performance might well be labeled law enforcement's crowning achievement of the twentieth century.

Yet the spoils are such and the temptations so great—and the organization's roots so deeply embedded in America's fabric—that the skimmings continue, the murders pile up, the extortions move on, gambling flourishes, the drugs flow, and each of us

continues to bear the burden of cost occasioned by the tax organized crime indirectly levies.

With the successful turnings and prosecutions, we now know
a great deal more about the less visible and less dramatic, but
infinitely broader, aspects of white collar crime and organized
crime, and their cozy relationships with the world of politics.

In this world sex, gambling, alcohol, drugs, and even, sometimes, tobacco (in terms of smuggling to circumvent taxes and in
the mendacities of internal corporate policies) become the most
frequently purveyed products. The undying allure of sin has
served as the handiest tool for the shearing of human sheep.

Guns, threats, muscle, and extortion become the vehicles of
enforcement—as well as lobbying, bribes, campaign contributions, jobs, and other favors.

The constant is profit, the variable the method employed—
with none of the inhibitions normally associated with civilized
society.

Sophistication—in terms of the education, skill, tactics, or
devices used in these criminal enterprises—stands in sharp contrast to the bloody and coarse characteristics of street crime. This
subtlety and lack of photographable obviousness lends a certain
aesthetic appeal, which deadens our outrage. It's a lot easier to
revile the rapist on the evening news.

RELIGION

Every good thing can be—and frequently has been—twisted
to some evil use. Religion can be transformed into a huckster's
fleecing of the gullible. The search for meaning can lead to mes-
merizing exploitations by cults. The conceit of having to believe in
something besides the temporal can—and has—led to death and
the destruction of families.[26]

In an age that delivers little evidence of either goodness or
promise, the pathetic longing for meaning frequently drives good-
hearted searchers into webs of darkness.

We will see how the human quest for life's significance can be redirected, by cunning mortals, into grotesque exploitations. At the end of the road is usually found sex, money, or—in its many forms and guises—power for the often charismatic manipulator of these instincts.

And, as we come, more and more and faster and faster, to resemble past decaying societies, our search for transient pleasure will lead to the creation of new icons and other symbols of our need to reconcile our lives with the search for some sort of cosmic significance.

Worship, however, doesn't have to be of specifically religious objects; it can be invested in celebrity or in other objects of adoration. Decadent societies tend to idolize those who bring it pleasure.

ENTERTAINMENT

America, as it nears the twenty-first century, could be described as a nation using its wealth for diversion. In its search for pleasure, the nation's idols became those who entertain us— movie stars, rock singers, athletes,[27–29] and stand-up comics. These are our celebrities. These are the rich and powerful. These are the examples we seek to emulate.

Not the keepers and transmitters of lore and values—our teachers and ministers—but those whose only task is to amuse or distract us.

Our materialism, hedonism, and consumerism lead us to elevate the world of entertainment to a national religion—and they lead, as well, to instructive lessons as we look into the mirror of pleasure and see our faces.

A discussion of our state, as the century ends, would not be complete without an examination of the society and its behaviors. A healthy society is altruistic; a sick one, hedonistic. The Ten Commandments established the essentials of what every human society considers to be moral, yet its receivers soon lapsed into the temptations of the golden calf. The push and pull between good and evil are always there and are present in the most moral and the most decadent societies. The question centers—again—on the tipping factor. Which is dominant? What is occurring faster, rot or renewal?

There is no barometer attesting to the health of a nation. There are no statistical tables to measure the spirit of altruism. The facts and figures can be helpful, but they are pieces of a mosaic whose image is rendered coherent by the combined mass of facts, anecdotes, impressions, analyses, and the distillations of artists who, unlike scientists absorbing data, become prophets through the absorption of these impressions, which lead to insights and which they communicate to us in the visions stamped on movies, plays, novels, essays, poems, and, yes, even rap lyrics.

Analyzing the subtler varieties of crime enables us to see the impact of mendacities, the influence of public relations types and spin doctors, the impact of the absence of shame or the saving grace of confession, the consequences of materialism and the temptations of the metaphysical, and the myriad other traps that lead a people astray.

The task is to make the reality of the threat vivid enough to lend the reader an appreciation of the danger he and his nation face. The problems ahead are daunting, but America retains the energy and skill to meet them, if it recognizes the peril and retains the will to combat it.

1

White Collar Crime

Some rob you with a six gun, and some with a fountain pen.
WOODY GUTHRIE

Just defining white collar crime can be slippery. Its clever, manifold activities drift into areas that border on political corruption or organized crime or, sometimes, even take on characteristics of street crime, such as when embezzlers feel themselves forced to kill to conceal their thievery. But it is one of the elegant hallmarks of white collar crime that its practitioners eschew dirtying their hands or engaging in much direct personal contact.

Some reasonably confident assertions can be made about white collar crime. It is criminal behavior undertaken for gain by individuals or corporations employing indirect techniques that require skills and education and that frequently involve complex financial transactions. White collar crime is the province of men and women in shirts, ties, suits, or tailored business attire. The image must inspire trust if that trust is to be violated successfully.

If the judge recognizes the defendant—either personally or as a familiar type from his own circle—and if the prosecutor is inspired to think of the unspoken prayer, "There, but for the grace of God, go I," it's a good guess that the prisoner in the dock is a white collar criminal.[1]

This sense of identification is not a trivial matter. Empathy implies both understanding and sympathy, which are important psychic forces in determining contested outcomes. The ability of the principals to identify with the defendant may easily segue into lenient treatment.

White collar criminals often command impressive resources—wealth, power, celebrity, status—which can be marshalled toward the desired result—exculpation. In a very real sense white collar criminals are part of the class/race warfare increasingly raging between the rich and the poor, white and black, suburban and inner-city.

An impoverished, functionally illiterate, addicted, unemployable ghetto kid who gets "summary justice" cannot help but resent the drawn-out battles and appeals the rich white defendant is able to mount. He is bombarded with media reports of the struggles of the mighty, while conscious of his own insignificance.

Our response to white collar crime could become a final validation of our commitment to a justice that is, at least theoretically, blind to race, class, or condition. Thus, if we were willing to treat white collar criminals as we do street criminals, the Constitution could be validated. This doesn't necessarily work out to identical outcomes—the banker, lawyer, accountant, or corporate executive can be punished through fines that may have a more salutary social effect than long-term jailings, in terms of restitution, for example, and they can be humiliated publicly, through the loss of a status that the more anonymous and humble street criminal never possessed.[2] But it is central to the validation that the penalties be defensibly proportionate and socially useful. Restitution to victims can go a long way toward mitigating the crime's impact.

Every study of white collar crime shows hugely greater monetary losses than in crime caused by street criminals. It is pretty futile to try to put dollar figures on what has to be a gross estimate, but there can be no doubt that violators of trust annually pocket many times the paltry billions realized by the muggers, burglars, robbers, thieves, and carjackers who have so terrified our nation.

The S & L scandal alone robbed the American people of hundreds of billions, without a shot being fired.[3]

It is, of course, the physical violence accompanying street crime, and its distinct personal nature, that triggers the public's fear and rage. In terms of total human suffering occasioned by the different crimes, it can be confidently asserted that the economic holocaust generated by bankers, lawyers, doctors, and other trusted, educated types far exceeds the damage done by our admittedly large and swelling tide of street criminality. But it is easier to hate and fear the black, the poor, the ghetto dwellers, and the sullen.

Looking at the S & L scandal of the 1980s offers an understanding of the universal—yet largely indirect—devastation created by untrammeled greed and unbridled arrogance.

The removal of controls, wrought by talented operatives lurking in power's lobbies and corridors and intended to favor one interest group at the expense of what used to be called the commonweal, served as the launching vehicle for the scandal. We will see how intensive lobbying led to the loosening of legal restrictions and controls that sent the S & L institutions spinning out of control, with a cost to every taxpayer that will last for decades.

The 1980s, a period of rapidly shifting economic fortunes—when the poor got trickled on and the old, white, rich, and suburbanites got to do a lot of the trickling—greatly accelerated the numbers and deepened the plight of the poor.

President Ronald Reagan arranged for a tax break for the wealthy and coupled it with increased Social Security taxes, not payments, for the workers. Whites fled to the suburbs with their new-found wealth. Cities decayed. The excluded were abandoned to the ghetto. The chasm widened. By 1995 President Clinton could unashamedly refer to an "underclass" three times in his State of the Union address. These utterances would have been unthinkably provocative only a few years earlier.[4,5]

The marvel was that the Republicans had been able to convince Joe Lunchpail that the tax breaks actually benefitted the production-line worker. How could a working stiff relate to a cut in the capital gains tax? Or to a reduction in income taxes at the highest levels? Or to an interest deduction up to $1 million on a mortgage? Or to raising the tax-sheltered estate limit beyond $600,000? Or to even consider a flat tax that exempted coupon clippers from any payment at all?

The answer may lie in the unremitting assault on "welfare cheats," food stamp recipients, Medicaid patients, and public housing residents—for which we might read the "underclass" or, simply, blacks. It seemed a very subtle play of the race card—and it worked.

Some of those left behind expressed their disaffections through riots, muggings, and such street crime specialties as drugs and violence. These cannot be excused, but it is imperative that the link be understood.

There is a connection between white collar crime and street crime, as the overclass waxes and the underclass wanes. The levers of power are pulled to aid the former and to punish the latter. The resulting alienation produces the nightly horror show on TV news, while white collar criminals continue their cunning and stealthy depredations.

TRUST

It is not a semantic accident that so many of our banks have "Trust" in their titles. That is what banking, at least theoretically, and certainly rhetorically, is all about. "Where your treasure is, there shall your heart be also."

Banking instinctively recognizes the centrality of trust to its success and actively exploits the recognition, in each of us, that controls, monitorings, regulations, and laws will not suffice. Trust requires the investment of confidence that those into whose hands we've entrusted (yes) our treasure can be trusted (again) to behave honorably, whether someone is watching or not.

The government, anxious to promote the growth of capital needed to fuel the innovations of capitalism—thereby creating jobs and prosperity—undertook the significant service of guaranteeing the safety of the first $100,000 of a depositor's capital. In exchange for this considerable, and virtually free, insurance policy, the government exacted the legally binding promise from the banks that they would use the capital according to established norms of prudence that resulted in "safe investments." Thus a bank would assess the value of a property carefully and make a loan—theoretically, at least—only at an amount the bank was certain it could retrieve from the ashes of a repossession or bankruptcy.

Not content with this gift, the banks then hired lobbyists to press for legislation relaxing the restrictions, while, of course, preserving the very considerable advantage of having taxpayers assume the risks.

THE BANK OF CREDIT AND COMMERCE INTERNATIONAL

It isn't easy to fathom why the Bank of Credit and Commerce International (BCCI)[6,7] was created, in 1972, by Aga Hassan Abedi. Longtime friends of Mr. Abedi spoke glowingly of his pride in having a Third World bank attend to Third World problems with Third World personnel and funds. Ostensibly, it was a financial institution intended for the most altruistic purposes—bootstrappism at its loftiest. It turned out, instead, to become perhaps the biggest fraud in world history.

It all began when an affable, mystical, worldly schmoozer born in 1923 approached Abu Dhabi's ruler, Zayed bin Sultan Al Nahyan, for a loan to establish an international bank. Aga Hassan Abedi was a secretive and eccentric mover given to twelve- to fifteen-hour speeches on the "cosmos, desire, and psyche" and who, unwittingly illustrating his penchant for the bizarre, once fired an executive for wearing the wrong-colored suit.

It is easy to imagine the ruler's temptation to run a vehicle in competition with intimidating Western institutions. The proposal seemed a logical extension of the oil emirate's desire for autonomy and independence, rather than forever relying on "colonial" expertness. The nation had a hard experience gaining mastery over its liquid gold and wanted to be a player in the banking universe, rather than the client it had been to oil companies. The Abu Dhabi ruling family wound up owning 77.4% of BCCI.

The bank incorporated in Luxembourg, a country with flaccid oversights. It was controlled through a maze of holding companies in the Cayman Islands, London, Amsterdam, and other sites. At its height BCCI was operating in 70 countries, had hundreds of thousands of depositors, and listed assets of $20 billion.

International banking has long been a highly lucrative industry, and competition for deposits and the use of such capital has been keen. Those with large sums to keep secret and protected naturally shop for countries that, like Switzerland, have made themselves into handy repositories for wealth, be it suspect or "old money."

Laws shielding the depositors and ensuring secrecy attract capital. Where cunning Latin American caudillos stashed their numbered accounts now become the refuge of drug lords. Huge sums from drug deals can be deposited, used in such cash-rich, marginal operations as casino enterprises, and then invested in legitimate business, like real estate. In the end the funds have been laundered into fungible acceptability.

BCCI numbered, among its clients, General Manuel Antonio Noriega—the imprisoned drug baron of Panama and its erstwhile ruler, the Central Intelligence Agency (which described its connection as "routine activities" without further embellishment), the Medellin drug cartel, the Palestinian terrorist Abu Nidal, organized crime groups in the United States and Italy, arms dealers, international terrorists and money launderers, and suppliers of aid to the Nicaraguan Contras and Afghanistan insurrectionists. BCCI rapidly developed into a convenient venue for clandestine international operations.

BCCI would provide a quick infusion of cash for nations needing to impress auditors evaluating applications for loans. It bribed public officials, misled auditors, circumvented regulators, and, ultimately, caused $12 billion in losses to mostly non-U.S. depositors. Many of these deposits were uninsured, and the thousands of losers, after years of litigation, had to settle for about 10 to 20 cents on the dollar and be very glad they'd been able to recoup that much from a wildly embarrassed Abu Dhabi royal family. As of September 1995 even this paltry return had not been paid.

Needing a foothold in America, BCCI ran into obstacles, in the form of regulations controlling foreign ownership of native banks. Characteristically, it moved, with practiced precision, into the corridors of influence that would grease the wheels of circumvention. It managed, in the 1980s and early 1990s, to secure the aid of figures at the very pinnacle of American power and prestige. It did so the old-fashioned way—by buying them.

In the early 1980s BCCI secretly purchased the largest bank in Washington, D.C.—First American Bankshares—as well as three banks in California, Florida, and Georgia. As a result, a former cabinet secretary, Clark M. Clifford,[8] and his protégé, Robert A. Altman, 47 in 1995, were indicted for deceiving regulators about BCCI's ownership of First American and for receiving commercial bribes.

Clifford, a genuine American icon and a prime capital power broker, had to resort to the humiliation of claiming to have been duped in a transaction that enabled him and his protégé to realize a $9.8 million profit in their dealings with BCCI. He and Altman had purchased bank stock, with money borrowed from the Arab investors, and sold it back to the investors at an inflated price. Clifford's only other recourse would have been to admit venality. He chose the rock, rather than the hard place.

In a months-long trial, Altman was acquitted and Clifford, 89 in 1996, avoided trial because of a heart condition. The Altman trial transcript was ordered sealed by the presiding judge.

Before public disclosure of Altman's involvement, but after its 1989 Florida conviction for money laundering, BCCI's power was such as to persuade Utah Republican Senator Orrin G. Hatch to deliver a speech, written by Altman, on the Senate Floor, defending and praising BCCI. He also pressed the Department of Justice to defend what had been a very lenient plea-bargain arrangement. A Senate colleague pressed the inquiry and criticized the plea bargain. With almost predictable inevitability the press later revealed that a supporter and friend of Senator Hatch was trying to secure a $10 million loan from BCCI.

From 1979 to 1991, more than 700 tips highlighting BCCI's catalogue of crimes flowed into the indifferent ears of American law enforcers. The Bank of England finally, in July of 1991, shut down BCCI for looting depositors of billions. The looters pocketed, spent, concealed, and otherwise stole much of the money entrusted to their care. Other nations panicked at the dimensions of the fraud and quickly moved to stanch the flow of red ink. The enterprise, at its peak one of the world's largest banks, collapsed in a heap. Although Guiness doesn't record these items, it was widely regarded as a record fraud, with losses estimated at $10 billion. Most of the financial records had been removed, just before the final Götterdämmerung in 1991, to Abu Dhabi.

As the New York City District Attorney pressed the case, he managed to secure 11 guilty pleas and recovered $1.2 billion in settlements, which more than paid for the few American depositors' losses and the costs of the prosecutions.

Stung by the international embarrassment and the financial losses, Abu Dhabi convicted 12 former BCCI executives on June 14, 1994, sentencing them to up to 14 years in prison and assessing fines of $9.13 billion, which no one expected to collect. The prisoners claimed to be destitute.

Aga Hassan Abedi, ill and bed-ridden in Lahore, Pakistan, was sentenced to 8 years, in absentia. The Pakistani government announced he would not be extradited. He died in 1995 at 73. On October 19, 1994, Swaleh Naqvi, BCCI's 61-year-old second in command and 20-year deputy to Aga Hassan Abedi, pleaded guilty to fraud and was sentenced to 8 years in federal prison and ordered to pay $255.4 million in restitution. Broke, he was not expected to pay and would be eligible for release in less than 6 years. Syed Ziauddin Ali Akbar, then 50, the former treasurer of BCCI, was released from an English prison and was arrested immediately upon emerging into freedom for extradition to New York in September of 1995.

In July 1994 investors and depositors sued Clark M. Clifford, Robert A. Altman, and 15 others for $55 million, demonstrating the importance of civil litigation in what are really criminal, if not easily prosecuted, cases. These scandals also spawned a new segment of the service industry—the tracers of hidden assets.

BCCI continued to produce reverberations, even after its demise, with further disclosures of wrongdoings, such as laundering drug money, by its branches.

It had all been very sterile, antiseptic, and abstract. Not one drop of blood spilled. There was no dramatic footage on the evening news of manacled prisoners, no bandages or body bags or even hysterical survivors—the staples of the format. There weren't even ghetto dwellers glowering at the bar of justice. There were only respectable, suited, talented, educated, smooth, revered, and recognizable figures, flanked by the most gifted advocates money could buy. Prominent statespeople would attest to the virtues of the accused, their paragon qualities would be extolled, admiring photographs of the accused with the mighty would be waved. Juries would look on in wonder. The vast injuries to savers, workers, the elderly, hopeful entrepreneurs, and other innocents were lost behind the welter of bloodless facts and glowing rhetoric. Carefully accumulated nest eggs had been robbed, and the victims were left to fight over the remaining crumbs—with most finally settling for fractions of their losses.

The BCCI scandal, however, proved the anecdotal illustration behind the massive, universal depredations of the S & L debacle. The latter proved they were all doing it, while the former gave face and form to who "they" were, by putting a face on the scandal. How could anyone's faith in the system survive such onslaughts?

Savings and Loans

A sleepy financial bywater mostly restricted to chancy, if lucrative, personal loans, Savings and Loans institutions were brought into the roaring mainstream of the nation's fiscal waters through deregulation, the cherished notion of those suspicious of all governmental controls.[9,10] Debureaucratizing S & L activities was pure Reaganomics—the loosening of the bonds that had restrained entrepreneurial and capitalistic energies.

The Depository Institutions Deregulation and Monetary Control Act of 1980 relaxed the restrictions on S & L activities— enabling these thrift institutions to expand greatly the areas of permitted investments. This heightened the possibilities of profit and growth but, as with most such activities, upped the risks. The kicker here, though, was that the risk would be borne by taxpayers who insured depositors' funds, up to $100,000 per location. Thus financial buccaneers could engage in dazzling transactions, with depositors' insured funds and the downside covered by the public. Depositors got their interest; the operators got their perks, bonuses, and huge salaries; and the citizens assumed the losses. And it was all perfectly legal. The activities of Charles Keating, described in the pages following, illustrate and personalize these activities.

The surprising aspect of the consequent debacle—in which there were, ultimately, 4,000 bank fraud prosecutions nationwide—is that the operators were too greedy and arrogant to be content with the free ride obligingly provided by a compliant federal government. We will see, in examining a variety of specific cases, just how mind-bogglingly vast the scandal became, as the estimates of the net cost to the public rose to the $150 billion range. There had never been anything to rival this economic tragedy in American life. It is a measure of the zeitgeist of the 1980s that insiders felt emboldened to expand beyond the ample new borders created by hustlers operating as bankers and lobbyists.

The S & L scandals prove a riveting tableaux of the incestuousness of profiteering professionals, daubed on the gargantuan canvas of history's greatest economic fraud. Painted in are the lawyers, accountants, politicians, corporate officials, and entrepreneurs—shifting roles, changing allegiances, and serving as so many Lego pieces in the creation of the massive pyramid of greed and theft.

In the S & L drama, one-time overseers defected to the higher-paying ranks of the overseen, while high-priced and ethically bound professionals performed skillful surgeries on the books to further the general cause of the client's gain. It was not seen as remarkable that the man nominated to head the Resolution Trust Corporation was revealed as having fought to get RTC work for his law firm. How much confidence could an industry, in which the supervised and the supervisors were constantly switching roles, inspire?

Denver's Silverado S & L[11] failed in 1988, at a taxpayer bailout cost of $1 billion, while accused of such misapplication of funds as using deposits to pay off the personal debts of the principal owner, the falsification of records to conceal huge diversions of funds, and the general employment of the thrift as if it were the private personal property of its officers—all while President Bush's son served as a director. The former chairman was accused of taking $458,000 for his personal use and won an acquittal of the charges in February 1993.

And the members of the Palm Beach Polo Club—part of a default in the S & L crisis—complained that the Resolution Trust Corporation had failed to follow through on an alleged promise to offer the members an advantage over the general public when the posh institution came up for auction. They sought an insider's bargain price before the properties would be submitted to a public auction, and failed. The superciliousness of participants in the crisis continuously illustrates the utter lack of introspection or balanced view among the overclass. It was quite legal to make an outrageous demand, but it brought new meaning to the chutzpah of the privileged.

The Centrust Bank of Florida cost taxpayers $1.7 billion. Its CEO, David L. Paul, used the bank's funds to purchase art for his home and diverted millions tagged for construction of the bank's emerging skyscraper to remodel his waterfront residence. He was convicted in November 1993 of racketeering and fraud. On December 1, 1994, Paul was sentenced to 11 years in prison and was ordered to pay $65 million in restitutions and fines. He claimed to be broke. It was the fourth-largest banking collapse in U.S. history. Prosecutors estimated a loss of $371 million on junk bonds that were later sold by regulators following the bank's demise.

The disposition of deflated assets became one of the defense claims of S & L pirates, as they loudly proclaimed that the investments would've bounced back, to higher values, if the feds had only been patient. These unrepentant swashbucklers invariably claimed that, given a little time, their investments would have perked up and provided a profit, notwithstanding the patently inflated prices at which they'd been purchased.

Around that time, the early 1990s, Ernst & Young, one of the accounting giants, paid the federal government $400 million to settle claims of improper audits. The failures swallowed 300 banks and thrifts, costing taxpayers billions. The bookkeepers not only failed to spot egregious flaws but also frequently aided—as we will see—in cooking the books.

Another accounting firm, Deloitte and Touche, paid $312 million in March 1994 for providing unqualified certificates for S & Ls on the brink of insolvency. Typically, in such cases, the firms admitted no wrongdoing and none of the principals would be charged; yet, in Alice in Wonderland fashion, they would still pay a whopping fine. The firms agreed to pay huge sums to the government, certainly the equivalent of a fine, while "acknowledging no wrongdoing in the matter."

Covering the institutions' ill health through false reports of profits was, as in the case of Midwest Federal, typical. Their over $800 million loss led to the conviction and imprisonment of its head and, also true to type, of several family members who'd been invited to dine at this sumptuous feast.

The Government Accounting Office announced that more than half (57%) of all cases of S & L criminal fraud in the 1980s occurred in Texas, with that state requiring 41% of the federal money used in the bailout.

Recoveries proved pitifully small. Prosecutions hardly existed. Bureaucratic turf battles and organizational problems at the Resolution Trust Corporation aided the general escape of judgment. RTC's boss, Treasury Secretary Lloyd Bentsen, was from Texas and campaigned against extending the federal statute of limitations to pursue S & L wrongdoers.

Every American would assume responsibility for $2200 as a result of the S & L bail-out. The bonds issued to pay for this debacle would be paid off over decades, thereby prolonging the agony and adding billions in interest payments.

Notwithstanding what seemed to be a sickening, muted, and pervasive sense of public helplessness over an incomprehensibly vast fiscal disaster visited on every single American, the halls of Congress remained active with lobbyists fighting "nit-picking" restrictions on banks and successfully resisting laws that would have made pursuit of malefactors possible. And the same bipartisanship that attended the deregulating initiatives that launched the disaster now presided over the efforts to bring wrongdoers to justice, through the defeat of such sensible measures as changing the statute of limitations to allow investigators to chase wrongdoers now protected by the mantle of untimely discovery.

While many players pirouetted onto the stage, one held its center and came to symbolize the S & L mess.

CHARLES H. KEATING, JR.

If an avatar for the S & L scandal could be fashioned, it would likely resemble Charles H. Keating, Jr.,[12] the man who, in 1984, at 60, bought the California-based Lincoln Savings and Loan and, over the next 5 years, turned it into a textbook case of fiscal prestidigitation that, as it happened, also made it, at $2.6 billion, the S & L tragedy's costliest. This sum ultimately proved the difference between the losses and the proceeds realized from liquidating the institution.

When first bought, Lincoln was a money-losing, small-time S & L. It was turned into a massive land and development speculator in the go-go 1980s by the most daring and outrageous of the fiscal pirates plying those sunny, greedy seas. Keating, in actions typical of the genre, invited his son and sons-in-law to dine at this table, which, over the next 5 years, resulted in more than $40 million in salaries and bonuses, a fleet of private jets, vacation homes, European jaunts, and an imperial style of life that included hectorings of the nation's most powerful when they failed to dampen the ardor of "meddlesome regulators."

The nub of the scheme lay in selling undeveloped land in Arizona at prices that were far higher (sometimes double) than the bank's own appraiser had listed for the properties. Depositors were induced to buy at these inflated prices through the offers of loans, to serve as downpayments (secured by the inflated value of the land), and the bank's promise to buy the land back, at a profit,

within a year. The loans and the land's purchase frequently occurred on the same day. The price—or value of the land—didn't
matter to those dazzled by the prospect of a quick resale back to
Keating's S & L.

Depositors in the S & L—those who put their savings up to
secure protected, conservative returns—were coaxed, by promised higher interest, to transfer their federally insured certificates
of deposit into junk bonds of the parent company, American Con-
tinental Corporation. (Those nifty tools of Michael Milken, through
which investors often were promised risky, lucrative interest rates
in exchange for the cash used to buy and retire the stock and take
ownership of the business, junk bonds were the equivalent of
buying a business with money borrowed on the promise that the
firm's future profits would subsidize payments of principal and
interest.) The junk bonds would be secured by the assets of Lincoln, which were, of course, inflated wildly on the books. At its
crash there were 17,000 bondholders.

Arthur Andersen, one of Lincoln's accounting firms, settled
charges of helping Keating cook the books for a $30 million pay-
ment to the government. The law firm paid $41 million for with-
holding information from regulators. Another law firm—Jones,
Day, Reavis and Pogue—paid $51 million for aiding Keating in his
frauds. The federal government's director of bank exams and
supervision, who had worked on Lincoln's case, joined this law
firm at the height of these activities.

As the scandal developed, bondholders recovered most of
their losses in lawsuits against Keating and his accountants and
lawyers. Remaining depositors were insured. The bag-holder
turned out to be John Q. Citizen.

Keating's defense was that vindictive regulators were out to
get him. Given a bit of time and freedom he'd have made it all up
was his claim. His lawyers argued that he'd practiced unsound,
but not illegal, investment strategies. It was truly amazing how
these worldly, experienced, canny operators found the temerity to
claim that they weren't crooks, but only fools.

Keating's federal trial lasted nearly two months, in 1992 and

1993. His earlier state trial had revealed Keating's unbelievable bullying of senators who came to be called The Keating Five (four Democrats and one Republican) for failing to stifle investigations by what he saw as pettifogging meddlers and bumblers waging vendettas against honest bankers. Keating hectored the senators mercilessly, upbraiding them as if they were errant boys, for failing to show sufficient vigor in stalling the investigation. His contributions to their campaigns were the mother's milk nurturing their reelections.

The testimony of associates ensured the conviction of Keating, his son, and assorted accomplices. The 1991 California trial having resulted in a ten-year sentence, the federal suit produced a concurrent twelve-year, seven-month sentence and a largely symbolic fine of $122.7 million. By then Keating had already served months on the state conviction. Legal costs, fines, and the fine combings of asset tracers had very likely left Keating broke—although one couldn't be certain.

Keating's daring, brash assertiveness, mastery of the corporate executive's aggressive style, and understanding of the nexus between government and business made him and his enterprise the paradigm of the age.

A numbed public silently watched the curtain stripped away, revealing the evidence of the skeptic's worst maledictions. They were all crooked. It wasn't just the occasional vice president or the rare president of the United States, the expected senator or the individual lawyer or accountant—it was all of them, national heroes not excepted.

Bitterness and cynicism leeched into the national fabric like some noxious stain. The electorate, and the large body of nonparticipants, reacted with the resigned gloom of those with nowhere to turn. The S & L scandals had been, to Americans, what the corruption of the Vestal Virgins had been to Romans. In a world without altruism, there is nothing to be done but to serve, and save, yourself.

At the bottom, the plebes were learning a few tricks of their own.

CONSUMER FRAUD AND FRAUDS BY CONSUMERS

General Motors finally apologized to Ralph Nader for questioning the safety of the Chevrolet Corvair, in 1966, and, over 20 years later, again tried stonewalling findings that the fuel tanks on pick-up trucks were positioned dangerously—leading to explosions on impact. In 1993 a jury held that GM knew of the flaw in the design and that it hid it from the public. Some critics charged that at least 300 had died in fiery crashes, until the design was changed, in 1988.[13]

Dateline NBC had, in November 1992, dramatically demonstrated the danger by filming one such truck bursting into flames on impact. The network was later humiliated by the disclosure that the event had been rigged through the deliberate igniting of the fuel on impact. NBC was, in their turn, forced to publicly apologize to GM and to its viewers.

Citizens translated these corporate pecadillos into their own behaviors. In Arizona a car would flank the victim's auto, while a confederate vehicle, in front, made a sudden stop. The pigeon would strike the vehicle and the occupants would claim injuries, working with cooperating lawyers and doctors on the scam. New Jersey authorities, suspecting widespread fraud, staged ten bus accidents throughout the state, in 1993. In one accident 17 bystanders clambered aboard after the impact to emerge and claim injuries. Some had been scanning police frequencies for reports of accidents. In six of the staged accidents, over 100 "ghost riders," doctors, and lawyers descended to file false claims. Even cops were found to be implicated. In 1993 a New York City bus was struck by a garbage truck on 125th Street. Within a month 18 people filed suit against the city, claiming they'd been passengers on the bus and had been injured. The bus had been out of service and parked, with no passengers.

A customer gets scalded by McDonald's coffee and collects $640,000 when she sues. What might she have gained if the coffee had been served cold?

As a result of so much fraud, the insurance premium dollar

for motorists in 1989, with about 25% not covered at all, broke out as follows:

- 27 cents for auto repairs
- 22 cents for administration, profit, and commissions
- 18 cents for pain and suffering
- 15 cents for medical care
- 10 cents for litigation costs.

And overseeing the vast insurance industry was an army of state legislators in bed with it—either through direct employment or as recipients of funds and favors.[14] These were the guys and gals who would be in charge of the "devolution" that Speaker Gingrich promised in 1995.

Even garbage and waste have value, as illegal dumping allows excessive profits and recycled materials get stolen. Food stamps have been bartered for drugs.

And there is reason to believe that, while exploiters exhaust every possibility to defraud, honest folks may be failing to assert their rights. It has been estimated that only 2% of actual medical malpractice results in lawsuits. It appears to be the frauds that are raising insurance costs, while creating deep worries over our "litigious society."

It's not only in the cities that we find widespread fraud. Farmers have inflated crop losses in storms. Large agricultural multinationals have created foreign corporations to enable them to circumvent our laws against trading with the enemy, allowing them, for example, to buy and sell Cuban sugar. Military contractors have defrauded the Defense Department—repeatedly—without a thought of the dangers to our fighters. Patriotism has fallen as much a victim to greed as religious fervor and solemn oaths have to hedonism.

A moon-walking astronaut was charged with defrauding investors and was made to pay $400,000 in fines. And his colleagues at NASA were, in 1994, subjected to FBI investigations involving bribes, kickbacks, and inability to account for government property worth billions. It appeared that not all NASA workers had the right stuff. In February of 1994 nine employees were charged. The prosecution failed and no convictions were obtained.

While many of these cases ended inconclusively, or with acquittals, the Justice Department had, by 1995, racked up an impressive total of bribes, kickbacks, frauds, and even dangerous sales of untested military equipment. In a 7½ year campaign, the Department convicted 64 government officials, consultants, and corporate executives from ten defense contractors and exacted $250 million in penalties.

Writers of newsletters engaged in "front-running," the buying and selling of securities, in advance, that they'd mention in forthcoming articles—never advising the subscribers of this conflict of interest.[15] In December 1993 the Internal Revenue Service estimated that Americans cheated their government out of $150 billion in taxes through the underground economy—not including drug dealings and similar crimes[16]—and ours was one of the lowest taxed of industrialized societies, hovering between 26.7% and 28.5% of gross domestic product from 1969 to 1991. Medical fraud in America is estimated to range between $50 and $100 billion.

Since 1980 the trend has been to lower income taxes for the higher quartile, resulting in America having the greatest concentration of income in the fewest hands of any of the advanced economies. One percent of U.S. households, with a net worth of at least $2.3 million, own 40% of the nation's wealth. The top 20%, worth $180,000 or more, own over 80%, leaving the other 80% of the population to fight over the remaining 20% of the wealth.

Government tax policies widened the economic breach and contributed to the unrest of those at the lower reaches. The malaise deepened with disclosures of fraud at the top and of an evil symbiosis and interchangeability that had our overclass shifting economic and political roles for private advantage.

And the collapse of communism—certainly an evil force—made its conqueror appear that much nobler.

2

Capitalism

There has never been an economic invention to rival capitalism. Its capacity for creating wealth is legendary. Capitalism is, in practice, the Darwinian loosing of human animals upon the jungle of commerce.

The cunning, strong, ruthless, innovative, energetic, and inventive survive. The weak perish.

The history of the twentieth century has been centered on the struggles of nationalism and political ideologies like fascism, communism, and democracy against a backdrop of economic forces that, left to their own devices, would either deaden all initiative or create a nightmare of monstrous winners and hosts of destroyed losers.

As the ideals of communism gave way to the corrupting evils of totalitarianism, the attractions of capitalism, as practiced in the varied environs of the wealthy West, became irresistible. A sort of tacit acceptance of the virtues of untrammeled capitalism began to take hold.

Nowhere was the power of capitalism's genius more centered than in the capital markets in which ownership of enterprises took the form of common shares, which were traded on the various stocks markets, thereby greatly expanding the participation of the masses.

The 1980s can now be seen as the decade of greed—for which we ought to read "unbridled capitalism."

Everybody was doing it, but in order to understand "it" we need to examine the behavior of some of the principal players and the vehicles they used or invented.

Crime is very complex human behavior. It often springs from inner desire or emotion. Sex, money, power, status, or celebrity are frequent motivators. Addiction to alcohol, gambling, drugs, or other substances is not only a frequent companion but is also evidence of a predilection for crime—evidence that should awaken others' impulse to investigate.

The need to rely on the integrity of others is obvious, but there is the concomitant requirement that their activities be monitored. Those supervising must also be alert to tell-tale signs of trouble—absences, changes in behavior, unexplained difficulties, alterations in health or appearance.

Our society could be likened to a race between rulemakers (legislators) and rulebreakers (criminals), as the regulators hustle to create new constraints and the inventive criminals find new ways to exploit or abuse their fellow humans. So much has to be based on confidence, however, that sole reliance on rules—and their enforcement—is a certain sign of societal disintegration.

Our lives depend on being able to trust our doctors, lawyers, bankers, brokers, and other service providers, and laws and regulations are present to proceed against the few who violate that trust. When that "few" become the many, no amount of supervision will arrest the slide.

While street crime tends to be primitive and direct—usually involving a personal confrontation, a palpable theft, or egregious harm—white collar crime is notable for its subtlety, cleverness, indirectness, inventiveness, and sophistication. Its scope is altogether too broad, variegated, and intricate to allow confident taxonomies, but it is useful and instructive to analyze paradigms in order to both appreciate its singular and labyrinthine nature as well as to better understand ways of detecting it, coping with it, or preventing it.

A simple—and, perhaps, simple-minded—axiom is "trust, but verify." If the human animal has displayed anything, it is a talent for abuse of power or violation of trust. If the history of humankind has taught us anything it is that temptation frequently overpowers the weak flesh of the most hallowed citizens. We've heard of priests succumbing to the allure of abuse of their charges, even in such refuges as Covenant House; we know of betrayals by public officials, bankers, lawyers, doctors, and other repositors of our esteem and trust.

It is noble and edifying to recognize genuine heroes, and few things are as uplifting as the sight of selfless sacrifice or silent, consistent devotion to duty. Great writers recognize the myriad forces working on mere mortals, while comic books serve up perfect paragons of virtue. Part of the meaning of life lies in dilemmas of vulnerable flesh, difficulties of will, and the seductive pull of corruption.

Frauds and embezzlements rely on concealment and cleverness. Discovery leads to analyses and the development of controls.

KIDDER, PEABODY & CO.

When Kidder, Peabody & Co. hired Joseph Jett, 33 in 1991, as a bond trader, it was taking on an MIT- and Harvard-educated promising young man with brokerage experience at First Boston and Morgan Stanley.[1,2] The hirer's judgment seemed confirmed as Jett propelled himself to stardom, with reported trading profits of over $150 million in 1993. This remarkable coup pleased a skittish corporate parent, General Electric, and resulted in Jett's being named employee of the year. He collected a $9 million bonus for his achievement.

Auditing systems were in place to monitor transactions involving billions of dollars. The industry smarted under disclosures that destroyed such venerables as E. F. Hutton and Drexel Burnham Lambert and that resulted in the jailings of such financial geniuses as Michael Milken and Ivan Boesky; they were crippled by huge fines and staggering legal fees. Singed, investment firms were determined to avoid the flames. General Electric's chief executive, John F. Welch, Jr., was famous for his belief in tough internal controls.

The financial world attracts many of the brightest minds in our society. If they were even mostly trustworthy, concealment of wrongdoing wouldn't be as commonplace as it is today, but the fact is that these talented folks exist on both sides of the ledger. The necessary alertness is lulled by obeisances paid the rainmakers. The need for profit and the greed fed by the possibility of huge bonuses fuel the myopia essential to the nurturing of hope. Who wants to be looking gift horses in the mouth?

Joe Jett went from impecunious unemployment to collecting millions in the space of months. To bolster his career, Jett invented nonexistent trades and had future interest payments entered as current profits in a computer system, alerted to this potential danger, that had been shut down by the scheme's perpetrator. The computer accepted the entries as current profits, and discovery was forestalled by accelerating trades to cover surfacing discoveries. In the end there were about 60,000 false trades entered in the system, involving $600 billion in phony transactions. The circumvention had been made possible because Jett was able to control the systems intended to monitor his actions.

Supervisors who might have detected the fraud hadn't bothered to check the books. Audits routinely reported all was well. Finally, the success was simply too good to be true and the first cursory glance confirmed the suspicion.

Joe Jett was fired. The bonus—which had been deposited in a Kidder account—was frozen, as the firm fought to recover it. Jett's boss and his boss's boss were forced out. Others were demoted or transferred. The investigating attorney Kidder hired prepared a report that was devastatingly critical of the flaccid to nonexistent supervision given Jett. On January 9, 1996, Jett was charged with fraud by the Securities and Exchange Commission (SEC), and the agency further reported that two of his bosses had failed to monitor his work.[3]

To everyone's surprise Mr. Jett had actually begun cooking the books much earlier than originally thought, only months after starting with the firm.

In one of life's delicious ironies, Jett hired Gustave H. Newman, the advocate who'd successfully defended BCCI's Robert A. Altman, as one of his lawyers.

General Electric, never wholly satisfied with its purchase of Kidder, sold it to the Paine Webber Group in late 1994. By then G.E. was itself defending its name against Justice Department charges that it had conspired with DeBeers Centenary A.G. to illegally rig the prices of industrial diamonds to increase its profits.

The charge of diamond price-rigging had been made by an employee who had been dismissed at G.E. His later recantation failed to stem the tide he'd set in motion. G.E. had, with near-miraculous prescience, agreed to settle his wrongful discharge suit against the company, provided him with retirement benefits, and paid his legal fees. The Justice Department nevertheless proceeded with its case against G.E., only to have it thrown out by a judge in December 1994 because the evidence, without his testimony, simply wasn't strong enough.

As audits proceeded in earnest, it developed that Jett had actually experienced losses of almost $50 million in 1993, which had been concealed amid the welter of phantom profits. Jett had created his own pyramid scheme, but Charles Ponzi, the Italian immigrant who became a Boston investor in 1920 and who lured countless pigeons to invest in his swelling get-rich-quick schemes—in which early arrivals received big interest payments and friends and relatives were sucked into the unwittingly set trap—had already lent his name to these scams.

As a result of Jett's prestidigitations Kidder reported a profit of $350 million in 1993 that never existed.

Had a crime been committed? The question would turn on whether Kidder would claim that the bonus paid Jett was, in fact, based on his fraud and, hence, a form of theft. The SEC's answer was yes.

G.E. shareholders suffered somewhat less than 25-cent loss per share. It was a fitting paradigm of such schemes—huge piles of cash that, distributed over millions of victims, actually amounts to only pennies of loss for each. This is the principle behind every exploitation of "the people" who may lose only pennies each for the enormous enrichment of some lobbyist's client.

Jett's supervisors spoke of the need for more careful screening in hiring practices, and, indeed, a check with previous employers would have shown that Jett had occupied junior positions and had performed undistinguishably in both. Jett's rise to chief of the government trading desk, from which he supervised 16 traders in the brief span of months attests to the powerful influence of his mendacities on his bosses.

The most interesting part of it all was that Joe Jett, an African American, consistently reported that, when the scandal broke, reporters and other interested inquirers repeatedly looked past him when seeking the scandal's central figure, automatically assuming him or her to be white.

Was Jett a lone rogue or a symbol of a pervasive problem?

In 1995 an executive vice president of Daiwa Bank confessed to having lost $1.1 billion over an 11-year period, during which he'd been trying to recoup a $200,000 loss. He said that he had sold bonds from the bank's portfolio and forged the records. Thus the bank, which thought it had $4.6 billion in bonds in its New York vaults, was actually left with $3.5 billion. Compounding the problem, Daiwa leaders failed to notify the authorities promptly and were forced into ignominious resignations. Tremors from the scandal would continue to dominate financial pages into 1996.

In the Baring Brothers Singapore office, a 28-year-old trader bet heavily that the Japanese market would rise and lost $1.4 billion when it descended, driving his ancient firm into bankruptcy. Charged, he was to be extradited to Singapore for trial. From prison, he later expressed amazement at his firm's willingness to forward huge amounts of money to cover his trades without checking on the transactions. This insightful fellow had likened the trading floor to a casino.

In 1992 an employee of Showa Shell Sekiyu lost $1.1 billion in currency speculations. Two of his superiors had learned of the losses, failed to act, and later resigned.

In 1987, another Merril Lynch employee took a risky position on mortgage-backed derivatives (which depend on the fluctuations in value of underlying commodities, such as mortgages or treasury notes) and cost his firm $337 million. He had ignored instructions not to do this. When caught, he was suspended from the industry for 9 months, but returned later to work for another firm.

What all of these individuals had done, by and large, was function free of controls and outside the boundaries of the legally permissible, investing huge sums and falsifying records to reflect a rosier picture.

The extent of the wrongdoings was mind-boggling. How many others were sweatily doctoring the books? What, if anything, had the monitors learned?

MICHAEL MILKEN

Who might represent the zeitgeist of the go-go 1980s? It would have to be one of the darlings of capitalism, who embodied the complex mix of virtues and vices, strengths and weaknesses of the tragic hero.

Surely it must have struck observers as absurd that so many clever, educated insiders, having been given the keys to the treasury by their political associates—who had relaxed the regulations sufficiently to allow perfectly legal speculations and personal enrichment—should have resorted to peculations instead. The greed and hubris formed the core of Greek tragedy, in which lack of introspection and humility inevitably led to the brilliant hero's demise.

It had all seemed so easy. The breaches were only temporary. Everyone was doing something, after all. The likelihood of discovery was remote, and the offenses were easily rationalized as trivial and explainable. "It's a jungle out there, Jane, please get me another martini."

Junk bonds have been around awhile, so Michael Milken, the 1947-born wunderkind of Wall Street, could not be labeled their inventor, but he sure brought them to new and wonderful uses.[4,5] Milken turned junk bonds into capital-raising vehicles for the takeover of promising—sometimes somnolent—cash-rich or cash-producing family businesses possessing strong potential for exploitation. And what vehicles they turned out to be.

Unsecured by the usual mortgages on tangible property, junk bonds plied the fiscal waters needed by desperate enterprises willing to pay premiums of 3, 4, or 5 percentage points of return higher than safer, secured instruments. Junk bonds served as a way of converting ownership of an enterprise from shares of stock (which received dividends from earnings that were taxed at both the corporate and individual levels) to debt in the form of bonds (which was a cost of doing business, the interest on which was not taxable to the corporation). Thus they changed—through their alchemy—taxable profits into tax-deductible expenses.

What better instrument for the Age of Greed than the junk bond? Sure they were risky, but where else could you get 12% to 15% on your money?

These exotica proved, for decades, the warrens of a few speculative gun slingers. The overwhelming majority of investors left these areas to the bottom fishers.

Milken, sensing the value of these devices, concocted a scheme to have his firm—Drexel Burnham Lambert[6]—participate with takeover artists. The raiders—friendly or hostile—would offer shareholders a premium for the stock. Investing little of their own capital, they raised the cash through floating bond issues paying very high yields. The bondbuyers put up the money with which the business was bought and hoped to collect high dividends and, eventually, their investment too, as the bonds were redeemed. A company's earnings would be used to pay off the loan (junk bond) that enabled the borrower to buy the business, instead of going as dividends to stockholders.

Tempted by the returns and solipsized by the reassuringly

familiar and solid names of the corporations involved—and doubly encouraged by the prestige of Drexel et al.—the bonds sold, the stock was retired, and the public corporation was taken private.

Drexel (and Milken) collected huge fees for handling the transaction; the raiders collected options, bonuses, salaries, and fees; and the bondholders—absent an occasional bankruptcy or default—collected hefty interest payments from corporate coffers. Sleepy companies were energized and cash cows got milked—or Milkened. The takeover rage seemed to be capitalism at its most robust—the Invisible Hand freed at last.

But was unfettered capitalism unequivocally good for the country? Might unfettered capitalism not result in child labor, worker exploitation, the impoverishment of the elderly, and the crushing of the weak? Wasn't it concentrating wealth among the top 1% in one of the fastest-developing economic chasms in modern history? Who paid?

Corporate raiders invariably moved quickly to exercise the right to renegotiate existing labor contracts—allowed in a change of ownership. The next steps would be reduction in labor and benefit costs, paring expenses, and a tight focus on quick returns, in order to pay the bond interest and even retire some of the bonds through redemptions. Parts of the business would be sold off. A lot of it looked like car-stripping—selling off pieces while hoping to keep the vehicle functioning.

Pension funds suddenly available to the new owners were pressed into the service of the new regime as sources of capital to be borrowed and plowed into the business.

But the real kicker lay, again—as in the S & L catastrophe—in the availability of the taxpayer as the fall guy and gal. While corporate earnings were taxed before dividends were paid, payment of debt (junk bond interest payments) was considered a cost and, hence, was deducted from earnings. It amounted to the personal equivalent of mortgaging one's house to the hilt, since the government would allow the interest payments as a deduction against income—one of the very few tax shelters left. Paying the house off—and burning the mortgage, an age-old immigrant dream—would, in the circumstances, be to burn money. Why surrender one of the few federal tax shelters left—the deduction of mortgage interest payments? Bond redemptions would, depending on profit or loss on the original purchase price, either be taxed as income (if profitable), or usable as a loss against other gains in such transactions. If there were no other gains, then a loss deduction up to $3000 could be taken.

The American treasury was deprived of the hundreds of billions in taxes formerly paid from the earnings of now debt-ridden corporations. The deficit had to be made up somewhere, and the first and best place to look was in the taxpayer's pocket.

One of the curious aspects of this tax break is that states haven't invented their own versions. Maybe it's symptomatic of the torpor normally attending governmental operations. The state equivalent to this form of financing would be, for instance, for a given state to center all its taxes on state income taxes (federally deductible), thereby shifting the cost from the citizen of Minnesota to all American taxpayers. Under this system, Minnesota, for example, would have no sales, property, or any other taxes and would collect all of its revenues from the state income tax, thereby providing its citizens with this deduction against federal income taxes. Minnesotans would be paying higher state income taxes, but few, if any, other taxes, and they would receive a large additional deduction on their federal income taxes. Since all non-federal taxes were once deductible from income, for federal purposes, the elimination of most of this deduction made state income taxes the last such shelter left.

Of course, in this takeover climate, research, innovation, new products, gradual growth, and long-range planning were not high priorities. Quick turnover and skimmings were. Just one buyout, the $26-billion purchase of RJR Nabisco in the late 1980s, would, it was estimated, cost the federal treasury $7 billion is not just foregone taxes but also in tax refunds of $2 billion for taxes paid on the earnings of the 3 years previous to the buyout.[7]

Thousands lost their jobs and many more suffered reductions in pay and benefits, as the labor–management pendulum swung, pronouncedly, toward the new masters.

But even away from the jungle's meaner warrens, there were the stirrings of unrest. Americans had long been used to the bureaucratic security and permanence of employment at America's giant corporations. Suddenly the blanket was withdrawn and layoffs, by the tens of thousands, were periodically announced by corporate titans. And, to the workers' shock, the stock climbed as increased profits emerged from the debris of broken careers.

At the top, directors got options and payments and golden parachutes and executives received obscenely large sums for their profit-enhancing skills.

Nothing better illustrated the uncontrolled energies of capitalism, or the greed of its acolytes, than the takeover frenzy made possible by Milken's ingenious use of junk bonds. Milken self-mesmerized into the conviction of personal infallibility and inviolability. He had earned $550 million in 1986 alone, and if this wasn't proof of superhuman status, what was?

Not content to profit hugely—in the end he'd pay $1.1 billion in fines and settlements and contribute another $350 million to charity and still retain a fortune of about $500 million—Milken wound up, in April 1990, pleading guilty to six felony charges that included conspiracy, aiding in the filing of false information with the SEC, aiding in the filing of false income tax returns, and related offenses. He also agreed to answer questions about his transactions and to help investigators pursue other frauds. In this service he proved less enthusiastic and helpful than the man who had trapped him, his erstwhile friend Ivan Boesky.

Milken reneged on his deal, and the Justice Department furiously insisted on a harsh penalty. On November 22, 1990, Federal Judge Kimba M. Wood sentenced him to ten years in a federal prison, to pay over $600 million in fines and other fees to the government, and to perform 5800 hours of community service. This was the harshest sentence by far.

Chastened by a sentence that outraged many colleagues, who produced irate letters to *The New York Times* and other outcries, Milken repented and agreed to cooperate. His sentence was reduced to two years of actual time. The rest of the sentence remained in effect. Milken's performance, as a help to prosecutors, proved mixed, but two additional convictions did result.

The Milken investigation began in 1986 when a big-time stock speculator, Ivan F. Boesky, pleaded guilty to insider trading and, in exchange for a lenient sentence of three years, agreed to cooperate. The man who would wind up suing his wife for support and a division of the $100 million in assets she allegedly controlled worked devotedly to snare the brokers who'd broken the law to do him favors—and succeeded.

In another irony, Milken—who had fought the charges and delayed the reckoning for many months—wound up pleading guilty the very same month, April 1990, in which Boesky was released. One was going in as his betrayer was going out.

In this inquiry, a baker's dozen of investment bankers, speculators, and other high fliers were convicted of white collar crimes involving corporate activities intended to profit the insiders at the expense of the herd.

Insider trading is, by definition, the exploitation of unknowing outsiders (general investors) by insiders acting on knowledge gained from their special role. Corporate executives or lawyers or such who are working on a lucrative merger are forbidden to trade on that knowledge at the expense of the investors not privy to such inside information. The activities of the white collar criminal can, however, span a very wide spectrum.

Using an unapproved pesticide can result in huge savings, but it can endanger the food supply. Commercial disputes can lead to murder plots. Defrauding cooperative housing tenants can lead to the impoverishment of seniors. Anything of value creates the temptation to steal. The ingenuity and variety of theft schemes are limited only by the scope of the human imagination.

Insiders have advantages that scream for monitorings and controls. Tracking an insider's violation can lead to multiple companies and to those who are generations far removed from direct contact yet are somehow connected to the principals. The takeover bid for Norton Co. involved nine generations of tippees, some of whom also participated—illegally, as well—in Accor's tender offer for Motel 6 Limited Partnership in 1990.[8]

Some underwriters brought stock to market in weakened states to guarantee the profits of other insiders selling the stock short. Hanover Sterling went out of business in February 1995 after bringing a number of firms into the trading market, only to see their values plunge—following the initial euphoria. That investors will gullibly buy initial public offerings (IPOs) without heeding the warnings that are legally required in the prospectuses argues either for the futility of trying to protect determined pigeons or for the need for government oversight in the face of soaring victimizations.

In the end there are fancy phrases, complex imagery, and labels such as "derivatives," "limited partnerships," and "IPOs," as well as inventions such as junk bonds, mutual funds, and leveraged buyouts, but the basics of trust and betrayal rarely disappear behind the façades.

Many, including Milken, emerged from prison to find the psychic or monetary reward in such didactic joys as lecturing on ethics. He might well be styled an expert, but it looks and sounds a lot like Charles Manson touting family values. He was, in late 1995, reported to be raking in millions in fees for advising his erstwhile associates on business deals. Wall Street's tortured ambiguity about its hero could still be found in literary discussions surrounding Milken.

At the close it wasn't hard to conclude that the criminals in this case emerged unscathed by the scythe of contrition. What was much more disturbing was the number of industry associates willing to champion such heroes and defend their conduct.

SALOMON BROTHERS

Venerable names succumbed, seemingly everywhere, to venal enticements.

Salomon Brothers was found to have made false bids in illegal efforts to trade treasury bonds between August 1989 and May 1991.[9] The resulting scandal shook the firm to its roots, causing resignations, firings, and the payment of $290 million in fines and penalties. The trader was sentenced to four months in prison, and the chairman resigned.

The tobacco industry obdurately resisted scientific findings of nicotine's addictive power and circulated internal memos demonstrating their guilty knowledge, all the while issuing reassuring and contradicting public statements. The irony was that the companies' use of the warning label affixed to their product since 1969—adopted over their bitter opposition—now served as a protective mantle against suits. The surgeon general's advisory that smoking was harmful was now used as fair warning to the consumer. Caveat emptor indeed, but the remedy had been hammered on the resisting tobacconists.[10]

Just as Michael Milken embodied the Tragic Hero of his time, and Salomon Brothers a revered institution brought low, Prudential proved the symbol of the loose corporate morals of the age.

THE ROCK

Few of capitalism's symbols capture the spirit of enduring reliability of Prudential's Rock of Gibraltar logo. The corporation's mantra of trust was garbled by the scandals wafting through the corridors of its brokerage subsidiary over a tortuously long period of the 1980s and 1990s.[11,12]

It all could be said to have started with Prudential's ill-fated attempts to please valued clients. When Texas' outsized Hunt brothers[13] set out to corner the silver market as the 1980s began, they factored in every possibility—production, inventory, usage, future demand, and even the needs of the photography industry. Their stranglehold tightened as their enormous wealth and status enabled them to leverage the necessary billions in loans.

The price of silver soared as the commodity's control appeared to be a certainty. As silver passed $50 an ounce, a funny thing happened—householders who had taken pride in the family's plate now trundled lovingly crafted pitchers, knives, bowls, and candelabra to smelters. Incredibly, the family plate was suddenly worth more as a melted blob than as a treasured heirloom.

The sudden flood of unanticipated silver stock—from an

unconsidered, but vast, inventory of household silver services—caused a reversal in the price spiral. It was a classic example of the power of market forces on a commodity's price. The perfect functioning of capitalism's genius of supply and demand factors undid its most febrile believers, the Hunts.

As silver's price plummeted, the Hunts' creditors made the equivalent of margin calls—only to find the Hunts scurrying for the protection afforded by the Bankruptcy Code.

The lenders, suddenly confronted with the hideous truth behind the joke that the person who borrows a thousand is owned by the bank while the borrower of billions owns the bank, included venerable Prudential. The Hunts had borrowed hugely, from The Rock and from a host of other lenders.

The tangle of suits that followed would extend over the next decade and a half, at the end of which lay an unhappy settlement and a lot of rich lawyers, accountants, and tracers of hidden wealth.

Emerging from this bitter and chastening experience, Prudential Insurance of America looked nervously about for a profitable vehicle. It found one in a good brokerage firm that seemed to be spewing profits by putting together and selling limited partnerships in tax-favored energy and real estate deals.

Entrepreneurs paid hefty fees to brokerage firms who could market and sell these products. And, in imprecise businesses such as real estate, who could challenge the assertion that a building that might sell for $100 million was put on the books as being worth $150 million? Such an assessment would greatly inflate the enterprise's book value and make it easier to sell shares in these partnerships at higher prices.

So, in 1981, Prudential Insurance Company of America bought Bache & Company, a brokerage firm that, the year before, had greatly expanded its limited partnership business.

Prudential Bache thus made its niche at the head of a line speeding to create the go-go 1980s. With executives who had been attracted to the quick and handsome profits at the helm, the brokerage pushed to sell not just risky, but flawed and fraudulent investments, with the Rock's assurance of safety and return.

By 1986 Prudential Bache settled a major suit, signed a consent decree, and acknowledged its failure to file appropriate compliance reports, while strenuously denying any criminal wrongdoing (one of the semantic niceties expensive lawyers regularly delivered to well-heeled clients). It wouldn't be until 8 years later that the company would finally admit it had broken the law, by which time most of its investors in these partnerships had been gulled into accepting an eight cents on the dollar loss.

As 1994 ended the parent company anted up an additional $365 million to defray costs of settlements with the hordes of defrauded investors. Prudential Securities also, on December 21, 1994, paid a huge fine for making illegal contributions to politicians—on both sides of the aisle—who were in positions to influence legislation affecting the brokerage.

Of course, for many Americans, it remained a lot easier to fulminate against the burglar in the tabloid than to generate any prejudice against all of these highly educated, articulate, sophisticated, and outwardly admirable leaders of our society.

The tortured path of Prudential wound over a 14-year span, cost hundreds of thousands of citizens their carefully accumulated life savings, and resulted in record fines and fees for the company—all of it fueled by greed and oiled by lies. When the disaster's smoke cleared, the culprits had been let off lightly and the victims were left holding the empty bag of their hopes.

The characteristics of the frauds were that they were system-wide, varied, and involved the highest executives, who suppressed information. In fact, the few in the organization who sought to sound the alarm—early on and later—were fired, eased out, or otherwise financially injured or submerged and, unlike the roseate hues attending our fairy tales on the screen, rarely emerged into the sunlight of prosperity thereafter. Ours is a society that punishes rightdoers severely.

By the time clients' lawsuits triggered SEC investigations, the damage had been done.

James J. Darr, one of Prudential Bache's key executives, had engaged in highly suspect sweetheart arrangements with firm clients at his previous employer. Warnings had been sounded as early as 1980, but his new boss was too dazzled by this supersalesman's productivity to do much but ensure the defeat of the accusers.

Darr pushed real estate-limited partnerships; took gifts, accepted special deals, and made profits; and received bonuses and high salaries. The deals soured and law suits followed. Darr had been aided by Clifton S. Harrison, whose 1967 conviction for bank embezzlement had been pardoned, on October 9, 1974, by President Gerald Ford, at the behest of Wall Street heavyweights. In hiring Harrison, Prudential Bache hadn't bothered to contact his former partner and concealed the information on his conviction—relying on the pardon as the ultimate absolver of guilt. Given the risk of being sued, former associates and employers have proved remarkably reluctant to report fecklessness or malfeasance. Protecting informers is not included in most proposals for tort reforms. Mr. Harrison spent lavishly on his clients and on himself.

The sale of partnerships in oil, gas, and real estate was premised on assurances of safety, guaranteed returns of 12%, and the promise of the preservation and return of the capital invested. As some of the enterprises foundered, Prudential Bache returned payments to investors—as distributions (or profits)—that were actually the investors' own capital. It was described, accurately, as nothing more than a Ponzi scheme.

This would be a running story, in the nation's press, for at least a decade. By October 21, 1993, Prudential Securities (the name had been changed) acknowledged unauthorized trades, lying about the risks and about the return on investment, failing to supervise the brokers, churning (purchases and sales to generate commission fees), pressuring clients to sign unwise agreements, and ignoring promises made to regulators and other mendacities. It agreed to pay $371 million to the SEC for distribution to 400,000 investors. Those who accepted this meager settlement (averaging $679 to each of 100,000 investors) had to agree to no further compensation and were precluded from any further recovery—even following the firm's criminal conviction the following year and the additional penalty of $330 million. By then Prudential exceeded the previous record of $650 million paid by the junk bond impressarios at Drexel Burnham Lambert.

As the scandal unraveled, new and different disclosures revealed just how widespread the abuses had become. Insurance agents were found to be functioning as stockbrokers—for which they had no license—and the firm's records had been doctored to conceal these facts. Signatures were forged.

The second-biggest producer of commissions was found to have engaged in forbidden practices with the accounts of wealthy clients.

The whistle-blower on inflated real estate investments was fired, sued Prudential, and was silenced from further outbursts by the terms of their 1994 settlement.

In 1988 a broker signed a wealthy alcoholic patient out of a nursing home and emerged with the sale of almost $700,000 in limited partnerships. When the patient's doctor complained, the broker, in 1992, fled to Guatemala with his fees and commissions, leaving the client with a loss and, adding insult to injury, a tax liability.

George L. Ball, the chairman and CEO of Prudential Bache from 1982 to 1991, landed firmly on his feet when he was named executive vice president at Smith Barney Shearson following these disclosures. A low-level trainee who'd rise to star status at E.F. Hutton & Co. before heading Prudential Bache, Ball had graced the rosters of Wall Street's whitest shoe firms. He eventually, in 1988, consented to a New York Stock Exchange censure for violating rules and securities laws at E. F. Hutton. When ousted from the Smith Barney Shearson firm in October 1993, he was reported to have another position lined up.

AS THE SMOKE CLEARED

As 1995 began, the time within which claims could be made was expiring. A total of 340,000 investors had socked $8 billion into 700 Prudential limited partnerships. Those pleading victimization had to establish that the investments were inconsistent with their objectives, that they'd been taken in, or that they hadn't been fully informed.

The big losers were those who failed to make a claim or who died unknowing. Next came the great majority of the 130,000 who bought energy income partnerships and who settled for $90 million in early 1994. As the deadline of January 10, 1995, neared, 152,000 investors had submitted claims, and 56,000 of them received almost $400 million. Even restitution produced losers.

Although Prudential dismissed another broker for trading without client authorization, the company fought both this and the preceding case and pursued a slash-and-burn legal strategy, until they were finally forced to admit widespread criminal wrongdoing—8 years after the crimes first came to light and fully 14 years after cogent and eloquent warnings had been sounded and ignored. In the kind of musical chairs that exist in such old boys' networks of channels and connections, former regulators and prosecutors were enlisted to defend Prudential's key executives.

The accounting firms regularly attesting to the soundness of Prudential's practices and books were sued in 1994 for $1.1 billion by victimized investors. Texas, Idaho, and other states sanctioned Prudential for victimizing residents. Prudential—outwardly acquiescing in civil penalties—loudly proclaimed criminal innocence while still, privately and behind the scenes, fighting every disclosure.

Finally, by June 1994, the leading executives were swept out. Months later, in October, the company capitulated and admitted criminal conduct. By then they claimed they'd changed top management, had cooperated with the investigation, and had compensated investors.

Not one person was held criminally liable.

These were crimes with hundreds of thousands of victims and unimaginably high social costs, but, because there hadn't been bloodied heads, body bags, or manacled prisoners on the evening news, the event slipped into the mists of abstraction. In the end, in 1996, Prudential had paid almost $2 billion in legal claims and costs from the limited partnership debacle.

By January 1996, Lehman Brothers Inc., Dean Witter Reynolds Inc., and Merrill Lynch and Co. were in negotiations with the SEC to settle claims that they had misled investors in the sales of limited partnerships in the 1980s. The total damage was estimated to be in the $100-million range for the three. Earlier, Paine Webber Group Inc. agreed to a $250-million accord to settle a similar SEC administrative complaint.[14]

The Prudential Insurance Company of America scandal illustrates a number of important points:[15]

- There is little hope for meaningful reform as long as individuals escape punishment. Hiding behind corporate skirts is bound to encourage further crimes.
- The importance of civil suits in rooting out wrongdoing cannot be underestimated and should not prejudice us against litigation per se. Prudential was able to resist criminal prosecutions for 8 years following the disclosure of widespread wrongdoing.
- Although the schemes are complex and sophisticated, they are rooted in such easily understood matters as lies, thefts, and misrepresentations.
- The symbiosis between business and politics requires constant surveillance.
- Anecdotes on the evening news are more powerful than the most sweeping array of figures. One person's tragedy has more impact than the abstract.

The victims were mostly the little investors, but the conniving human mind was also capable of mulcting those at the higher reaches.

RICH AND POWERFUL NOT EXEMPT

The extension of life and the infirmities that accompany the geriatric experience expose many once competent and powerful persons to the exploitation of greedy "caregivers."

Doris Duke,[16] the billionaire heiress to a tobacco fortune, made her butler the executor of her estate when she died. His profligacy led her family to sue to wrest control of the empire from his grasp. As the tangled suit swept tortuously through the courts, into 1996 and well beyond, only the intended major beneficiary—a philanthropy to ease human suffering—suffered the absence of the treasure intended for its use. The butler settled for millions in 1996.

Charles Lindbergh's 89-year-old widow, incapacitated by strokes, was embezzled out of $250,000 by the person the family had hired to pay her bills. Unlike many such cases, in this one the family insisted on a criminal prosecution to protect others. This was both wise and rare.[17]

TAKING A BYTE OUT OF CRIME

The advent of the Information Age—in which cards, codes, and numbers replace coins, bills, and checks—has also transformed crime.[18,19] The mugger's take is now even more paltry, while the hacker who knows how to use information is enriched.

A cashless society and the concomitant need to transfer sums in a river of wealth has made the interception and redirection of such a flow a highly lucrative area.

In October 1993 Spectrum Information Technologies Inc. stunned Wall Street with the announcement that John Sculley, the former chairman of Apple Computer Inc., would become its chief executive. In March 1995 the former president of Spectrum and nine others—including his wife, son-in-law, and nephew—were indicted for a fraud scheme in which they had charged 300 companies in 23 states as much as $40,000 each to secure lavish investments in their fledgling enterprises with a Saudi prince and investors in Hong Kong and Switzerland. The total allegedly bilked was over $6 million between 1988 and 1994.

Disillusionment, in the form of a letter advising the client companies that they hadn't met Spectrum's investors' requirements, followed, and was succeeded by indictments for fraud.

That a supersophisticate like John Sculley could have been taken in by this sham—however briefly—is a cautionary tale. The indicted Peter T. Caserta and his group allegedly sold Spectrum stock at a huge profit on the news of Sculley's appointment.

Spectrum's market value then plummeted from nearly $1 billion to $43 million and closed at 56 cents a share on March 23, 1995.

A hot product can create demand pressures that evolve into sophisticated and massive schemes of fraud. For example, the popularity and limited supply of Honda vehicles in the 1970s and 1980s produced lightning-fast sales at premium prices. The value of Honda dealerships soared. One dispenser of these franchises collected $2 to $5 million in bills stuffed in envelopes or wrapped in newspapers from 1977 to 1992. The recipients of these treasured franchises became instant millionaires. But with utter predictability, the soaring profits produced bribes, kickbacks, and the creation of a corrupt culture that resulted in scores of criminal convictions.[20]

THE CORPORATE CULTURE

Too many publicly traded enterprises are operated as private fiefdoms by executives and boards presumably pursuing the stockholders' interests while actually lining their own pockets.[21] In these conspiracies they've been shielded by corporate secrecy and the skillful ministrations of professionals—lawyers, accountants, public relations flacks, and such—hired to facilitate the fleecing, or at least to acquiesce to their masters' interests. Such tangled webs cause the public's mind to fog over and seek relief on beery couches offering sports diversions and other distractions.

In 1992 an executive of Archer–Daniels Midland,[22–24] a giant food company, approached the FBI with allegations of a price-fixing conspiracy with its competitors. The whistle-blower taped a series of corporate conversations that led to a government investigation that was continuing three years later. The inquiry caused the company to undertake an internal investigation, which discovered that at least $9 million of corporate money had been found in overseas accounts controlled by some executives.

In the days following this disclosure, the whistle-blower was charged by the company with stealing the money; the company fired him and accused two others. Another executive was dismissed in October 1995. Those fired or forced out claimed that the $9 million had been paid with the knowledge and consent of their superiors. Whatever the outcome, it was clear that lack of oversight—internally and externally—had led the company astray.

While we entrust our treasure and freedom to accountants, bankers, brokers, and lawyers, we entrust our bodies and minds to doctors and academics. Because we feel that they are ostensibly driven—and maybe even inspired—by higher motives than crass profits, we tend to expect higher levels of morality from doctors and teachers.

3

Whom Can You Trust?

The most disquieting effects of white collar crime lie in the betrayal of trust by practitioners in such hallowed institutions as medicine, law, religion, and other exalted professions. These highly rewarded and regarded guilds require deep and extensive training and preparation. The professions are marked by the loftiest moral aspirations and are characterized by their devotion to altruism. The rest of us surrender our treasures, our persons, and our hopes to the ministration of these talented and privileged experts.

The evidence seeping through the cracks in these edifices creates the unease accompanying a society coming apart. This restiveness is reflected in vague slogans like "decline in family values" and is, equally vaguely, often described as a sort of "societal malaise."

CHARITY AND NONPROFIT

Even organizations entirely reliant on the high opinion of voluntary contributors—whose very existence depends on the confidence of the public—are not exempt from betrayals.

The man who led The United Way[1] for 22 years was convicted, along with two principal aides, of looting that charity to subsidize a lavish lifestyle that apparently required more than the $463,000 in salary and perks he received in 1992. The three were charged with stealing over $1 million, were convicted in April 1995, and were sentenced to seven years in prison. That part of the thefts involved maintaining a teenaged mistress—by a CEO in his sixties—added to the tawdriness tarnishing an organization that sought to help millions across the nation and that pitched a lot of its appeal to couch potatoes watching professional football on television.

While this poisoned the very well-springs of altruism, the nation was further sickened by the turmoil wracking the most important fighter of racism—the National Association for the Advancement of Colored People.[2]

In the NAACP's case the abuses involved the board chair depleting the treasury to support a luxurious lifestyle and the settlement of a sexual harassment suit against the organization's CEO. The latter scandal was attempted very covertly, but news leaked out. Both officers were ousted in acrimonious battles, and the odor lingered over a once-revered organization.

With two hallowed institutions that are desperately needed to alleviate the plight of the poor, the downtrodden and ill, and victims of racism now stained beyond much hope of cleansing, where could a citizen look for untainted vehicles of altruism?

Foundations, colleges, hospitals, human service charities, and even religious groups were, in 1995, reporting salaries in the hundreds of thousands for CEOs. It was careerism run riot. And this from the very people supposed to lead the battles to serve humankind. Scandals permeated the charity fundraising industry as embezzlements—such as that of a group that worked to cure Parkinson's disease—surfaced in 1995, further chipping away at altruism. Added to this were the high administrative costs connected to fundraising, which made contributors even warier.

BEHIND THE HEADLINES

Rarely do scandals and tragedies strike out of the blue—they more frequently emerge from the gray of greed and attempts at quick profits.

A Harlem building collapses, killing three tenants, in March 1995, and the hitherto largely ignored records reflect complaints, failed inspections, and other signs fairly screeching for correction.

Behind the deaths lay neglect, avarice, and the opaque realities created to conceal the truth. The resulting inquiry revealed solid connections to officialdom: expert knowledge of the labyrinth of the real estate industry and smart lawyers concocting clever defenses.

Behind all this lie half-done repairs, papered-over flaws, and frauds that are not always directly traceable to identified victims or disasters. The constants are that victims and disasters will occur, but the variables are whether the connections between cause and effect can be established.

Dummy corporations, bribes, faked documents, and other strategies are intended to blur the link between the mangled bodies in the rubble and the greedy operators who set the collapse in motion. Ironically, though, the event is almost certain to produce legislation that specifically addresses the tragedy in question—thereby adding to the tangle of regulations lending employment to the experts, but neither enhancing the public's safety nor making the process more responsible.

MEDICINE AND ACADEME

As President Bill Clinton pressed for healthcare reforms that contained the threat of "socialized medicine," doctors scurried to ally themselves with giant health-providing corporations and began behaving like entrepreneurs as they invested in home-care providers.[3] One company, T2 Medical, reported that the number of doctor investors had risen from 650 in 1988 to over 2200 in 1992. The potential for conflicts of interest, as doctors lock-in the prospect of referrals to such companies, is vast. A 1991 New York City study found that home-care providers charged up to $9000 for a month's supply of an intravenous food supplement that cost $1300. It was obvious what such gouging was doing to medical costs.

Some university medical schools have combined with drug companies and other outside interests to promote drugs and treatments, which greatly enriches professors while raising conflict-of-interest questions that center on the school's reliance on objectivity and neutrality as it evaluates, tests, and experiments new methods and drugs. Some have promoted the sale, use, and distribution of drugs not cleared by the Food and Drug Administration—patently illegal behavior, but undertaken under the noble rubric of medical altruism. This rationale, however, is undermined by the millions of dollars involved and the sometimes tragic results.

The University of Minnesota's antilymphocyte globulin (ALG) drug was used in transplants to combat organ rejection and was sold widely despite being considered experimental and not eligible for such dissemination. A far-ranging inquiry was launched, by the FBI and other federal agencies, in December 1992. Guilty pleas and indictments came down in August 1995.

As if to prove how the loftiest objectives can be debased to the crassest outcomes, the world-famous transplant center of the University of Minnesota was rocked again, in 1995, by charges that its revered practitioners had concealed information on nine deaths, had lied about the costs of producing a "miracle drug" to enhance profits, and—inevitably—had failed to pay the requisite taxes. The trial began on January 16, 1996 in Minneapolis.[4,5]

Here was the very citadel of Hippocrates, the intellectual jewel of the state devoted to medical research and highly publicized miracles, corrupted to the lowest personal purposes.

With the revelations came the dismaying evidence of a callous indifference to the fate of dying patients. Instead of behaving like an institution devoted to education, training, and research, the prospect of enrichment led the school to act entrepreneurally—turning some of its teachers into millionaires. Lack of oversight, greed, and administrative reluctance to investigate many warning signs—dubbing each disclosure an isolated incident—led to a broad scandal engulfing the entire institution, tarnishing reputations, and worse. The former head surgeon was acquitted in February 1996, but not before apologizing on the stand for a series of fiscal errors, oversights, and excesses. The reputation of the once-eminent university's transplant program had, by then, been irretrievably muddied.

In still another University of Minnesota case, the school's top child psychiatrist, Dr. Barry Garfinkel, was convicted of filing false statements on his research into an antidepressant drug, Anafranil.[6] His faked reports to the FDA undermined the integrity of the drug-testing system. He'd been turned in by an associate who'd been pressured to file false reports.

Occasional cases, such as the doctor convicted of murder in 1995 for his reprehensible indifference to human life and incompetence in performing an abortion in which the patient died, reveal how flaccid the licensing oversight over many professionals can be. This doctor had, as long as a decade earlier, been shown to be grossly negligent, yet had gotten off with a meaningless brief suspension.

In contrast, in 1995 Dr. Benjamin Spock, at 92, decried the erosion of spiritual values. He cited violence, divorce, teenage pregnancy, and the decline of standards relating to respect, compassion, and understanding. He very shrewdly observed the symbolic importance of manners, dress, and art in depicting the decline of values.

Using an 1863 law (the False Claims Act) that enabled the federal government to grant a reward of 15% of the full recovery of a fraudulent charge to the whistle-blower, the universities of Utah and California, in mid-1994, paid $1.6 million to settle charges that they had helped a faculty member cover up scientific misconduct. The researchers had falsified information about the immune substances produced by the body when the skin is burned. Under the agreement, the scientist had to publish both letters of retraction in journals that had published his ersatz articles from 1978 to 1984 and corrections of articles published in four journals from 1985 to 1987.

Rockefeller University,[7] one of the world's premier scientific research institutions, only recently rocked by a falsified data experiment scandal that shook the nation's scholars, was shaken again in 1994 by a series of unscholarly deeds that put the school on knife-edge. Threatening letters, poisoned sugar, open bunsen burners (creating the threat of an explosion if a match is lit or a spark emitted), and arsons terrified and sickened the most eminent researchers of the age. Although suspicion centered on a culprit early, no evidence had been adduced to produce an arrest. In the earlier case, repeated warnings and several lethargic investigations failed to uncover falsified data on an important experiment into immunology. It was only following the dogged pursuit of a determined scholar and the pressures of a suspicious politician that any substantive reforms were undertaken. The seemingly abstract search for scientific knowledge had its inevitable casualties.

Researchers in Cold War experiments exposed patients to intense radiation to test how much soldiers might endure in battle. Had the patients been informed? Had the treatments been, as doctors claimed, based on cancer research or on military necessity? However the cases were decided, it was clear from these and other incidents that the exigencies of the Cold War and the absence of oversight had tempted those in power—military and medical—to sacrifice means for ends that they had decided were worth the sacrifices.

In another mixing of medicine and politics, Baxter International Inc., the world's largest medical supply company, was ordered in 1993 to pay a $500,000 fine and $6 million in penalties for cooperating with Arab countries in their decades-old economic boycott of Israel. In an effort to escape an Arab blacklist, Baxter revealed, to the Arabs, details of its dealings with and charitable contributions to Israel. Safeway Stores Inc. paid almost $1 million in 1988 for cooperating with the boycott. Thirty cases were settled in 1992 for a bit over $2 million.

Jewish groups praised the actions.

The complexity behind criminal conduct may, in some cases, never be understood. How can the reported behavior of Dr. Orville Stone be explained?

Seeing patients for almost three decades—with no hint of impropriety—he apparently sent cancer tissue he had saved from patients for diagnoses that would raise the amount that insurance companies paid for treatments. Thus he'd be reimbursed at about three times the rate for removing noncancerous moles. He was reported, by five former employees, to have begun this practice in March 1992. In December 1992, the 61-year-old dermatologist walked in front of a huge rig and was run over and killed instantly.

In another case, Sepsis—a deadly bloodstream infection—was thought treatable by a new antiinfection drug, Centocor. In the early 1990s the drug was distributed in Europe—long-noted and frequently extolled for the speed with which it allows the introduction of new drugs to the market. American patients have been traveling to Europe and Mexico to get medicines not approved for distribution in the United States by the FDA. Shrill cries rose for its use, but the FDA requested an additional clinical trial.

In early 1993 the company, Centocor, said that the "data reflect[ed] an excess of mortality" among patients treated with the drug. They omitted numbers of deaths. The stock plunged from $11.12½ to $6.62½, after having flown as high as $60.25 in 1992.

Another drug maker, Bolar Pharmaceutical, saw its co-founder sentenced to 5 years for submitting fraudulent records to the FDA to obtain approval for the use of low-price blood-pressure treatment drugs.

In another case, National Health Inc. submitted false claims for tests they had assured doctors were free. They'd manipulate doctors into requesting tests for cholesterol and iron storage and submit bills as high as $18 a test to federal agencies. National's CEO pleaded guilty to two felonies in December 1992 and faced up to ten years in prison. The company agreed to refund $111 million to the government.

The Office of Technology Assessment, a congressional agency, conducted a study of drug companies that showed "excess profits"—even allowing for research, advertising, and distribution costs and risks. Even the growth of generic alternatives failed to stem the upward climb of prices and gains. Medicine, it developed, was an easy area for hidden profits, and the nation had the medical bill to prove it. Federal officials estimated that $80–$100 billion of the nation's $900 billion expenditures on healthcare in 1993 may have been due to medical fraud.

In the escalating battles between treaters and patients, Courtscan, a sort of medical practices record provider, promised Philadelphia doctors "complete litigation histories of patients, in 60 seconds or less" for $80 a month. This would enable doctors to screen patients who might be "malpractice prone."

In yet another scandal, C.R. Bard Inc. pleaded guilty to more than 390 counts of fraud and human experimentation for selling untested heart catheters, the result of which was one death and 22 emergency heart surgeries. The company agreed to pay $61 million to the recipients of the devices. Six company executives were indicted separately. Catheters, of course, are tubes that are inserted in blocked veins to facilitate the flow of blood, a sort of human Roto-Rooter. The FDA charged that the company had concealed critical negative information as it marketed its product.

In the Bronx, New York, junkies were given drug prescriptions in exchange for scores of sonograms they had to submit to and hand over. They were selling records of their bodies in exchange for prescriptions that enabled them to get drugs, much as alcoholics regularly sell their blood for cash. The records were distributed to radiologists, who would submit them to the state's Medicaid program for payment. The owner of M.S. Medical Associates was charged with stealing over $500,000 from the government. New York State had, as of late 1993, charged 40 persons with stealing more than $5.3 million in radiology and ultrasound frauds, creating a rare instance of symbiosis between street and white collar criminals.

The risks facing street criminals and their clients or victims are reflected in New York's Rikers Island prison population of 14,000 inmates: a quarter have syphilis, another quarter are mentally ill, and more than three quarters are drug users. There are 140 inmates with contagious tuberculosis. Of the women inmates, 27%

are HIV positive, 30% have sexually transmitted diseases, and 10% are pregnant. Jail is frequently their only opportunity for health-care, parenting classes, or drug treatment.

When the National Institutes of Health conducted a clinical trial of a drug to treat hepatitis B, the experiment ended disastrously, with the deaths of five of the 15 patients. Additionally, two of the ten survivors required liver transplants. All of this was simply a tragedy: The real problem stemmed from a government doctor's suspending the treatment to one of the survivors because the patient complained that his reports of toxic effects of the drug had been ignored for months. The National Institutes of Health organized a committee to investigate the charges. Depriving the patient of needed treatment appeared to be a new way to punish whistle-blowers, not to mention its effect on the public's confidence in its government.

Increasingly, doctors are being accused of sexual molestation of patients being examined or of the helpless patients who have been drugged for treatment. This violation of trust has its echo in the sexual exploitation of innocent youths by Catholic priests, in sexual harassment in the workplace, and in egregious abuses by highly placed officials. And yet, the world is so constructed as to require all of us to place our fates and bodies under the control of others whom we are forced to trust. The notion of being sexually molested while recovering from an operation, for example, is an unsettling thought that gets the herd shifting restlessly in the meadow.

In upstate New York, nursing home officials discovered a comatose woman's swelling stomach. This beautiful 29-year-old had been in a coma since an automobile accident a decade earlier. Examination yielded the incredible finding that she was pregnant. The rapist had not been identified as of the moment of discovery in January 1996. Another anecdote of the risks surrounding even those who are helpless and "protected."

A generalized abstraction comes with the comment of the state's Attorney General—who is charged with such inquiries—who reported that his office receives 1000 complaints about abuses in nursing homes each year.[8]

The New York Times reported that a university hospital secretly tested pregnant women for drug use and coerced them, under threat of arrest, into treatment. From 1989 to early 1994 over 40 women were arrested in South Carolina in an attempt to protect the fetuses. The experiments were widely criticized as violating the confidentiality of the doctor–patient relationship and raised the issue of informed consent (the women had all signed releases when beginning pregnancy treatments as a condition of such treatments). A collateral question, not raised in the controversy, was whether this constituted a violation of the Fourth Amendment's prohibition of unreasonable searches.

The end—protection of unborn babies—was noble; the means were patently abusive. It was another good example of what can happen when good intentions are not carefully evaluated. This is worth noting because the wrongdoing had been undertaken in the name of protecting the fetuses. Criminal means will alter the loftiest ends.

In April 1994, National Medical Enterprises Inc. agreed to pay $362.7 million to the federal government and admitted to seven charges of fraud and patient abuse. The corporation was alleged to have held patients who did not need psychiatric hospitalization against their will until their insurance coverage ran out. More than 50 doctors were said to have referred insured patients in exchange for kickbacks. The company acknowledged it had been overzealous in its pursuit of patients. The company also faced a flood of lawsuits from shareholders, patients, insurers, and, of course, the government. A former executive pleaded guilty to bribery and kickbacks and agreed to testify against colleagues. Two of National Medical's founders resigned and other top executives left in the wake of the scandal.

Referrals—indicating the potential for a corrupt partnership between drug suppliers and doctors—have often proved tempting routes to unworthy enrichment. An Edina, Minnesota, pediatric endocrinologist, three officials of Caremark International, Inc.[9–11] and the corporation itself were indicted in August 1994 for engaging in a referral-for-kickback scheme that netted the Edina doctors over $1.1 million.

Dr. David R. Brown was charged with referring patients to the company, resulting in millions in sales of Protropin, a synthetic human growth hormone to treat glandular disorders. The payments were allegedly disguised as research grants. Both Genentech and Caremark executives were acquitted of making false payments in October 1995, but Dr. Brown remained under charges.

In another case, Caremark was sued for grossly overbilling an insurance company in connection with the treatment of AIDS patients in Atlanta. In that case the treating doctor received from 25% to 33% of the patients' charges. The treating doctor advertised in a gay publication and was recommended by AIDS sufferers. One patient, who had a $1-million policy, was advised to get his drugs from Caremark, using a predesignated pharmacy. He never saw a bill until he lost his job and the bills arrived at his home. The amounts were staggering. He and other patients were dismissed to charitable care when the policies were drained. The company denied the charges. Caremark Inc. paid $161 million to settle the patient-referral kickback scheme. Critics used the case to illustrate some of the factors driving American health costs skyward.

An entire economy has developed around the treatment of AIDS. Diet supplements hold out the promise of retained health—unethically, if legally. Exploitations range from the practices described here to the gamut of questionable commercial ventures that seem to hold out the hope of health, but that take care not to overstep the bounds of legality.

The American public was increasingly exposed to disclosures outlining the most egregious misdeeds in a profession hitherto assumed to have been pursuing the highest-minded objectives. Everywhere one turned there came more evidence of the slippage.

The National Cancer Institute knew, for three years, that the data submitted in connection with a treatment that changed medical approaches to breast cancer were false, yet it failed to act until prodded by the threat of a congressional investigation in 1994. Tens of millions of taxpayer dollars were spent on this fraud, yet the agency did little to investigate, nor did it insist on the publication of corrections.

In a case that demonstrated the creative heights that the inventive might scale—again without breaching the law—a doctor precluded the publication of articles critical of his client's interests in a prestigious medical journal while writing, and ensuring the inclusion, of his own apologia.

Dr. Peter H. Schur helped write an article defending breast implants and, as editor of *Arthritis & Rheumatism*—an eminent publication in the field—had it included in the February 1994 issue. Dr. Schur had rejected two papers critical of implants, which were later published elsewhere.

While engaged in all these professional pursuits dealing with enormously controversial and widely litigated medical questions, he neglected to mention that he'd been employed by lawyers representing implant makers.

This may not have been a breach of law, but it certainly looked like an act of sophistry.

On December 20, 1994, doctors Peter Schur and Matthew Liang agreed to resign from the largest study of the safety of breast implants because of their work with the lawyers defending manufacturers of the implants.

The concern expressed centered on the "appearance of a conflict of interest," not, a spokesperson hastened to reassure, because of any wrongdoing.

The breast implant controversy, ironically largely centering on narcissism raised to heroic proportions, finally spawned its own cottage industry of clients, doctors, and lawyers suing the implant manufacturers.

A consumer advocate group charged, in 1994, that Upjohn & Co. had falsely reported on side effects of a sleeping pill, Halcion,[12] that the company knew to be serious. The corporate spokesperson called the initial failure to report the side effects a mistake that was later corrected.

The paranoia and severe anxiety experienced by 30% of those tested were not reported to the FDA by the manufacturer. Britain, Belgium, the Netherlands, and other countries forbade the sale of Halcion. The FDA said that Upjohn sacrificed users' safety for additional sales. Lower doses of Halcion and using it fewer than 14 days made the drug safer, but FDA investigators cited an internal corporate memo that stated that limiting usage to 14 days halved the sales.

A manufacturer of prescription creams and gels was cited by federal marshals in mid-1993 for having rodents and insects at its plant, threatening contamination. A total of $700,000 worth of stock was seized. Yet, there were skeptics who found the government too intrusive, too large, and too irrelevant to the daily concerns of American entrepreneurs. It was, they often said, another good example of how bureaucrats "interfered with capitalism's wholesome energies."

Advances in medical technology have led to criminal charges for the destruction, or illegal commercialization, of genetically engineered cells. In one case, the motive was simple jealousy, or revenge against a competing scientist. In the other, it concerned the commercial use of a patient's cells for the treatment of other sufferers without the donor's permission.

As genetic and cell engineering enter the explosive uses expected just ahead, the temptations will grow exponentially. All recent evidence points to the all-too-real threat of abuse by once-revered professionals.

Lay persons have joined the parade of medical criminals by cunningly tampering with on-the-shelf patent remedies. That such tamperings frequently victimize unintended targets to cover the killer's true purposes seems to trouble the perpetrators little. The practice, first popularized in a sensational tampering with Tylenol, resurfaced in Tennessee in late 1992, when a 51-year-old man died from sodium cyanide poison contained in a crudely sealed packet of headache powder. Earlier, in August 1992, a husband was charged with trying to kill his wife with cyanide cold-remedy capsules to collect her insurance. The tampering led to a nationwide recall of Sudafed. As it happened, the wife lapsed into a coma, but recovered. Two other Tacoma, Washington, area purchasers were not as fortunate. They died. Such schemes require innocent suffering, such as the purchase and use of the substance by a stranger, to mask the killer's true design. The intended victim is meant to be one of a number of targets "unknown" to the poisoner. The suspect actually testified in the survivors' lawsuits against the cold remedy's manufacturer.

The man who built Phar-Mor Inc.[13] into a 300-store chain grossing $3 billion annually was charged, along with two other executives, with fraud and conspiracy. They were alleged to have inflated the company's worth to secure loans and investments. The total estimated to have been embezzled was just under $500 million. Inventory was alleged to have been overvalued, account receivables were overstated, and liabilities were understated. The money was assumed to have been used to finance the founder's odd attempts to gain acceptance and popularity through such ventures as a minor league basketball team, a 14,000-square-foot house, personal extravagances, and other attempts to impress. The company, privately held, was not subject to the usual scrutinies reserved for publicly traded corporations. The big losers were those who loaned money or who were owed for services or materials.

Mickey Monus, 45 when the scandal surfaced in 1992, had built Phar-Mor as a deep-discount drug store that bought huge quantities at special prices and sold them at big savings. Despite profits and growth, he was charged with altering the books for at least 6 years before the 1992 announcement of bankruptcy and the discovery of the fraud. His trial ended inconclusively, and he was tried again in 1995.

Some suggested that the massive fraud may have been caused by nothing more heroic than a nerdy guy's need for the adulation of his neighbors. He seemed to have, at least partially, got it, as the jury judging him couldn't agree on a verdict. Finally, in May 1995, he was found guilty and was later stunned to receive a sentence of nearly 20 years in prison. By then the toll was millions embezzled and over $1 billion lured from investors. His chief financial officer and his vice president pleaded guilty and testified against Monus.

EMPIRE

Those who protected the ill against ruinous costs—the insurers—were not themselves above maximizing gains by minimizing concern over their clients.

Lacerated by sudden, catastrophically costly medical crises, Americans invented nonprofit medical insurance that would pool and distribute the risks among contributors. Thus was Blue Cross born, in the mid-1930s, to cover hospital costs. It would be followed by Blue Shield, for doctors' fees, years later. By the early 1990s, there were 70 Blue Cross/Blue Shield organizations, covering 68 million Americans and processing Medicare for 30 million more.

The largest, Empire Blue Cross and Blue Shield (Cross and Shield often merged), covered almost half the population of the state of New York, or 7.6 million people. This figure declined precipitously in 1993 to 7.1 million, as a result of increased fees that drove many to other programs and left a host of clients bereft of any protection.

Altruistically providing a desperately needed service, these other programs were not organizations that inspired a lot of oversight or control, with totally predictable consequences.

Granted tax-free status, the insurers' fees and regulations were established by the state legislature—inviting the sprouting of lobbyists. Required to insure any applicant—ill or well—and at the prevailing cost (called the "community rate"), these organizations complained noisily of competitive disadvantages and fought hard for rate increases.

Empire, classically, testified how the ill health of its poorer clients created disproportionately high costs, which tended to drive out the more lucrative corporate accounts that brought thousands of healthy workers into the pool. Empire testified that they were losing their profitable clients to cherry-picking competitors.

Although Empire obtained discounts on rates it paid for hospital services, it registered a loss of $250 million in 1991–92 and a total loss of $600 million between 1987 and 1992. It attributed the losses to the defection of healthy customers and the costs connected to caring for the poor and ill that they were forced to admit.[14]

The 1992 legislature required other insurers to adopt community rates and forced them to accept high-risk customers. It also allowed Empire to raise premiums 25%.

Disturbed by troubling accounts of waste and mismanagement, the U.S. Senate, in 1993, launched an inquiry that quickly produced evidence that Empire had exaggerated its losses on community-rated clients and understated losses on the desirable corporate accounts. The investigation found that Empire had been misleading the New York State legislature for years.

Among the abuses discovered were gifts to employees that totalled $1.1 million from 1988 to 1992; the use of limousines and chauffeured cars for commuting; the rental of a corporate apartment, at $48,000 per year; the gift of free medical insurance, for life, for directors serving ten years or more; lavish presents; a personal security system for the chairman; and such perquisites as annual weekend seminars in luxury sites for board members. In an eerie reprise of Louis XIV's court, a masquerade ball required an expenditure of $3000 for masks.

All of this made the board very compliant to the CEO's wishes. The inside joke at Empire centered on the two sets of books kept—one for the dissemination of data to a few key operatives and the other for such popular consumption as the press, the public, or the organs of government. Empire's accountant—Arthur Andersen—supported Empire on the source of its losses before the state legislature. The Superintendent of Insurance, Salvatore Curiale, proved less than curious about Empire's slips and slides.

Empire's CEO, Albert Cardone, the recipient of all of the corporate largesse—and a $600,000 salary per year—was ousted in May 1993. The chief financial officer and two aides were fired in July 1993 for destroying documents and filing false data. That they had lied, thereby confirming the most prejudiced archetypes of the poor and excluded, and had followed policies that ultimately left thousands stripped of any protection seemed lost amid a welter of charges.

Louisiana, Maryland, and Colorado were found to exhibit lavish spending, poor management, large salaries, storied perks, and inept billing practices that failed to properly collect money due the organizations and that regularly allowed the use of unauthorized providers of medical care.

Mississippi's CEO earned $700,000 per year.

The West Virginia system collapsed in 1990, leaving 51,000 persons with unpaid medical claims.

Meanwhile there were no shortages of corporate planes, fancy trips, club memberships, and other client-financed, but not client-aiding, privileges.

And yet, these protectors of Americans' health had been cunning enough to avoid the errors of the Savings and Loan sharks. These executives broke faith, but not the law. They took what they could and, mostly, carefully avoided crossing over the line that led to jail. They had not in the main, though, lost their chutzpah, as they whined about being discovered and ousted. They also lent their talents to the interdiction of any attempts to provide all Americans with basic health services in the big debate of 1994.

Medicine continues as one of the sacred cows of our society. Much is made of the fact that we have the best medical care in the world—and we do. Less is made of the fact that we also have the worst—at least for those at economic interstices. And nothing at all seems to be made of the fact that we have the costliest system and continue as the one industrialized nation that doesn't provide all of its citizens with medical protection.

We do all this because our system is driven by the Darwinian logic of our capitalist society, which does very little to temper its distributive cruelties while doing a lot to fan the flames of its competitive energies.

Forgotten in all this is that sickness causes all of us to suspend our normal cautions and thrusts us onto the mercies of persons and systems on which we must rely, without the protections all other advanced nations provide their citizens.

As 1995 was closing, the American government was seized by a paroxysm of worry over spiraling health costs that threatened disaster. A frantic search to arrest the steep rise was underway as the sacred cow of Medicare came under beady-eyed, green-shaded scrutiny. The would-be reformers knew there was fraud and that a very large portion of any person's lifetime medical bill would be rung up in the first six and last six months of life, but the problem was approached with the caution borne of the knowledge that seniors don't forget, and they vote.

Medicaid produced such grotesqueries as driving its clients to hugely expensive emergency rooms for routine care. That there was a crisis, across the board, seemed beyond dispute.

WHAT MIGHT BE DONE?

With our most admired citizens exposed and our most cherished institutions convicted, how is integrity to be preserved?

Two things are needed for a moral society—virtue and controls.

As the charms of an unblemished life and the value of an unsullied name decline, the deficit must be addressed by ratcheting up the negative incentives keeping persons and institutions from faltering. The strategies employed to ensure the integrity of society should include:

- The need for corporate democracy:
  - Greater shareholder involvement in deciding major issues.
  - Deeper participation by knowledgeable, independent, and representative directors.
- The need for regulations:
  - Governmental involvement in ensuring product safety, fiscal integrity, and the maintenance of a healthy environment.
  - Recognition of the folly of thinking we can devise both a fair and a simple tax system—the graduated income tax is complex, but fair, and ought to be used to limit rapaciousness at the highest economic reaches and level the economic playing field; the sales and flat taxes are simple, but terribly unfair in the disproportionate weight with which they fall on the poor.
- Lobbying and electoral reform:
  - A lobbyist register and gifts listed and limited to no more than $100 a year.
  - Election campaigns paid out of tax dollars, with maximum expenditures listed for different offices.

- Use of sting operations to uncover frauds.
- Requiring audits and holding auditors accountable for their accuracy.
- Consumer protection laws to prohibit frauds and require truth and accuracy.
- Requiring disclosures of investments by those touting stocks or other vehicles for making money.
- Licensing persons who trade in public trust:
  - Should include background investigation.
  - Check with previous employers.
  - Financial, criminal, and personal history.
- Recognizing the value of free market dynamics, but also the danger of "purism":
  - Elimination of regulations, controls, and "government interference" will accelerate rapaciousness and spread fraud.
  - Laws and regulations should be aimed at fraud and danger—not at "excessive profits."
- Encouraging competition.
- Rewarding and recognizing whistle-blowers.
- Involving the media in attacking wrongdoing.
- Socially useful punishment:
  - Restitution, fines, and community service.
  - The importance of shame—negative publicity and public humiliation are more important than generally realized.
- Eliminating personal bankruptcy that permits asset-protecting loopholes.
- Using statutes similar to the Racketeer Influenced and Corrupt Organizational Act to proceed both criminally and civilly.

What the history of the last 20 years has displayed is an alarming erosion in America's integrity—whether that centers on honored persons or hallowed halls. If the descent is to be arrested, we are going to have to question the effects of a social, economic, and racial system that is creating sharpening division between an overclass and an underclass.

4

Politics

Is there any profession in American life that has sunk as low as politics in the people's esteem?

The jibes of stand-up comics, the targets of satirists, holders of elected office are high on any list of the most scorned among us. That the legal profession—a frequent companion of public office—should share a parallel assessment shouldn't surprise us. The two professions, politics and the law, go together. It is no happenstance that elected officials are dubbed lawmakers.

Polls attempt to establish what statistics cannot measure, such as levels of confidence, degrees of trust, weight of skepticism, or prevalence of cynicism surrounding any institution or idea. Americans are angry at their government and mad as hell at its component parts.

Why is this and how has it come about?

Whenever we are called to analyze an event as vast as the decline of a civilization, the temptation is strong to search for the cataclysm. It is insulting to think that the life of a great nation can be changed by the sullen grievances of one of its least significant citizens. To this day we find it at least psychically unacceptable that a worm like Lee Harvey Oswald could alter the course of this great ship.

Yet the reality is that societies are sharpened or dulled more by the quotidian acts and numberless mundane transactions of the colorless minions than by the epic feats of a few heroes. As millions of cells fight daily battles within our bodies, the onset of disease occurs at the unknown moment when the forces of illness experience an imperceptible shift in their favor.

What drives a people to look first to private gain, following centuries of focusing on the nation's destiny or the family's progress? There is always corruption—and always reform and good works—yet societies start disintegrating when the inner rot of decadence begins to outpace the rate of regeneration.

Americans are increasingly fond of blaming the media—especially such offenders as rap songs, violent or sexy movies, or consumerist television—for the corruption of the nation's soul, but wiser observers might hold that the arts reflect our society more than they shape it. Our creative geniuses are, like Cassandra, prophets, and, like Priam's daughter, often cursed by disbelief. Socrates, after all, was executed because he "corrupted" the youth of Athens through his subversive insistence on examining forbidden questions. We harbor the conceit that we have no forbidden questions, but it is absurdly simple to prove that there are many areas of life that remain inviolate to our scrutiny.

As with the arts, it is altogether likely that politics and those who hold elected office are nothing more than mirror reflections of who we are as a people. Why is it that no one ever says that if we are to have better leaders we'll have to become a healthier people? It is no accident that the executed Socrates forever enjoined his fellow citizens to look within first. Instead Athenians found it easier to force hemlock on him.

The temptation to blame outside forces is irresistible: the need to look within is easy to resist. Thus do we rail at politicians and lawyers for looking after themselves, when we clearly need them to look after the public good and search for justice.

In examining public life we will be analyzing individual misdeeds that, when added up, amount to what was quoted earlier: "Everybody cheats—you'd be a fool not to."

What has proved increasingly difficult for our leaders to grasp is that the major forces pulling at them are the lobbyists seeking millions at the expense of a public that stands to lose pennies. The lobbyist is there—charming, flattering, helpful in elections, and grateful—and the people are an absent abstraction; many of them don't bother to vote and make little effort to remain even minimally informed. The lobbyists' spin doctors have learned how to manipulate the information to make it palatable even to those it is intended to harm.

Multiplied enough times, the visceral sense takes hold that you'd better grab what you can, while you can. Humans are terrifyingly susceptible to the allures of panic flight or uncontrolled graspings. The appetites are always there, nudging to be sated. So, are we more or less honest and devoted to the public weal than we were in 1795 or 1895? Or are we more or less obsessed with hand-wringing self-excoriations today?

In the corporate world we've seen how the "everybody's doing it" syndrome has created the need for tighter controls and more sweeping and draconian monitorings—at precisely the time when these "hamstringings" are being broadly attacked by those being restrained. The catch-phrases are, "Government is evil— let's neutralize and diminish it," and "regulations are cumbersome and serve only as excuses for bureaucrats to shackle capitalism's energies."

What is the natural consequence of the broadly held view that government is evil?

Programs are attacked not on the basis of their effectiveness, but simply because the government can't be trusted to do anything.

And yet, even in this nihilism there is a touching faith in building more prisons, hiring more cops, and appointing tougher judges.

The acceptance of these contradictions precludes the debate without which real understanding becomes impossible. And it will never occur to those pouring resources into these unquestioned black holes that they are perfect replicas of their predecessors' actions in supporting a huge defense establishment. The connection between crushing defense expenditures, hiring more cops, and building more jails—and the growth of government— seems never to occur to the advocates of these policies who simultaneously oppose bigger government.

Where is the examination, the introspection, the search within?

What the litany of wrongdoings illustrates is America's passion for action and aversion to thought. The Vietnam hawks were doers, the critics were wimps—or so ran the wisdom of the day.

Despite being, potentially—in terms of the breadth and depth of the material available—the best-informed people the world has ever seen, we are pitifully unwilling to ask the hard questions necessary to find our way to the truth. For decades we accepted the labeling of The Evil Empire without cavil. Now we embrace the charms of capitalism without regard to its cruelties, excesses, or crimes.

The debate in Washington, D.C., is not over values or social, economic, or racial justice; it is about which party will deliver what the American people seem to want—not what they need, but what they want. It is the mistaking of pleasing with serving.

Despite lip service to family and community values, many of those running for office fractured their families, avoided serving their country, betrayed spouses, or otherwise violated the very principles they espouse so fervently. Ronald Reagan was the first divorced person elected to the presidency. It would be an instructive lesson in public morality to survey all presidential aspirants for the incidence of divorce, service to country, connection to suspect enterprises, and actual wrongdoings in their backgrounds. The chances are that, whatever is disclosed, our sense of outrage is now so diluted as to inspire the question, "So what?"

Many have been tainted by connections to meretricious deals. Few have had the grace to bald-facedly acknowledge truth, preferring to rely on the prestidigitations of cunning public relations experts.

Bob Dole's presidential campaign revealed a 1995 letter from a potential contributor that said: "I know I can't afford enough to get Italy. But how much would I have to give for New Zealand? Could you please send me a complete price list?"[1]

It was all pretty laughable, except that the writer had served as envoy to the Netherlands after a $100,000 contribution to the Republican Party during George Bush's 1988 campaign.

Solemn oaths are taken in the name of attacking welfare cheats, and the cities are happily abandoned. The ghettos are furnished drugs and alcohol—but not jobs, schools, or hope. Corporations receive lavish legal concessions in exchange for their contributions, while some betray the nation by trading with the enemy or circumventing the most passionately held convictions of our people—such as our frustrated fury over the actions and words of regimes such as Iran's.

"If the salt shall lose its flavor, wherewith shall it be savored?"

If our leaders sacrifice our interests for their private gain, where can we turn for help?

The massive abandonment of the ballot by a people aware that our founders—and subsequent generations—risked, and sometimes lost, their lives to ensure it; the rise of cults and sects promising answers to a troubled people; and the escape into the delusions of entertainment and sports all presage flight from what used to be called *American ideals*. Even our describing every event, whatever its character, in terms of whether we "enjoyed" it or not subconsciously transmits the message that all transactions are to be evaluated on the basis of the pleasure they deliver or withhold. Blacks, never as politically active, were, in the 1990s, even less so.

The fact that the 1992 presidential election was the first in American history in which suburban votes outnumbered urban depicts the shift in power from the city to the suburbs, from black to white, from poor to relatively prosperous.

A glimpse along the political landscape reveals a barren desert of values. The world's most powerful club—the United States Senate—today contains men and women who have been accused or proved guilty of a dazzling array of wrongs. And they leave office loudly proclaiming not just their innocence, but also their nobility. Whatever the nature of these wrongs, the indirect but ultimate victims were the people. Is the behavior of Caligula relevant because of the suffering of his victims or because of its impact on the people of Rome?

Would it have be altogether too hyperbolic to claim that the general mood of Americans toward politics is a thinly masked frustration that has its expression in massive disgust and withdrawal?

How else to respond to the actions of the New York state senate's new majority leader? Senator Joseph L. Bruno theorized in early 1995 that black and Hispanic New Yorkers "are the people that got their hands out. They are the ones fighting for welfare." A storm of criticism produced a tepid apology to "those people that feel offended." He, nevertheless, stood by his tough assessment. *The New York Times* fully reported the development and, in another inquiry, revealed that Mr. Bruno's son, his son-in-law, his brother, and his daughter all found jobs paying from $34,000 to over $73,000 on the New York State payroll.

The newly elected New York state attorney general—the state's preeminent law enforcer—swept out the old and installed friends, donors, allies, and the powerfully connected in posts formerly unpoliticized upon taking office in January 1995, carefully skirting outright illegality.[2]

A study by the Consumer Federation of America and Common Cause, issued on August 31, 1995, found that one in five members of state legislatures serving on committees regulating the insurance industry had professional ties to the industry as employees, accountants, lawyers, or in other positions.

No, or few, abuses were found in states with tough conflict-of-interest laws, while flagrant conflicts were evident in states without such restricting legislation.

These were, of course, the persons writing the laws for the regulation of the insurers.

In another New York State case, an executive of Sweet N' Low pleaded guilty to making illegal political contributions, in federal court, on April 12, 1995. His company lobbied against the banning of saccharin, a key ingredient in its sugar substitute, and one that the Food and Drug Administration had found, as early as 1977, could, in large doses, cause cancer. Congressional legislation resulted in a suspension of the FDA's ban.

And, as the 1995 Congress cranked up, a new assault on the Endangered Species Act was underway. This 22-year-old effort to reverse or mitigate the ravaging of nature was about to suffer the attacks of corporate interests frustrated by "tree huggers."

On the other side of the scale were deforestation, smog, a burning river, the spoliation of public and private lands, Appalachian coal mines scarring the earth, and a global warming that served as an ecological Sword of Damocles over the planet. In the push–pull world of environmentalists and free-booters,[3] the latter were about to have another turn at bat.

The Secretary of Agriculture was forced from office because of gifts from corporate interests with ties to Arkansas and the Clintons. The secretary would confidently assert—as the allegations surfaced—that he'd be cleared. In late 1995 the Energy Secretary was accused of spending public funds on improperly monitoring press coverage of her agency and on lavish travel spending—with atrocious record-keeping of these uses of taxpayer dollars.

The Secretary of Housing and Urban Development was fighting charges that he lied about payments to a former mistress in seeking appointment to the cabinet.

The Secretary of Commerce was repeatedly charged with suspect connections to slum housing projects and loan defaults and was, in 1995, the target of investigations by the Justice Department, the Federal Deposit Insurance Corporation, and congressional Republicans. All of these ceased with his tragic death in a plane crash in Croatia in early 1996.

The Transportation Secretary was cleared of allegations that his firm had received funds, for investment, from Los Angeles transit officials managing a pension fund when it became clear he was headed to Transportation and would be in a position to help with the building of the Los Angeles transit system. The secretary had severed ties with the firm bearing his name and had sold his stock at a loss. His actions stood in stark contrast to the cloudier dealings of some of his colleagues in the cabinet.

President Bill Clinton's nominee for Attorney General was humiliatingly withdrawn when it was discovered that the nation's top law enforcer might be a law violator herself, having hired two illegal aliens for child care and household help. For a President who'd promised a break with the sleazy past, it seemed an ugly echo of his predecessor's failed efforts to appoint as Secretary of Defense, in 1989, a senator alleged to have engaged in excessive drinking and womanizing.

Such other reversals as the call for the Surgeon General's resignation following statements that seemed counter to national policy on drugs and sex education, seemed much more a continuation of business as usual than the break with the special interests promised in Clinton's campaign book, *Putting People First*. The Surgeon General was finally driven from office for suggesting that masturbation might be taught as safe sex.

Even when the new administration was doing the right thing—as when it cleaned out the White House travel office in 1993—it appeared to be doing it for all the wrong reasons. It came out that a distant relative of the president had sought the ouster of the employees in order to profit from the lucrative travel business of newspeople and staff accompanying the president.

The head of the travel office was later indicted for theft of travel funds, but this vindication of judgment came too late to burnish the White House's reputation because of the motives perceived as motivating the "reforms." The head's acquittal on November 16, 1995, again raised the question of the appropriateness of the White House's handling of the event. The suicide of the deputy legal counsel on July 20, 1993, included a note in which he expressed worry over criticism in handling the travel office case in the days before his death.

The impression of inconsistency, disarray, and disappointment deepened. The expectations raised by the president's campaign were further diminished by his own perceived inconstancies and desire to please. As he sought to dismiss a press aide, it became embarrassingly clear that she extracted important concessions and delayed her departure. He was perceived to have waffled the gays-in-the-military issue tortuously. His concession to staffers and strident politicos was seen as a tendency to cave in under pressure. There was a reprise in his meanderings over the budget and whether to press for a tax cut, attack the budget deficit, or reduce government's involvement in the lives of Americans. On all these issues the president was seen as "turnable." His campaign had contained ringing calls for reform and change. As he neared the end of his term it was he who was seen as changeable. Even defense spending—an area in which the nation had looked to the dovish views of the Democrats to perhaps extract the elusive "peace dividend" from the morass—proved a disappointment as Clinton joined the hawks and seemed very anxious to make peace with a military he'd once scorned. He announced a $25-billion increase in military spending over the following six years as 1994 was ending.

The contemporary echo lay in his tough law-and-order stance and his hiring of 100,000 more cops without real debate, analysis, or discussion. Clinton was not going to let the Republicans paint his Democrats, or his administration, as being soft on crime. He proposed, and signed into law, a huge increase in spending on cops, prisons, and other accoutrements of the criminal justice system and greatly expanded the reach of capital punishment. The usurpation of local authority and the centering of all these expenditures, programs, and laws on the nation's capital somehow never entered the discussion over "big government and Washington interference."

Clinton's mindless, reflexive reaction in both cases—the military and crime—reflected a troubling suspicion that no particular philosophy lay at the core. The one sincere undertaking—universal healthcare—became his most humiliating defeat and probably confirmed his instinct to malleability.

His predecessor, George Bush, had presided over scandals in the Department of Housing and Urban Development (HUD) that, in 1996, resulted in a former cabinet officer, James Watt,[4] pleading guilty to a misdemeanor to satisfy what had been a 25-count felony indictment, reduced to 18; the incarceration of the treasurer for tax fraud; the ouster of a chief of staff as abuses of power such as travel perks for private errands surfaced; the sudden exit of officials accused of improperly searching the passport file of candidate Bill Clinton; and his own son's involvement in the S & L debacle.

And Iraq-gate, a sale of arms to a regime that became our enemy, involved the crimes of statesmen rather than self-enriching criminals at the top and wound its way through both the Reagan and Bush eras. A wonderful example of the cynical world of realpolitik.

Before that, there had been Watergate,[5] Vietnam[6] and its duplicities, and the ouster of a vice president. It seemed that only decent, hapless Jimmy Carter fulfilled the failed dreams of Americans for honor in office, and he was repudiated as inept; his mesmerism with the Iran hostages and apologies for such achievements as the Panama Canal treaty and transportation deregulation didn't help.

The contrasts between the scandals were wonderfully instructive. Watergate illustrated the dark, fascist suspicion of democratic processes entombed in the paranoid breast of Richard M. Nixon. Iraq-gate reflected the genial indifference to piracy that a good-natured Ronald Reagan brought to public and, very likely, private life. Bush, the quintessential caretaker and good corporate soldier, continued that toleration, in which, in both administrations, private gain and criminal governmental actions comfortably coexisted.

The Reagan–Bush years constituted the triumph of rugged individualism, capitalism, and the importance of winning. Neither regime seemed to engage in the tortured introspections of Carter or in the half-concealed sympathies for the underclass that peeked out from under Clinton's bushel. A philosophy that operated on the notion that all was fair in battling the Evil Empire wouldn't be expected to be particularly finicky over such ethical lapses as those that led to the indictment of the Interior Secretary or the ouster of the Attorney General—among other peccadilloes suffered by a band that will likely be judged, by history, as being among the most corrupt in history.

In just about his final act in office, in December 1992, President Bush pardoned six Reagan officials who had been criminally charged in the investigation relating to the secret and illegal sales of arms to Iran and the use of the proceeds to clandestinely support the Nicaraguans fighting the leftist government. It may all have been high-minded attempts to circumvent democratic processes in the name of fighting communism, but the profoundly subversive actions on the nation's institutional workings seemed to go unnoticed. And, it must be said, there was some measure of personal emolument involved as the line between personal expenditures and legitimate government payments sometimes got blurred.

That the funds got laundered through secret bank accounts reflected the interconnections between government and corporations needed to make such conspiracies work. The mostly successful cover-up of the Iran–Contra scandal involved, according to the Special Prosecutor's report of 1994,[7] the destruction of evidence, lies, and the withholding of testimony by senior officials. By the time the trail got too cold to follow, it was clear both presidents, Reagan and Bush, had knowledge of the activities. The national security adviser attempted suicide as the case was unraveling. In the final analysis the cover-up worked, and the American people were left with the vision of serious wrongdoing at the highest reaches of government going unpunished. One of the principal villains painted himself a hero, wrote a book, raised millions, and almost got elected to the U.S. Senate. He was defeated by a candidate who had been accused of partying suspiciously, bugging the conversations of a rival, and womanizing. None of it could have been called an edifying spectacle. The voters of Virginia learned what it meant to confront a Hobson's Choice.

Rather than outrage, a defeated air of fatal inevitability characterized the public's reactions to the numbing disclosures. The events dripped at the granite of public faith, gradually carving a niche in which evil could flow. As it deepened, the danger to the block of public trust deepened with it.

And still, that very public had resoundingly rejected the reborn Christian innocence of Jimmy Carter, favoring the glitzy smoothness of Ronald Reagan instead. It seemed the selection of a

CEO over a wispy dreamer to guide our destiny. Nice guys did finish last, and there was a heavy price to be paid for ensuring that result.

Bill Clinton brought his own baggage to his troubled presidency. First came the assaults on his patriotism, as his objection to the Vietnam War was transformed into draft-dodging. If he'd accepted prison, rather than Oxford, forgiveness might have accompanied the nation's new understanding of that tortured conflict. By the time he was asked if he'd ever done drugs, his waffling was etched in his answer that he'd smoked a bit of marijuana in England but had "not inhaled."

This was followed by charges of infidelity, but these lost steam when his wife stood by her man. The rule on such shenanigans appeared to be that the nation would accept whatever the wife would. After all, if, in the face of such resoundingly public humiliation, the spouse could say, "It's okay, I'm with him," and, however skimpy the fig leaf, accept his explanation, then the public would too. The operative rule was to not make infidelity the litmus test of character, as Gary Hart had done. Casting the gauntlet down in front of the Fourth Estate was to challenge that institution to dig hard for the truth.

The ticking bomb in Clinton's suitcase was Whitewater,[8] and, like the timepiece's tick-tocking in *Treasure Island*, its ominous reminders were, in a way, worse than any explosion. Whitewater and its associated deals—involving real estate developments, the raising and using of campaign funds, the accuracy of tax returns, a killing in the commodities market by Hillary Clinton, and even such minor stuff as favoring relatives in the travel office brouhaha—proved stark reminders of what might be called the sharp practices of these yuppies. It was as if the nation engaged in a semiotic exercise—among the entrails of past actions—for the omens pointing to the nature of a leader's character. Even Carter's own presidency had not been spared some taint, as his crony and budget director, Bert Lance, was driven from office amid charges about his questionable acts as a Georgia banker and his involvement in the earlier-mentioned BCCI scandal.

Whitewater looked like The Long March through Clinton's

presidency. Casualties occurred periodically, along the way, including Clinton's successor as governor of Arkansas.

A second indictment in August 1995 seemed closer to home, as the Clinton's partners, the McDougals, were charged and, along with the governor, convicted. Their response seemed to be the key to whether the inquiry would reach all the way to the White House.

Friends and aides pleaded guilty to one or another crime; others left office or got shunted into less visible roles, and one, as we've seen, committed suicide. And yet, it was a stealthy march, as the scandal inquiry wound along in stately quiescence for years. The Whitewater special counsel plodded on, curiously undisturbed by a Republican senator who had publicly salivated at the prospect of highly visible hearings. Alfonse D'Amato had had his own problems over utterances that proved offensive and over letting his brother—whose conviction was reversed on appeal—use the senator's office, name, and stationery to impress a client and garner a fee.

D'Amato's sudden acquiesence to delay hearings should have been a very ominous sign for the president. The appointment of a replacement as special counsel—now a Republican—certainly satisfied the senator's desire to push the inquiry all-out. By August 1994, Kenneth W. Starr was gearing up an investigative force that included 100 FBI agents. In a year he'd have a bunch of key figures convicted, including Clinton's successor as governor. The final act curtain was going up. Senator D'Amato's hearings on White House issues began in 1995 and continued with an interruption, conveniently, into the election year following.

Occasional disclosures or such action-spikes as guilty pleas became the thunderclaps emerging from Whitewater's darkening clouds, but the event seemed to just chug along at what looked like an inevitable, unavoidable, and unhurried pace. Polls reflected public ennui on the issue, but such calm could be deceptive. Frequently, the American people appear to be willing to let events take their course, so long as a course has been set. Expressions of outrage tended to be triggered by inaction—rather than by slow or not readily visible action.

The gavotte of Whitewater assumed a languorous rhythm. There would be an accusation or indictment, followed by ferocious claims of innocence; then would come a plea bargain—in which guilt would be asserted, *sotto voce*—and a deal to reach the next higher rung struck. It wasn't a "Stairway to Heaven," and there was no angelic chorus—only a grim and relentless ascension. In the confused wake of White House wanderings lay the suicide of Vincent Foster; the conviction of Webster Hubbell, the governor, and the Clintons' close associates; and gathering clouds over the Arkansas clan.

The effect of Whitewater and all the disclosures surrounding Clinton and his aides would only contribute to the prevailing public cynicism. The people—who railed at feckless caretakers or silently withdrew—never, somehow, harkened to the Socratic injunction to look within. Perhaps a better people would send a better class of person to our ruling councils, but this doubt never seemed to intrude into the thinking of the critics who found it much more fun to wish a pox on "all of them." In a democracy it appeared that people got just the type of government they deserved. Would it ever occur to the viewer that his representative was more representative than might be, superficially, imagined?

While the national landscape got writ large with the accounts of official wrongdoing, the less dramatic and visible local scenes did not reflect a morally inspiring, or even slightly contrasting, image.

THE LOCAL SCENE

Away from the Beltway the picture is no more heartening.[9] A successful candidate's political guru first asserts, then denies, that he'd spread cash around the African-American community to keep voters home. He attributed his remarks to "cynicism" as he repudiated them. His candidate had won and became the governor of New Jersey. The guru later tied up to Senator Robert Dole's bid for the Republican presidential nomination, but had to quit because of another public gaffe, this one offensive to Jews. He was finally driven to the ultimate extremity—the publication of a memoir.

Meanwhile, the Newark city government was being investigated for corruption and its schools system became the third that had to be taken over by the state's Education Department. Other New Jersey leaders—mayors and council members—joined the line-up of convicted felons. The spectacle at City Hall in 1996 was such as to confirm the wildest speculations of the most cynical citizen. The mayor stood by an aide in whose home investigators found $150,000 under floor boards and who was now indicted for accepting bribes.[10,11] Even the losing governor was a target of an inquiry into the handling of state bond business. Simultaneously, the State Commission of Investigation narrowly averted extinction in a 1994 vote of the legislature.

Across the street Pennsylvania's Crime Commission was decommissioned, in June 1994, after a quarter of a century's investigations of organized crime. In Philadelphia Frank Rizzo's mayoralty was followed by W. Wilson Goode's, and neither left office with their reputations enhanced—or the city much improved, by any observer's standard.

In Chicago, ex-convicts and former gang members claimed prior experience in urban ills as they ran for the city council in 1995. They lost, but vowed to return and "take us some power."[12]

Chicago aldermen complained of harassment by the federal government, which offered them bribes for such long-simmering problems as illegal dumping—often in poor neighborhoods. They felt unfairly singled out.

The federal prosecutor had a response—that as long as officials accepted these bribes, the government would go on offering them.[13]

In Alabama the part-time preacher who became governor was convicted of illegally converting money for his inauguration in 1993. Across the way, in Georgia, officials overseeing airport operations were convicted of accepting bribes to favor a business that was supposed to help minorities. In Missouri the former attorney general admitted to misapplying state funds. In Oklahoma the governor who'd pleaded guilty to a misdemeanor for encouraging a contributor to give more than the maximum ($5000) to his campaign refused to resign as a grand jury recommended he be impeached. The governor of Arkansas was convicted over campaign funding in 1996.

Even squeaky-clean Minnesota had its Minnesotan scandal, as hosts of legislators faced censure and worse for abusing phone-calling privileges. Its senior senator pleaded guilty to defrauding the government in August 1995 and decided against running again. He'd teach ethics instead, still proclaiming his innocence, despite having pleaded guilty. And, of course, there was the usual parade of officials arrested for driving while intoxicated and theft who had, in other circumstances, vigorously espoused the tough law-and-order stance we all loved so well. As the legislature recessed in 1996, its proud reputation lay in tatters.

Louisiana is worthy of its own book, in a history going back at least 100 years to the scandalous collapse of its privately owned lottery, in 1894, amidst a welter of charges of bribery, fraud, and corruption. It would be 70 years before New Hampshire was emboldened to kick off another round of lotteries in America. And Louisiana politicos were, in an echo of 1894, caught up in a wide and spreading scandal, again involving gambling payoffs, in 1995.

New Orleans police were, in the 1990s, regarded as little more than an out-of-control band of criminals from whom the public frequently sought protection. At least one murder plot was hatched over the police radio. The tape of the call was used in the prosecution of the killer of a drug informant the cops wanted eliminated. A cop-killer suspect was beaten to death in a police stationhouse and the city paid his family a whopping settlement in a civil lawsuit. The police, under a sort of federal receivership, as the feds investigated the many charges of wrongdoing, was arguably the country's worst department.

In Michigan, Detroit became the nation's paradigm for the results that fecklessness in office and middle-class flight could produce. In Kentucky a parade of legislators, lobbyists, and other public figures were filmed, by federal investigators, offering and pocketing bribes in connection with horse track betting and the regulation of hospitals. Citizens were treated to a ceaseless flow of evidence relating to widespread corruption in office.

In New York every election seemed to bring new charges of illegal contributions, extortions of firms doing business with government agencies, and calls for investigations. The innocent appeared to be those called on to handle the cover-ups, since they hadn't initiated the crimes but were simply impressed into the service of suppressing inquiries. In quick succession, the political bosses of Brooklyn and the Bronx were convicted and imprisoned for frauds connected to bidding contracts and other political corruptions, while the Queens chief spectacularly committed suicide to avoid disgrace.

In New Jersey the prosecutor in Somerset County was indicted on 33 counts that reflected allegations of such misdeeds, over 13 years in office, as tax fraud, extortion, and blackmail.

Across the river, the long-serving prosecutor in Rockland County was forced from office amid disclosures of an affair and the use of government officials as chauffeurs and gofers to facilitate trysts.

How many prisoners, languishing behind bars, got sent there by these officials? What might they be thinking?

New York City's head of health and hospitals resigned suddenly, in 1995, for "personal reasons." There were sympathetic cluckings over having suffered interference from City Hall. This public handwringing was followed by the disclosure that the head's former administrative assistant had charged him with sexual harassment.

But the crowning glory of governmental hopelessness had to reside in the nation's capital, where the convicted (for drug use) and discredited former mayor was able to persuade the voters that he was at least better than the incumbent and was returned to office. By the spring of 1995 he was fighting charges of misusing campaign funds.

Washington, D.C., in 1995 was also instructive for the futility it demonstrated for reliance on cops for safety. Easily the most heavily policed metropolis in the nation–with about three times the usual ratio of two cops for every thousand citizens, and lots of other police and law enforcement agents walking its streets—it was also the most violent. The irony that he could look out on the most heavily patrolled urban center in the country and see the homeless camping out in Lafayette Park seemed entirely lost on a president who, faced with appalling crime levels, called for more cops and never mentioned the underlying plight of the underclass producing all this misery. That he'd made repeated references to an "underclass" in his 1995 State of the Union address at least confirmed his familiarity with the problems, even as he averted his official gaze from such unpopular acknowledgments.

The obvious decline of the core cities was palpable evidence of the sort of service our officials were providing. Los Angeles became a case in point but was not, in any form, unique. When the malfeasance and misfeasance got mixed in with the nonfeasance of the front-line workers—protected by unions and civil service regulations from being held accountable for even the most egregious acts of official ineptitude—the rising tide of public despair, expressed in their withdrawal or cynicism, seemed unstemmable.

But how were those who'd fled to affluent suburbs faring?

Orange County

While we normally anticipate that it is individuals who will betray our trust, there are dramatic examples of institutions abetting the flight of public confidence.

Local government units finance capital projects with bonds that are backed by the "full faith and credit" of the issuing agency. This means that an important civic need can be met by officials who borrow the money for the project from citizens who rely on the government's avowed determination to meet its obligation to pay interest and redeem the principal eventually. The entire process is predicated on trust developed over decades of performance. Even New York City, in the awful fiscal crisis of 1975, laid off many thousands of cops rather than default on a single bond.

Orange County, California,[14] used its unencumbered funds to speculate wildly in the financial markets—with such enormous strings of success as to garner accolades and re-elections for those claiming credit for the coups. When the market predictably soured, recriminations flew. The fiscal wizard suddenly claimed ignorance and announced himself the dupe of Wall Street sharpsters. The county sued the broker that had handled the transactions.

The county treasurer was indicted on a wide array of charges relating to lying, falsifying records, and other attempts at deception. He pleaded guilty and left office.

So far the scenario had played out fairly enough, without much serious damage to public trust, beyond the actual scandal. The kicker came when Orange County hired a cunning lawyer who would erode the solemn contract entered between the government and the investing public by declaring bankruptcy, challenging the claims of bondholders, and defaulting on the obligations.

The lesson would not be lost on those relying on the full faith and credit of governmental agencies. An old and neglected industry blossomed—the insuring of municipal bonds against just such possibilities. This, of course, added to the costs of these instruments—a cost that would naturally be borne by the taxpayers, who would also bear the heightened interest rates the now suspect bonds would be forced to pay. And this was one of America's most affluent communities, collectively thumbing its nose at bondholders.

The total lost, by taxpayers, was nearly $1.7 billion. In January 1996 the Securities and Exchange Commission issued a report describing frauds and deceptions by a wide array of public officials who consented to the sanctions imposed, without acknowledging guilt. The charges included inflating the value of the pools that backed the bonds, from 158% to 292%, and other deceptions.

There was no evidence of personal enrichment revealed, so what did the officials get out of this? For one, political success in elections. For another, the plaques, dinners, honors, and other blandishments accompanying success and that cause many political flowers to blossom. And, for a third, very possibly the sort of indirect benefits that get expressed in ways not constituting a quid pro quo, but still leading to enrichment.

Orange County had lied to its citizens and, when discovered, declared bankruptcy and sued those they now blamed for bad advice.[15,16]

But unforgiving market realities would teach Orange County—and a lot of innocent bystanders—that there were high costs connected to such arrogancies. Everywhere Americans turned, evidence accrued to confirm the baleful speculation that "they were all crooked or corrupt."

CONGRESS

The view at the House of Representatives was no more reassuring. Ousted Democrats inflated staffer's salaries to ensure a final bonus before exiting in 1994. The money, allocated to run the offices, belonged to the taxpayers and should have been returned to the Treasury. That a perfectly legal way had been found to line bureaucrats' pockets only fueled the people's fury.

A Speaker of the House driven from the title—and office—by allegations of wrongdoing relating to circumventing earning limits by coercing hosts to buy his book was followed by another—of the opposite party—who found himself forced to cancel a book advance for the incredible sum of over $4 million, offered by a publisher who would, only a couple of months later, become the beneficiary of a huge tax break and who had a lot of regulatory judgments coming from federal agencies. A colleague was convicted, in August 1995, of sexually corrupting a minor and promptly declared his innocence and announced he'd appeal, of course. He resigned and entered prison in October 1995.

Other representatives, such as the 1994 Speaker, were simply voted out, without taint, while some, like the powerful chair of the House Ways and Means Committee, lost while under indictment for theft. He fought the charge and lost, going to prison in early 1996, unrepentant.

Newspapers and radio and television stations carried charges of fraud, misuse of campaign funds, and other sales of office. While the Democrats tended to be involved in graft, theft, and other crimes characteristic of big-city machine politics, Republicans tended to favor corporate interests and to break the law in terms of such abuses of power as Watergate and Iran–Contra. The former seemed more at home on inner-city streets, while the latter preferred the more comfortable warrens of clubs and board rooms. The troubling constant, however, was the unvarying predilection of officeholders to place themselves above the law, whatever their party or professions of devotion to the public good.

Junkets to exotic places are routinely scheduled, even for outgoing office holders, as a final perquisite and are labeled as "fact-finding trips to aid in governmental functions." That they're no longer asked to discharge these "functions" troubles the beneficiaries little. And they leave with generous pensions and even, in some cases, the right to appropriate campaign war chests.

The abuse of free mail privileges by Congress is rarely even a subject for commentary. As with the swallows of Capistrano, all can look forward to a blizzard of messages from their elected representatives just before election. As of the end of 1994, four representatives were under indictment for accepting illegal gratuities, statutory rape and other sex charges, embezzlement and fraud, extortion, and tax evasion, and one senator for abuse of his expense account—to which he pleaded guilty. And a convicted former representative announced he'd seek his old seat in 1992.

Personal enrichment, through admission into lucrative investments in which the risk is frequently minimal and the returns astronomical, has become one of the benefits of office. Prosecutors use the lore gained in office to enable drug lords to circumvent justice as they join the defense team. The military–industrial complex has demonstrated what a lucrative shuttle it can become for compliant government officials.

Called The Millionaires' Club by many, the U.S. Senate is not only an attraction for the wealthy but is itself the creator of wealth. Political power is rewarded with invitations to participate in sure-shot deals, book contracts, honorariums, and such hidden gifts as junkets, meals, and the emblems distributed at conferences in the guise of "little mementos." And then there is the sale of access that comes from leaving office and becoming a lobbyist. Inquiries produce a march of facts attesting to abuses centering on cash, position, sexual exploitations, and other familiar sources of human pleasure.

Priapism, Power, and Pelf

Brazen defiance seemed to be the reflexive response of every accused politico. The American public was rarely treated to contrition or shame; it got, instead, bold-faced determination to tough it out. Even when guilt was proved, it would invariably be accompanied with such commonplace evasions as "legal costs," the power of vindictive prosecutors, or the excuse that it hadn't been such a big deal, anyhow, and it hadn't been repeated in recent years, etc. etc.

In Minnesota, former two-term Senator David Durenberger finally pleaded guilty to falsifying expense claims. His plea, in August 1995, came over 5 years after the Senate denounced him for bringing the body "into dishonor and disrepute." Durenberger's behavior was an echo of the antics of his colleagues, known as the Keating Five.

But for abuse of power, naked exploitation of office, and betrayal of trust, the cup would have to be granted to Oregon's Senator Bob Packwood, whose stonewalling of charges of having made unwanted sexual advances to scores of women and girls over a period of many years became the very symbol of the use of office for the purpose of pursuing a secret and abusive agenda.[17]

That many of the victims fell into the trap because of trust or some sort of economic dependence underlined the horror of attacks from a totally unexpected source. It became clear that many of the targets suffered permanent harm from Packwood's thrusts.

For Packwood, sex, power, and money served as nexuses for the pursuit of salacious instincts. On one level a respected and effective legislator, Packwood, the evidence claimed, was also a Mr. Hyde, using position to work his will. The charges and evasions consumed years and enabled Packwood to remain at the epicenter of power and influence as he stalled the process. In one case he won delay of a news account that would have threatened his re-election; the damaging report came out after his narrow victory.

Senators rose in defense of their colleague as he fought the charges. In the end, Packwood's reluctant colleagues voted, in the Ethics Committee, 6–0 to expel him from the Senate—the first such ouster in over a hundred years. And it came only after relentless pursuit by the victims, who were pressured and excoriated along the way. Then his friend, the Senate majority leader, attempted to keep him on the payroll another three months or so, but was finally pushed to get Packwood's resignation on October 1, 1995.

The Ethics Committee's report ran to over 10,000 pages of evidence and alleged that Packwood had altered documents he'd submitted, taken advantage of women dependent on him for jobs, and pressured lobbyists to provide consulting fees to his ex-wife to reduce his alimony payments.

What was perhaps most revealing in this paradigm of the genre of abuse of office was the mind-set reflected in his diaries. Packwood strove to avoid a direct favor in return for an accommodation. He could not afford to have his vote linked directly to a gift from a lobbyist, so his efforts centered on the avoidance of the dreaded quid pro quo that signalled an outright sell-out.

The proliferation of lobbyists seeking access in order to gain advantages for their employers is eloquent testimony to the likely prevalence of favors akin to Packwood's in the corridors of power. And every accommodation to a specific interest must come at the expense of the general interest.

Following his resignation, Packwood announced the creation of a political consulting business, in Washington, D.C., to advise clients on legislation and how to lobby congress. In declining to rule out a future in politics, he cited the then mayor of the city, Marion Barry, who'd overcome a drug conviction to return to office.

Meanwhile, across the street, in the highest moral edifice of the state, the view was not altogether edifying either. Sitting on the Supreme Court was at least one member whose purported lascivious penchants had provided the nation with public theater for months. There was nothing very vestal in American institutions as the century closed.

Where President Carter spoke of a national "malaise," President Clinton found it irresistible to utter that the country was in a "funk."

O tempora! O mores!

Given the parade of extortionists, sexual abusers, thieves, and other criminals at all levels of government selling-out to the well-heeled private interests, how could the public respond with anything but a cynical withdrawal and a stance of a "plague on both your houses?"

The irony was that so many whose lives were laced with sexual adventures, family break-ups, draft evasions, and other tokens of self-interest or worse should be invoking fervent religious images as driving their desire to serve. The devil quotes scripture to his purposes.

And then there were disclosures in which a senator faced public charges of attempting to have a safety inspector fired for hassling a friend's small airline, only to have the event explode when the airline suffered a crash on February 24, 1994. The pilot and three federal doctors from the Indian Health Service were killed. The event was the subject of a Senate ethics inquiry. In November 1995, the panel voted to clear the senator and issued a terse statement that seemed short of total vindication.

How many such behind-the-scenes acts fail to be discovered because of the absence of a paper trail and the lack of a link between the tragedy and its cause?

The Keating Five—senators who lobbied hard on behalf of the man later convicted of massive S & L fraud—escaped with minor rebukes from the Senate's notably clubby Ethics Committee. Others escaped on technicalities and through the second-bites-at-the-apple available through costly appeals and reversals of convictions. Our leaders were part of a system in which the rich and powerful could escape even criminal convictions, while impoverished addicts faced mandatory sentences of draconian dimensions, without hope of escape.

And with so many perks, gifts, opportunities to participate in initial public offerings (of stock), junkets, meals, favors, jobs, honorariums, contributions, book deals, and a veritable cornucopia of other goodies, the really amazing thing was that the arrogance of position inspired so many to break the law anyway. Our leaders could, frequently, be trusted to have discarded not only their moral compasses and any sense of loyalty to the people, but, along with these, any sense of constraint upon their actions.

The day did not seem far off when legislators might claim the support of voters because of their first-hand familiarity with the criminal justice system.

JUDGES

Surprisingly, the federal bench seemed to be relatively clean and free of the scandals attaching to so many elected officials.[18] It is still very rare for federal judges to be removed for cause or to be accused of crimes. This may be due to the rigorous inquiry and scrutiny into their background that precedes appointment. If we held the selection of officials seeking election to the same standards, we might well end up with a better class of people among our rulers. But the parties undertake no screening, relying on the press and opposition to discover any warts in their stalwarts.

Even at the state level, where the standards are clearly lower and the appointments subjected to less rigorous scrutiny—and where appointments are frequently naked political payoffs—the bizarre actions of the convicted former chief judge of New York state are widely seen as aberrations.

Total purity cannot be wholly claimed. Supreme Court justices and federal judges were revealed, in March 1995, to have accepted lavish trips and luxurious accommodations from a legal publishing firm on whose activities they frequently ruled.[19]

It was quite legal, but it blurred the lines. The publisher had created reward vehicles, of suitable subtlety and discretion, with which to curry the courts' favor—and the firm had many cases going through the courts in which large sums hung in the balance.

When the search for awardees for the firm's prizes and the high-sounding conferences were stripped away, we were left with the vision of clever entrepreneurs who had honed the skills of seduction to a very fine edge.

NATIONALLY

At the highest levels, the stakes are weightier and the actions are less tawdry. The cupidity of a vice president driven from office is widely seen as unseemly—as if to say, what need is there for that? What must inmates for lesser crimes have thought when a statue to this man was unveiled in the U.S. Senate in the spring of 1995, and without any visible dissent or expressions of outrage?

The sins at the top tend to be the crimes of hubris. After a 19-year-old lawsuit is lost, the former national security adviser reluctantly holds that he "regretted having ordered the illegal wiretap" of a White House aide's phone. Even the confessions of a Vietnam hawk fail to convey any sense of contrition, as the thought of a principled resignation is eschewed. He could not, more than a quarter-century after his "wrongs" (his word), bring himself to hold his loyalty to the American people higher than his personal loyalty to his boss. This is the corporate ethic at work in the highest councils of our national life. He still didn't get it.

With the money pressures that television advertising impose on any political campaign, the search for funds becomes the barometer of success or failure. Our system pressures candidates to get the money and run, and only opponents and the press really monitor the activity. The rest of us hardly know the identities, rarely bother to vote, and expend our energies on the standings in the sports pages.

In the pressure cooker of American political life, results are all that matter. Actions are justified by the thought of all the good that can be done when office is achieved, by whatever route—a Faustian bargain that, like that of Faust, inevitably results in payment to the piper.

We have created a political system in which money rules and have forced the contestants to secure these funds as best they can.

It is an invitation to chicanery, and one that, given the general decline of civic and family values, we cannot afford and they cannot resist. The loss of public faith makes the nation ever more vulnerable to the easy promises of demagogues.

Yet some would argue that the political landscape has grown noticeably less polluted as a result of civil rights laws, the end of segregation, sexual liberation, the increasing rights and power of women, and the loss of hypocrisy that shielded awful cruelties and abuses—in the home and in the workplace.

These observers of the half-filled glass deserve an answer.

The plight of blacks has, by such statistical measures as teenage births to single women, appearance in prison and nonappearance in school, disparities in income with whites, homicide victimizations, welfare receipts, unemployment, and almost every other measure of progress, worsened.

Income disparities between the overclass and the underclass have widened since the abandonment of the War on Poverty in 1980.

And how would Americans respond to the query of who, in public life, represented the models of rectitude they could hold up to their children? Could we, like Lot, fail to find any good people in our Sodom?

The fact is that a society, like an organism, both degenerates and regenerates all the time. The key question is, which is happening faster? And the response can only be found in a welter of statistics, observations, analyses, or opinions that, in sum, become subjective conclusions.

One might see the declines in smoking, the reduced imbibing of hard liquor, and the growth of fitness as hard evidence of reform. Others might see narcissism or, granting the point of virtue, might overwhelm the findings with a flood of negatives.

Polls do show a decline of faith in our leaders and institutions. We have had scandals throughout our history, but nothing on the scale of recent years. And, even given the old boys' network of backscratchings and winking silences of the past, the fact is that we are being inundated with exposures of corruption and abuse of power.

Only 44.6% of all eligible Americans voted in the crucial 1994 national elections. Those earning $50,000 or more voted at the rate of 60.1%. Whites voted 46.9%, blacks 37%, and Hispanics 19.1%. These figures deepen the impression of a bifurcating society.

Nowhere is the analogy of modern America to Caligula's and Nero's Rome more dramatically and eloquently demonstrated than in our political arena.

REFORM

The first and foremost lesson is that we are sending people who are both representing us and representative of us to our ruling councils. In order to get a better class of rulers, we will have to concern ourselves with harsh questions centering on economic, racial, and social justice.

We need electoral reforms:

- Democrats and Republicans need to choose candidates more carefully—creating search committees to induce wise and honorable citizens to run.
- Campaign financing should be reformed:
  - Government should refund any citizen's contribution up to $200, on submitting proof.
  - Totals spent should be legally limited.
  - No individual contribution of over $2000 should be allowed for any office.
  - No cash contributions should be made by political action committees.
  - All contributions must be meticulously recorded and filed with election officials.
- Candidates should file detailed tax and financial disclosures.
- Candidates should submit comprehensive background information on filing to run.
- The two-party system is essential to the democracy and ought to be encouraged and preserved.

- The role of the media, especially as muckraker, is central and should be extolled and encouraged.
- The government must be made more efficient and more effective. This means doing it better and cheaper:
    - All local governments should be consolidated into one county government for the area. This gets suburbanites to work on the problems of the cities they've abandoned.
    - Term limits of 12 years must be imposed for all offices.
    - There should be unicameral legislatures in state houses.
    - Productivity and performance need to be extolled over sheer numbers. The point is not to hire more of anything (cops included) but to use existing employees more effectively.
    - Civil service must be reformed to permit hiring qualified minorities and other victims of discrimination and to fire the unfit. Government service must be subjected to the same rigors as those that exist in the private sector.

Politicians are the gate-keepers to the rules that order our lives. As such they are the most inviting targets for those seeking an edge—legitimate or otherwise. Those seeking these edges are ready to spend for the benefit. In this equation, it is the people who lose.

5

Organized Crime

White collar and street crime must first be defined if they are to be understood. Distinctions are important to the development of real solutions. Both a class and a race distinction must be made, since street crime tends to be the province of the poor, urban, largely black, and excluded underclass, while white collar crime felicitously conveys the notion of a white, educated, suburban, prosperous overclass. There are, as we've seen, important exceptions, but these mainly tend, by their comparative rarity, to prove the rule.

Muggers use guns and embezzlers use computers. The former go for hundreds, while the latter have been known to plunder hundreds of millions. The differences are such as to lead to the conclusion that a solution for one would have absolutely no effect on the other.

Organized crime[1] has similarly tempted taxonomy. The professional commentaries and scholarly literature are loaded with references to the provision of illegal services, continuing devotion to the organization and permanent employment, a hierarchical structure, and rigid codes of conduct—with strong sanctions for enforcement. There is the sort of shifting that characterizes the metamorphosing of legitimate corporations, as adjustments are made to a changing environment and economy.

While organized crime once bootlegged alcohol—it, in fact, proved the vehicle to undreamed-of success—it was able to shift into bootlegging cigarettes or drugs. The individual entrepreneur—the call girl—made organization obsolete. The focus on prostitution turned then to pornography and, when Hollywood preempted this field with sexy movies that, nevertheless, satisfied the Supreme Court's insistence on some "artistic merit," then segued into child pornography. When gambling was largely legalized and operated by governments now fiercely jealous of their new domain, organized crime evolved into loan sharking, union takeovers, and such legitimate businesses as waste hauling, construction, fish mongering, and trade shows.

Gambling continued to be a lucrative and substantial profit center in places where sports betting remained illegal. It also served as a source of customers for the loan sharking operation, as bettors inevitably got in over their heads.[2] And the gains inherent in fixing events were not ignored either, as the mass of indictments charging rigging of harness races in Yonkers, New York, made clear in August 1995.

So it was not really difficult to distinguish organized from white collar or street crime. The first required a continuing commitment to criminal activities by a largish group of employees who were tightly bound in a secret, permanent conspiracy, from which the only separation was death. White collar and street crimes tended to be largely the work of loners. Brokerages, accountancies, insurers, attorneys, and doctors rarely bonded in continuing criminal conspiracies. Their crimes tended to be ad hoc succumbings to opportunities and temptations. It might even be held that the overwhelming majority of white collar and street criminals are, except for the odd moments of depredation, honest folks. The same cannot be said of the mobsters; they are totally and consistently immersed in criminal pursuits. What, then, is the impediment to a clear definition?

THE MAFIA

Just as it is politically incorrect to describe street crime as the province of impoverished black males—and, by adopting this ostrich approach effectively precluding any hope of a constructive remedy—the challenge of describing organized crime can be seen when we study the attempts of scholars and law enforcers to define it.

Typically there are descriptions of the organization and of the activities we will explore, followed by a tortured and pathetic meandering that ends up with a wimpered word—Mafia.[3]

Yes, there have been—and continue to be—tongs and other organized criminal groups in America's Chinatowns,[4] but that is just the point—they rarely emerge from their ethnic enclaves. And yes, there are large-scale operations—such as drug dealings—that require organization, and, yes, there are even street gangs that fit the usual descriptions of organized crime, but these are mere temporal or geographic islands in a national sea of criminal activities.

There have been disclosures of organized crime in Chinatown, where native mobsters assigned territories, protected gambling dens, dealt in drugs, and collected $30,000 to smuggle Asians into America, frequently requiring them to perform sexual services in payment of passage. And they have kidnapped and murdered their clients. Using fraternal, social, and business associations—tongs—as fronts, these criminals exploited connections to politicians and corrupted cops.

The ethnic, cultural, and language barriers made infiltration difficult, but a series of indictments in June 1995 clearly indicated that investigation was possible, even when the crimes were narrowly confined to Chinatown. Like the early Mafia, the Chinatown thugs found it safer to remain within the familiar waters of their language and culture.

Today's mafiosi are the generational successors of the Sicilian immigrants who began—as such groups inevitably begin—by squeezing their country-folk. The ethnic nature—actually Sicilian—of what was described, publicly, for the first time, by an unprecedented turncoat, Joe Valachi, as *La Cosa Nostra* (this thing of ours), actually served to protect the organization from infiltration or treachery. We will see, however, that there is no such thing as absolute inviolability.

The Mafia had nothing much to fear, from without, for most of this century, but one never knew when that could change, and complacency was always dangerous. And we shall see that change the feds did—following the rather timely departure of the Federal Bureau of Investigation's master in 1972.

Even allowing for the comfort inevitably creeping into the organization as a result of the all-too-benign neglect of the feds, there were serious challenges keeping mafiosi on their toes.

These struggles were, classically, internecine. The money was such as to inspire the rawest competitions. Bursts of war left casualties, but a confused public—not provided, at least until 1951, with any real information on the Mafia—could, at least, experience relief that these guys mostly killed only each other—in unfathomable corporate writhings.

The battles for control involved treacheries, plots, cunning strategies, and the pressuring of intimates and even close relatives into betrayals. If they typically arranged murders through the ministrations of a trusted associate who sold out and led you into a trap, how would loyalty be measured and assured?

In fascinating twists worthy of any Borgia stratagem, brothers lured siblings to their deaths. The continuing fights for ascendancy in organizations where the ruthless ruled led, periodically, to tremors that surfaced as dumped bodies, until a temporary succession was settled on.

The Machiavellian nature of Mafia organizational dynamics necessarily placed the highest emphasis on loyalty. The safest thing is to bring a son or two into the business and have them succeed you. The rewards are huge, and the risks, at least until reckoning day, easily pooh-poohed.

Every liaison has a fealty value. If ties of blood or marriage could not be contrived, then Godfatherhood would have to do. The need was to fasten the member to the group by as many ties as it would take to resist severance.

The disguises of respectability were often so deft that officials and respected corporate types would swear for the integrity of mob leaders fronting as hardworking, devoted industry figures. Even the busing of children was found to be controlled by Mafia unions, who sold real estate to the union fund at wildly inflated prices, diminishing the pensions of drivers. The cost of building in New York was estimated to be inflated by at least 10% because of the Mafia's control of the unions.

This double life, in which mafiosi pose as trade union leaders or corporate heads, has gulled many unsuspecting colleagues to come to the defense of exposed mafiosi. Such connections have also served as vehicles to the corridors of political power.

LAW ENFORCEMENT

With all the drug dealing, gambling, corrupting of unions, and intimidation and extortion of honest businesses, how is it possible that the Mafia was able to hold untrammeled sway for about three-quarters of the twentieth century?

Where were the cops?

The crimes were there to be seen and felt and smelled; bodies made periodic appearances, and it was certain some folks knew, or had seen, something. How came it to be that nothing—absolutely nothing—was done? How was the Mafia able to murder, extort, deal drugs, take over the nation's largest union, and become a vast empire-within-the-nation without their occasionally losing some soldiers in the battle (except those they themselves dispatched)?

The answer lies in the name of the one man who might have done something, but chose to chase rural bandits, reds, and personal targets—J. Edgar Hoover.[5]

With perhaps three or four exceptions, the nation's urban police departments are simply not equipped to deal with highly complicated, sophisticated, secretive criminal conspiracies that characterize white collar or organized crime. Infiltrations, turnings, electronic surveillance, the mastering of documentation that requires expert analysis, the devotion of scarce resources for long periods of time, the need for effective laws, and the complexities of asset seizures all work against America's cops making a dent in either white collar or organized crime. Police agencies are local, fragmented, and too small and limited to mount serious assaults on deep, continuing, well-financed conspiracies. The large ones—New York's, Los Angeles', Chicago's and others'—simply haven't bothered, beyond some organizational obeisances to public demands for action, such as the creation of innocuous intelligence units, which become little more than archivists and chroniclers of the more obvious depredations.

Other federal agencies can attack some segments—such as the Securities and Exchange Commission on stock fraud: the Bureau of Alcohol, Tobacco, and Firearms on eponymous violations; the Secret Service on counterfeiting; and the Drug Enforcement Agency on narcotics, but these tend to be compartmentalized and specialized.

THE FEDERAL BUREAU OF INVESTIGATION

The closest thing we have to a national police is the Federal Bureau of Investigation,[6] which has the broad authority to enforce a wide variety of federal laws. A national mandate ensures their capacity to look everywhere and not be hampered by state borders or jurisdictional factors. A highly educated, well-trained, carefully selected, and handsomely paid force of investigators provides the personnel equal to the complex challenges afforded by white collar and organized criminals. A generous budget furnishes the resources needed to conduct long-term, difficult inquiries, reward informers, protect witnesses, and gather evidence.

So, where was the FBI as the Mafia grew from the ethnic confinements of its local terrors to a national menace?

How was organized crime permitted to swell and prosper, fueled by the billions generated during the 13 years (1919–1932) of Prohibition?

Why were the Mafia's comfortable adjustments, during the Great Depression, permitted to proceed without interruption?

How did the Mafia manage its transition to Las Vegas, its takeover of the Teamsters, and its intrusion into unexpected nooks and crannies of the daily lives of Americans without significant opposition?

The answers to these questions lie—as every study and commentary either explicitly avows or timidly suggests—in J. Edgar Hoover's deep-rooted belief that his agency's involvement in such pursuits would endanger its integrity. That is the more generous view. Others would add that the John Dillingers provided the publicity resulting from easy successes and the Red Menace represented a threat that no American would risk opprobrium in defending. And there was the matter of the personal aggrandizement, through the accumulation of data on individuals, that would be useful in securing their support on votes, when needed.

The Hoover and post-Hoover eras offer, without doubt, the most dramatic contrasts in law enforcement efficacy in the history of the Republic, yet his public relations skills and political astuteness and power were such as to mesmerize the nation to the opposite conclusion.

While street crime festers and grows unabatedly and white collar's temptations suck more and more professionals into its orbits, the battle against organized crime, over the past 23 years, has been the law's most conspicuous and brilliant success. The FBI's prosecution and imprisonment of organized crime's leaders and soldiers—since Hoover's death—have proved an uninterrupted string of coups that have the Mafia reeling and waning.

The History

Notwithstanding the body count, the explosions, the occasional tax fraud prosecutions and a steady drumbeat of violent incidents, the FBI, as late as the early 1950s, denied the existence of a Mafia or any other national crime syndicate. Sure it was a shock to see the brain-splattered corpses of mobsters machine-gunned on St. Valentine's Day 1929 by Al Capone's minions in a Chicago garage—but it was all safely distant from the reader's life.

The FBI's denials were echoed by Italian-American groups smarting over prejudice and remembering the lynching of 11 Italian Americans in New Orleans in 1891 because they were reputed to be mafiosi. Following Hoover's lead, and very likely intimidated by his fearsome presence in their profession, America's law enforcers also denied a national syndicate's existence—a convenient stance—and many scholars took up the chant.

Yet it was becoming too transparently clear that Charles "Lucky" Luciano and Meyer Lansky—one of a coterie of Jews who were allowed in as partners of organized crime and who played central roles in the Murder Incorporated of the 1940s and the Las Vegas casino developments—had, in the 1930s, forged a national crime organization with a board of directors (the Commission), assigned territories, used Murder Incorporated as the enforcement arm, and legitimized successions and authorized coups. It even approved the elimination of a favored member whose slipping mind was evolving from embarrassment to threat. Some might have called this rub-out an enlightened form of euthanasia.

That stonewalling by Hoover—who was, in fact, the FBI—could follow the disclosures of the 1951 Special Committee to Investigate Organized Crime in Interstate Commerce was remarkable, since Senator Estes Kefauver had identified 24 families or groups and had established a record of activities in gambling (in and out of Las Vegas), loan sharking, narcotics, labor unions, corrupting politicians, exploiting legal enterprises, and generally operating a national empire that, it was then estimated, grossed $50 billion, with $15 billion in profits.

Hoover's resistance took another blow when a New York state trooper happened upon, in November 1957, what was a top-drawer enclave of mafiosi in Joseph Barbara's home in Appalachia, New York.[7] The event was attended by about 60 (some may have scurried into the woods as the raid began) Italian Americans, almost half of whom were related by bonds of blood, marriage, or Godfatherhood, the ritual bond of choice.

The summit was called to justify the October 25, 1957, assassination of the dreaded Albert Anastasia in the barber chair of New York's Park Sheraton Hotel by the infamous Gallo brothers, who were acting on the orders of Vito Genovese. There would be a review of the rationale and, Genovese fervently hoped, an organizational blessing on the act. It came.

Ironically, this was the same Genovese who was reputed to have gunned down the labor activist and fascist-foe Carlo Tresca on the streets of Manhattan, as a favor to Benito Mussolini. One never knew when one would need such a boon repaid, or when—as happened to Luciano—one would be returned to Italy. That such an act could be pulled off with impunity was eloquently reflected in the paucity of wit or results produced by the lackluster investigation into the murder of this well-known militant. Tresca's flirtations with the left made him a less sympathetic victim to his fellow Americans.

Then, in 1963 and before Senator John McClellan's Permanent Subcommittee on Investigations,[8] mafioso turncoat Joseph Valachi added La Cosa Nostra to America's lexicon. That Robert F. Kennedy was the counsel asking the questions of Valachi and such others as the Teamsters' Dave Beck and James R. Hoffa would have far-reaching consequences for the Mafia's future. Just as Hoover was the key impediment to battle, Kennedy became its foremost, and most effective, goad.

Kennedy had, earlier—in 1960—authored *The Enemy Within*, an account of how the Teamsters were taken over by the Mafia, mostly focusing on the activities of its then president, Dave Beck. Kennedy clearly saw the need for a nationally centered effort against organized crime.

A Presidential Commission

As the growing murmurs over "crime in the streets" reached a crescendo in the 1964 presidential election, the winner, Lyndon B. Johnson, probably wondering if Barry Goldwater might be onto something, appointed a President's Commission on Law Enforcement. In February 1967 it produced a seminal document titled "The Challenge of Crime in a Free Society."

The experts were prescient in citing Robert F. Kennedy as an activist in the battle against organized crime and were typically reverential in their tepid hint at "a lack of coordination and interest by some Federal investigative agencies." They were not about to defy the mighty Hoover, yet they could not deny the evidence of their experiences and studies.

The report described organized crime's involvement with unions, its need to corrupt politicians in order to function, and how its activities affected the daily lives of millions of Americans, who were mostly unaware of the effects and indifferent to the growth of organized crime. Its study of the interrupted 1957 Appalachia Convention revealed that nine were in the coin-operated machine business, 16 in the garment industry, ten owned grocery stores, 17 owned bars or restaurants, 11 were in olive oil or cheese enterprises, nine were in construction, and others were in auto agencies, coal companies, entertainment, funeral homes, ownership of harness and race tracks, linen and laundry firms, trucking, bakeries, and waterfront activities. They did, indeed, cover the waterfront.

The report offered a series of recommendations, many of which would surface in the Racketeer Influenced and Corrupt Organization (RICO) Act.[9] They sidestepped the "Hoover problem" by calling for federal assistance to local agencies and the creation of a federal centralized information office and encouraging the Justice Department to undertake research. The report ends with the eyebrow-lifting observation that "The extraordinary thing about Organized Crime is that America has tolerated it for so long."

In the mid-1970s the entire scene was framed by Mario Puzo's brilliant roman à clef, *The Godfather*, which offered intimate perspectives into the internal life of a Mafia family and its friends, enemies, and perils. The book and the movies that followed proved the accuracy of the view that the true artist is really a prophet. The revelations flowing from the defections of the 1980s and 1990s demonstrated the accuracy of Puzo's portrayals.

SICILY

However powerful the American Mafia became, it never reached the awesome, government-challenging levels it achieved in its Sicilian cradle. There it could not only vie with established authority, but it could also frequently supersede it. The Mafia's reach and strength have been such as to strike down the officials sent by Rome to tame its muscle—however many bodyguards were assigned or however elaborate the precautions taken.

General Alberto Dalla Chiesa was murdered, with his wife and bodyguards, in September 1982—shortly after being sent to clean out the Mafia. Ten years later, in May 1992, the Mafia blew up a highway to kill Judge Giovanni Falcone, who had led the maxi-trials of mafiosi in the mid-1980s. This was a crime that so shocked Louis Freeh, the FBI's new director, that he went to Sicily to vow to "root out" the Mafia. What a departure from his famous predecessor's posture!

The massive trials, the indictment of a former prime minister, and the defections all seemed to point to an historic break with Italy's silent toleration—if not involvement—in this cancer.

Between these outrages, and after, the Mafia continued to work its will.

The "capo de tutti capi," Salvatore (Tito) Riina—sentenced to nine life-prison terms—nevertheless lived as a fugitive for 23 years, until his capture in Palermo on January 15, 1993. He came from the town made famous by Puzo—Corleone.

Riina, 65 in 1995, married, had four children christened, and stated that he attended church regularly during his "absence." He styled himself a humble worker who knew nothing of criminal activities—least of all any that might have earned him the sobriquet "The Beast." His capture resulted in a series of art gallery bombings in retaliation. His 53-year-old brother-in-law, captured in Palermo in June 1995, was alleged to have urged all-out war against the government. It was clear he, at any rate, felt they had a chance of cowing the authorities into submission. And why not, since, as the trial of a former prime minister alleged in 1995, the Mafia's power had reached into that very office?

The connections to politics—and especially the Christian Democrats who ruled Italy during most of the postwar years—reached all the way to the top. The corruption of government made the Mafia virtually inviolate in Sicily, and, in many ways, the source of real power on the island.

Outraged by assassinations, drug dealings, governmental futility, and criminal impunity, and perhaps inspired by the American example, Italy began a crackdown on the Mafia in the mid-1980s and sustained the effort, if sometimes fitfully, into the 1990s. The effort acquired such unexpected allies as Pope John Paul II, who condemned the Mafia in a 1993 visit to Sicily.

The Mafia's connections to the Catholic Church were as troubling as their cozy relations with politicians. A Church poll revealed that only 35% of Sicilian priests had publicly addressed the Mafia issue; 53.6% said they never did so, and 10% didn't respond. The prelate of Monreale was dubbed the "Mafia bishop." In November 1994 a lamb, with its throat slit, was hung outside the door of a priest who had criticized the Mafia. Another was shot and killed, in broad daylight, as a warning.

America's fear of communism had led to the development in Italy of a single party government that, unchallenged over the years, found it easy to slip into the lucrative embrace of mafiosi, who got the voters out, provided the funds, and made life convenient. The path had been eased by the flight, or absence, of a governmental structure—except for the Mafia—as the Allies conquered Sicily in 1944.

Over the next half-century the Mafia would become Sicily's "Shadow Government."

THE AMERICAN MAFIA

In the United States, the Mafia broke out of its ethnic ghetto with the arrival of Prohibition. It never wholly abandoned its connections to those it felt the need to employ to secure prosperity and safety from intrusion. Liaisons with black or Hispanic groups—made necessary by the drug trade or the numbers racket—

and with a clutch of Jews—needed for their expertise in gambling and Caribbean contacts—tended to be temporary marriages of convenience. Since the biggest danger came from rival groups, the issue of fealty became paramount. And the profits were such as to command generational loyalty to the family's businesses.

Why did the Mafia thrive in New York and Chicago and not in Minneapolis? The answer probably lies more within the parameters established by corporate interests than in the efficacy of law enforcers. A corporate sector that identifies with its community and that has no appetite for illegal services will simply not attract those ready to exploit weaknesses. In the Midwest the corporate titans tended to be locals with deep roots in their communities.

New York's market was so rich it had to be divided among five groups—the Genovese, Lucchese, Bonnano, Colombo, and Gambino families.

The leadership of these groups had been killed, imprisoned, driven into flight, or forced to the unsavory expedient of feigning insanity. Vincent Gigante,[10] 67, reported that God spoke to him, wandered the streets in a bathrobe, and employed psychiatrists to declare him unfit for the trial the feds were insisting upon. He is alleged to run the Genovese family. His survival allowed his group to thrive, at the expense of the four other largely rudderless families. But even the Genoveses were put to rout by the FBI in 1996.

Membership was estimated to be down to 850 made members in 1994, from about 1000 in 1990. Indictments and convictions fell like rain upon mobsters at all levels of the organization. Additionally, the jailings were creating power and talent vacuums others rushed to fill, leading to street warfare for control and, some held, a dilution of managerial talent at the top.

The leader of the Philadelphia mob was indicted, with 23 associates, in March 1994. Amazingly, half of these pleaded poverty and accepted court-appointed counsel. Three chose to cooperate with the prosecutors, and one pleaded guilty outright. Earlier, in 1988, the then leader was sentenced to 69 years as he was convicted with 18 others.

This prosecution was made especially notable by a number of

unusual factors—first, the FBI had bugged the office of the group's lawyer and had captured incriminating, and terrifying, testimony. The attempt to invoke lawyer–client confidentiality foundered on the charge that the lawyer was acting not as an advocate, but as a confederate. Second, one of the principal witnesses for the prosecution—a former executive in the gang—wasn't Italian, and, finally, the strict protocols of gang life—one of which holds that the families of targets remain untouched—were breached when, on October 5, 1995, the turncoat's brother was murdered in Philadelphia in an apparent attempt to silence the witness. The 35-year-old victim had declined the offer that his brother had accepted to be a part of the Witness Protection Program.[11] The developments were, despite the awesome display of power reflected in the daytime rub-out, actually a dramatic indication of the organization's disarray.

New Jersey's mob shrank to 50, from 200, from 1990 to 1994.

The New England mob leader was arrested in Florida, in August 1995, following two years on the run. He'd been recognized when his face had been shown on the TV program *America's Most Wanted*.

The feds secured about 300 convictions from 1990 to 1994, and the numbers were climbing as the center failed to hold.

And yet, the 90-year-old man who gave the Bonnano family its name secured the attendance of actors, biographers, priests, college instructors, and celebrities at his birthday celebration in Tucson on January 14, 1995. Earlier the apparel industry honored the man convicted of corruption and racketeering, who was forced to abandon the garment trucking business he'd headed as a part of his plea bargain.

The cost of everything, from virtually every item in a building's construction to Italian bread to a restaurant meal, bore hidden mob taxes in New York City. It may have been thousands of individual small amounts, but the prices resulting were frequently 20% to 50% higher than in nonmob cities.

Trade shows, shippers, restaurant owners and others able to move found it cheaper and easier to do business elsewhere. And these were the legitimate enterprises. In such darker areas as loan sharking, money laundering, skimming, or drug dealing the mob's fangs were bared earlier and oftener.

John Gotti

Every age needs a paradigm. Prohibition had its Al Capone, the Godfather era its Lucky Luciano, and the flashier 1980s and 1990s its John Gotti.[12]

Apparently untouchable, the failed prosecutions in three cases (one turned out to be on the basis of a $60,000 bribe to a juror who was later convicted) led to Gotti's being labeled the "Teflon Don." Nothing stuck. He'd succeeded to the leadership of the Gambino family when its head, Paul Castellano, was rubbed out in midtown Manhattan on December 16, 1985.

John Gotti had, at only 44, hit the jackpot. Unimaginable power and wealth were centered on him. His relatives and allies had cause to exult—his enemies had ample reason to tremble. The rest of us might find relief in knowing we were removed from his orbit, at least directly. But were we?

Who was to know when they encountered this powerful, secret society? A chance meeting or a driving incident might escalate horrendously. Hadn't an architect for a mob boss' lavish house who complained of late payments been found dead, his body covered with knife and burn wounds, in 1989? And hadn't Gotti's own son been run over and killed by a neighbor who was taken away, never to be seen again? Quotidian events or ghastly accidents took on ominous dimensions when the Mafia was involved.

Then, in 1991, the wholly unthinkable occurred: Gotti's number two, Salvatore (Sammy the Bull) Gravano, 50 in 1995, facing lifetime in prison, defected. When it was over, Gravano had testified in seven trials and had persuaded guilty pleas in what would have been six more. He helped secure 30 convictions of 23 mob leaders, five corrupt Teamsters officials, one New York City detective who had functioned as a mole, and the juror who had refused to convict Gotti in exchange for a bribe.

But Sammy the Bull's greatest caper came in dramatically confronting his dreadful boss and testifying against him for nine days. "Teflon" became "Velcro," and the charges stuck. On June 23, 1992, John Gotti was sentenced to life in prison, without the prospect of parole, for murder, conspiracy, gambling, obstruction of justice, and tax fraud. He'd spend 23 hours a day in an isolated cell and try to run the family from prison through his son and brother. It remained to be seen how long this arrangement could last.

Gravano—despite complicity in 19 murders and other crimes—served less than five years in prison and slipped into the mists of the federal protection program. Notwithstanding the exculpation, the government had been dealt an offer it could not have refused—and turned it into one of law enforcement's finest hours. The public would have to come to understand that prosecutors would not be likely to find nuns, professors, or other highly regarded citizens with the sort of information it takes to convict Mafia bosses.

Appeals failed and Gotti had to cling to the hope that his lawyers would find a way to free him. It was beginning to look like a very long shot as 1996 wound along, but organizational restiveness had still to surface, in the usual form of street warfare, for control.

ETHNICITY

Italian ethnicity cannot be retained as the idée fixe behind organized crime in America. It is a shifting tide in which the vacuums created by vigorous enforcement get filled quickly by nimble, greedy acolytes of every national description awaiting their chance.

The disintegration of the Soviet Union loosed a flood of entrepreneurial energies, some of which inevitably took the shape of criminal acts.

In February 1995 a loan-sharking ring on the Lower East Side of Manhattan was found to have its roots in a bakery whose customers needed cash. The Russian émigré owner gradually created a ring that, after ten years, had close to a half-million dollars "on the street" (as loans), charging 120% or more interest a year.

Another group of Russian emigres was indicted for concocting a complicated scheme involving home heating oil (which is not taxed) and the virtually identical diesel fuel (which is). The 25 accused had an elaborate web of companies that bought heating oil and sold it as diesel—through dummy corporations that would be folded and carted off as the authorities approached—pocketing the taxes they collected.

As if to demonstrate their prowess, another Russian ring allegedly tapped into Citibank's computers and effected the transfer of $10 million to their accounts around the world. All but $400,000 was recovered. One suspect, working for a St. Petersburg trading company, was arrested in London in May 1995, and at least three more arrests were expected.

In another twist in April 1995, the attempted assassins of a trusted Mafia associate of John Gotti turned out to have Hispanic surnames. And in a clear-cut Mafia hit on two brothers on August 29, 1995, in the Bronx, which resulted in the killing of one and severe wounds to the other, the two shooters were described as black. There would not have been more telling portents of the Mafia's recruiting problems than these bizarre events, given their penchant for sticking with their own. Formerly, such assignments were tests as well as objectives and were a way to bring the organization more tightly together.

RICO

So it was becoming clear that—accelerated by the death of the director—the feds were finally beginning to get it.

The passage of the RICO Act in 1970 was not, at first, the boon it was to become to law enforcement. Aided by an expansive Supreme Court ruling of RICO's reach in 1981, the feds were, by the mid-1980s, using it as a scythe with which to mow the Mafia. RICO provided stiff penalties for connections to a "criminal enterprise" or to a criminal "commission" that functioned as a criminal enterprise and provided for civil processes that enabled the takeover of such organizations as corrupt unions and allowed for asset seizures.

RICO gave the feds jurisdiction over extortions, conspiracies, the use of interstate or foreign travel in racketeering (defined as a criminal enterprise), gambling violations, money laundering, and use of mails and provided immunity for witnesses.

Indeed, it could be said by the mid-1990s that RICO suffered, if anything, from such a surfeit of success that its existence would be threatened by overuse. Energetic prosecutors employed it against all manner of conspiracies—such as white collar or political crimes—that had very likely not been envisioned by the legislation's framer.

By 1995 most knowledgeable observers could agree with experts who had concluded that the FBI had been extremely successful in its assault on the Mafia because of its commitment to long, costly, complex, undercover investigations; use of wiretaps and bugs; employment of RICO; use of witness immunity and protection programs; asset forfeitures and infiltrations and turnings. The assessment contrasted with the Justice Department's concession, in 1977, that its "effort against Organized Crime … [could] be better planned, organized, executed and directed." What a difference a few years and some new faces would make!

In Italy, a shaken people began massive prosecutions and what looked like serious investigative efforts to challenge the Mafia's power. It seemed more than likely that they'd been influenced by America's example and, since the demise of communism, no longer had to rely on the Christian Democrats for protection from the Red Menace.

The adaptable, exploitative, opportunistic, and inventive nature of the Mafia is best illustrated through examining some of its activities—particularly in sectors normally seen as legitimate enterprises.

The Mafia has shifted its attentions from alcohol to gambling to unions, as legal and social shifts imposed the need for adjustments. Bootlegging gave way to Las Vegas, which involved the takeover of the nation's largest union, whose pension funds served to bankroll the building of casinos. The entry of government into gambling as operators, the end of the use of cash, and the widespread use of credit cards hastened the mob's departure from Nevada.

Nevertheless, as late as September 1995, Salvatore Carollo, the reputed boss of the New Orleans mob, and four associates pleaded guilty to defrauding Bally Gaming Inc.—a maker of video poker machines. Alan Maiss, Bally's former president, pleaded guilty to having video poker dealings with an unlicensed person.

So the connections weren't totally severed.

No one can really cite the Mafia's greatest success, but control of the International Brotherhood of Teamsters certainly would be included in any catalog of candidates for this dubious distinction.

THE TEAMSTERS

Founded in 1903 to organize horsedrawn deliveries, the International Brotherhood of Teamsters (IBT)[13] spread with the first transcontinental delivery of merchandise, by truck, in 1912. A Minneapolis strike led to four Teamster deaths and 50 picketers shot on "Bloody Friday," July 20, 1934. The strikers prevailed and the industry was rapidly organized.

The growth of interstate trucking and the activism of such leaders as James R. Hoffa led the IBT to the position of the nation's largest union by 1979, with nearly two million members. And, shipping a large percentage of America's goods over the road, the union possessed the fearsome capacity to paralyze the nation.

The IBT had, in the late 1950s, been kicked out of the AFL–CIO for its mobster ties. It was readmitted almost 30 years later, but not before four of its presidents were convicted of federal charges of corruption and alliances with the Mafia.

It was Jimmy Hoffa, whose two-fisted style symbolized the heyday of the Teamsters, but it was his predecessor, Dave Beck, who frightened the country with the threat of a strangling nationwide strike and stirred the authorities, with a lot of prodding from

Bobby Kennedy, to begin cleaning it out. This particular Augean stable took 20 years to tidy.

Beck, president from 1952 to 1957, preceded Hoffa—as leader of the union and as a prison inmate. Hoffa ruled from 1957 to 1971, but the last four years of his leadership were spent in prison for jury tampering. His carefully selected stand-in came, with fatal inevitability, to savor the emoluments of power and betray Hoffa. President Richard Nixon commuted Hoffa's sentence, on the proviso that he not seek to return to the union. The support of the Teamsters for Nixon and other Republicans became one of the more curious legacies of this fandango, with fateful consequences for the truckers as it allowed their expected ally, Jimmy Carter, to break their grip on the nation's arteries. The Teamsters became stalwarts in Ronald Reagan's two successful presidential campaigns.

Hoffa, restive and unable to resist the pull of power, attempted a comeback and notoriously disappeared in 1975. His middle name could have served as his epitaph—Riddle. In 1996 his son, James Phillip Hoffa, 55, would run for the presidency of the union. And, interestingly, Hoffa's daughter became a judge in St. Louis.

The enormous distance traveled by the Teamsters from the legitimate concerns of traditional labor were never better illustrated than in the life of its 1984–88 president, Jackie Presser. Presser, who died of cancer in 1988, embodied the conflicting forces at work within the union: he was its leader, a minion of the Mafia, and an FBI informer. Embellishing on the challenges inherent in those roles would beggar the imagination of the greatest fantasists.

By Presser's time Teamster membership had declined to 1.4 million, which was the total as of 1994. A number of factors led to the decline in the strength of the Teamsters and to the cleansing of the ranks. These were not accidents, but the deliberate acts of players seeking defined objectives.

Concerned over the power of the Teamsters, the escalating costs of trucking, and its effects on spiraling inflation, a Democratic president with no reason to be beholden to what would normally be labor allies deregulated the trucking industry in 1980.

Where the Interstate Commerce Commission allocated routes and rates—creating monopolies that enriched both union and management—President Jimmy Carter allowed the entrance of all competitors, who would be free to charge whatever they could get.

The sudden explosion of competition drove costs, prices, and wages downward and brought great numbers of nonunion truckers into a previously organized monopoly industry. What delicious irony that a Democratic president, usually sympathetic to labor's calls, would find himself free to realize an important economic objective, without having to worry over having offended a labor ally.

Soon thereafter the Justice Department sued the Teamsters, under the civil provisions of RICO, alleging racketeering penetration. The union caved in and, in 1989, agreed to a decree that permitted the direct, secret election of its leading officers by the rank and file (instead of carefully chosen delegates to purportedly rigged conventions). The process of cleansing the ranks of underworld figures and puppets had begun. By 1995 about 400 Teamster officials had been ousted on corruption charges. Fifty locals and one joint council were under RICO trusteeships. A reform president had been elected in December 1991 and, although at first moving with glacial slowness, finally got in gear and started making substantive reforms by 1995, such as taking over corrupt locals and replacing mob leaders.

By the mid-1990s a mechanism had been put in place to monitor the Teamsters, some highly publicized figures were deposed, and a union whose coffers had served as a Mafia bank was returning to the ranks of respectable labor organizations. A long nightmare of violence, extortion, and murder seemed finally to have been brought to an end.

OTHER UNIONS

The labor movement proved a lucrative vehicle for Mafia enrichment through the creation of paper locals who would sign sweetheart contracts; vote for the right slate of officers; provide

no-show jobs; condone thefts, extortions, gambling, loan sharking, and drug dealing on the job; provide employment for organization members; use pension funds to finance criminal activity; or
engage in whatever other depredations human inventiveness
could devise.

As the waterfront got milked virtually dry—the Mafia still
does business there, but on a reduced scale—activities shifted to
airports, convention centers, fish markets, and other sites. Con-
tainerization (the use of large, sealed containers to prevent thefts
by dock workers) came too late to save the port of New York as
other cities took over the business.

Newspapers, more perishable than fish, became targets for
thieving and extortionate deliverers' unions. From 1987 to 1992
union members reportedly stole 10,000 copies of *The New York Post*
every day and resold them to distributors.

Every American pays mob taxes, either in the form of heightened trucking costs, manufacturing payoffs, construction bills, the
price of fish, and any other commodity affected by mob control.

If the restaurant patronized has to pay exorbitant haulage
fees, the price of the meal will reflect this cost. If manufacturing or
shipping costs are artificially inflated by mob rakeoffs, the garment's price will include the additional tariff. If nine must be hired
to perform the work of three, the operators will use other cities or
pass on the costs to consumers.

The operations of the Jacob J. Javits Convention Center[14] in
New York produced such costs as to push the city into fourth
place, behind Chicago, Atlanta, and Montreal, after leading the
race for trade fair business. The Javits Center was described as "a
cesspool of extortion and mismanagement" in a 1995 *New York
Times* editorial. It had opened two years late and $111 million over
budget in 1986. The center rapidly developed into a center for
political payoffs, shakedowns, and such other abuses as would
leave no room for the honest worker or the unconnected little guy.
This economic jewel was speedily transformed into a symbol of
corruption, verifying the most cynical suspicions. Every study,
whether by overseers of the Teamsters or the New York state
comptroller—or the media—verified widespread corruption.

In the Alice in Wonderland world the Mafia often feels compelled to profess it inhabits, its reputed representative at the Javits Center—who controlled carpenters' jobs, oversaw no-show jobs, and negotiated contracts—called it coincidence that he'd had 372 beeper messages from his brother-in-law, a top leader in the Genovese family, between January 1993 and July 1994, in addition to scores of personal encounters the union official labeled as happenstance.

That this key operator owned no car, appeared in worker's clothes for a hearing (rather than his customary high-fashion tailoring), and dealt only in cash was also supposed to have been accepted as unremarkable. On September 29, 1995, he was expelled from the Carpenter's Union for associating with organized crime figures.

How all this affected the little guy became evident when 2700 applicants showed up for about 500 coveted union jobs at the Javits Center, in July 1995, when the rolls were finally loosened from the Mafia's iron grip. An additional 300 would be hired in August. Those with mob ties or criminal records would be excluded.

These hitherto invisible workers had been the losers, as was a city whose economy was severely impacted by the artificially added costs that made the center uncompetitive. Additionally, the Carpenters' Union treasury had been depleted and about 40% of its 24,000 members remained unemployed, while only a handful prospered. The government successfully pushed for a secret ballot, involving all members, in the election of a president in July 1995. The incumbent, running for a second four-year term, had collected over $360,000 in salary in 1994 and had his relatives all over the union's payroll.

When the City of New York threatened investigations and reforms at the Fulton Fish Market, arsonists burned it, on March 29, 1995, destroying financial records and sending a very clear message. The market remained operational but was beset with labor strife and other harassing tactics. Although owned by the city—which had long ago abdicated any responsibility for running it—the market was shot through with bust-out operations (in which fish would be ordered, sold, and not paid for, with the seller fleeing with the proceeds), ghost tenants, unauthorized subleases,

and extortionate loading, parking, and unloading fees and procedures. And the city was getting $268,000 a year in rents that were
estimated to have a market value at least ten times higher. The
slippery nature of reform was illustrated on April 18, 1996, when
the *New York Times* reported that one firm licensed to haul fish was
itself being investigated for wrongdoing.

Still, it appeared that the mob's iron grip over the market was
loosening as the tough ex-federal-prosecutor-turned-mayor ener-
getically fought the mob from his new perch, even taking on the
mob's historic control of the cement industry in Manhattan, in 1996.

Mayor Rudolph Giuliani also attacked the finances behind
the annual Feast of San Gennaro in Little Italy. Ostensibly a tribute
to a heroic figure in the Catholic Church, the feast was subjected to
an inquiry that revealed that the persons running it had been paid
$66,000 in 1994, with only $7697 going to charity. The city insisted
on a monitor in 1995, or there would be no license. The dollar bills
affixed to the statue of the saint would now go to the Most Pre-
cious Blood Church, and it was expected that the money would
not be siphoned off to organized crime's coffers, as in years past.[15]

With decades of official neglect opening the way for Mafia
entry, the reforms taking hold in the 1980s and 1990s had a tough
path to follow. At least four national unions, with millions of
members, were listed by federal authorities as controlled by
mobsters—the International Brotherhood of Teamsters; the International Longshoreman's Association; the Hotel, Restaurant Employees, and Bartenders International and the Laborers International Union of North America.[16]

Legitimate, corporate waste-haulers were beginning to break
the Mafia's iron grip over that industry in the New York metro
area. But there was a way to go, here and even in the disposal of
toxic wastes, where the mob continued its stranglehold in some
areas.[17]

And there were, of course, unions—such as the United Mine
Workers and others—with histories of awful crimes relating to
battles for control, sabotage, or other violence that had nothing to
do with the Mafia and everything to do with pursuing ambitions
through criminal means.

But the federal government's assault on organized crime and its activities in the labor movement had raised it miles from such depths as the April 5, 1956 blinding of labor columnist and muckraker Victor Riesel, whose relentless attacks on labor goons and union racketeers led to an atrocious assault in the busiest locale of Manhattan. The man who reportedly threw the acid and sauntered away was found dead, on Mulberry Street, three-and-a-half months later, with a bullet in his head and the identity of his employer locked in his dead heart. A month later, however, the FBI arrested eight men and revealed that the assault had been the work of garment center hoodlums determined to silence Riesel's voice—on the air and in his daily newspaper column. They failed, and Riesel continued to preach reforms and uncover scandals until his death, at 81, on January 4, 1995.

In a way, Hoover had been right—it was tough to fight the mob, but he couldn't have been more wrong than in foregoing the battle altogether.

Bob Kennedy burnished the family name more brightly than any other member by bravely insisting that the battle be fought. By launching the assault he performed a greater public service than even his illustrious brother had.

The FBI—especially some devoted insiders who waited patiently to take on the mob, and then did it with élan—deserves great credit for delivering the greatest law enforcement triumph of this century. Their efforts led to union reforms, the sapping of organized crime's strength, and the unexpected decline of the Mafia. They even encouraged similar efforts in its Sicilian birthplace. While street, white collar, and political crimes wax so threateningly as to endanger the very Republic, the battle against organized crime has shown what can be done by a resolute government acting with the people's support.

And while street, white collar, and organized crime strike at identified targets for specific interests, terrorism strikes randomly to achieve political ends. As we shall see in the next chapter, while the United States has been relatively free of this scourge, recent history reflects the very disturbing possibility that this hiatus may be ending.

6

Terrorism

Violence works.

The intelligentsia, rightly persuaded to the moral rightness of peace and negotiation and appalled by the carnage produced by force, has managed to convince the world that the use of violence is wrong. Through its legal and social mechanisms, it invests only a few with the right to employ violence—the police and the military—and controls its expressions rigorously. This approach is, in the main, the correct one, if society is to avoid holocausts, yet we forget, at our peril, that the Holocaust was stopped by the unleashing of incredible violence against its practitioners.

It is an anomaly of American life that we condemn violence in our rhetoric yet admire it in our art and worship it in our sports, without ever giving voice to our atavistic sense that it can work. And we enjoy the fruits of violence in our independence from Britain, in the acquisition of the Southwest, and in our successes in wars.

Americans understand the need to monitor and guide violence through laws and political actions and believe in its some-time efficacy, without saying so.

The police arrest those who break our rules, often violently, and our military imposes our national will externally.

Terror is the violence available to those seeking a political objective, without possessing the legal mechanisms to achieve their ends. Terrorists often segue into fathers of the nation.

King George III undoubtedly thought our foreparents terror-ists. Israel's rebirth was made possible by persons who bombed, burned, and killed and then led the nation.

Kashmiri separatists in India effectively killed tourism in that famous region when they beheaded a Norwegian in July 1995. The government resisted demands for the release of imprisoned ter-rorists, but the economic effects of the methods employed were palpable.

Groups seeking a political objective, such as the creation of a new state, the freeing of imprisoned associates, the granting of some right or ability to act, and the attempt to discourage a policy—or any of a host of possibilities that envision the achieve-ment of a political or social goal—frequently resort to terror.

Terror implies the use of violence to frighten the target into submission, or, usually less likely, to actually defeat the opposition by destroying it—typical of movements seeking independence from a colonial power.

Given the hugely complex interconnectedness and interde-pendence of modern society, targets abound—in the form of water or power supplies, transportation, or other artifacts of the modern state.

The constant in terror is the use of illegal violence by a person or group seeking a social, political, economic, cultural, or even personal aim. Terror can be described as a violent assault on society for the purpose of realizing an objective. By striking ran-domly, the necessary sense of predictability and safety is under-mined and society is spooked, with the terrorists hoping it will be sufficient to obtain concessions.[1]

Endless examples exist—the Irish Republican Army in North-ern Ireland, the Irgun in the old state of Palestine, Basque independ-ists in Spain, Moslems in Afghanistan, and the endless array of splinter groups in every hemisphere, from Tamils in Sri Lanka to Tutsi and Hutu in Africa. These are, in the main, however, national groups fighting in their own lands.

Then there are the rogue nations, like Libya's regime and other states characterized by the U.S. State Department as promoters of terror, who employ clandestine violence internationally as a real—if unstated—form of national policy. These nations harbor other nations' rebels, traffic in the nether regions of illegal arms traders, finance attacks on regimes they dislike, and otherwise seek to "destabilize" their enemies.

International terrorism can take such bizarre twists as attacking American sites because of our aid to Israel or bombing an airliner out of the sky in retaliation for a punitive military strike. Terror might be described as the weaker opponent's response to a more formidable foe.

Terrorism can take a very personal form, as in the attempt to extort ransom in exchange for safety, in the case of a man caught with explosives who planned to injure subway passengers if his demands were not met, or in the case of the Unabomber. It can also be an expression of simple grievance by a disturbed person, as it was with New York subway system's Mad Bomber in the 1950s, who turned out to be a sad loner with a grudge, not against the subway, but against the agency that provided its power.

While the United States has been a haven to organized crime, fallow ground for embezzlers, and a virtual nirvana to the street criminal, the nation has been generally free of the sort of terror that surfaces as explosions in cafés in Europe, the mowing down of bus passengers in the Middle East, the assassinations in Asia, the genocides in Africa, the exquisitely varied forms of violence in Latin America—such as that practiced by the uneponymous Shining Path guerrillas of Peru—or the politically inspired carnage occasionally flashing on our screens or dotting our newspapers.

For reasons as complex as why the Mafia thrived in Chicago and not Seattle, the end result is that America has, for most of its history, been relatively free of terrorism, with emphasis on both "relatively" and "recently."

Terrorism in America has usually and fairly inevitably mirrored the political angst of the age. Mainstream protest movements, whether pacifist, anti-Vietnam War, Civil Rights, extreme right, left wing, or whatever, invariably harbored extremist splinters dissatisfied with the crawling pace of change and determined to accelerate it.

It is lost on most Americans that one of the few effective ways to combat terror is to infiltrate the mainstream group and drift off with the splinters who break away. Any study of the activities of New York City's Bureau of Special Services—the New York Police Department's intelligence arm—in the 1950s and 1960s will reveal that criminal conspiracies were repeatedly interdicted in just this fashion, and without breaking the law in order to enforce it.

The public's abhorrence of such spying techniques—etched deeply and vividly by Hoover's excesses as he chased his phantoms—made infiltration of political groups politically unpalatable and legally impracticable, even when no law barred such approaches.[2]

The result of such acquiescence to fashion were tragedies such as the Ruby Ridge, Waco, Oklahoma City, and World Trade Center disasters and the train derailment in Arizona in the fall of 1995. In earlier times such groups—militant activists of both extremes of the spectrum (we mustn't forget that the Bureau of Special Services infiltrated the American Nazi Party too)—were monitored from within, and their criminal conspiracies were nipped in the bud.

Religion has, as often as politics, served as a vehicle for extortions, sexual exploitations, brain washings, and other criminal abuses, and it has not hesitated to use terror, as Japan discovered, to its horror, with the gas attacks in its subway system. The radical elements in the Islamic, Protestant, Catholic, Jewish, Hindu, and other religions have demonstrated the potential for violence in the most benign organizations.

INTERNATIONAL TERRORISM

The U.S. government, which has been tracking international terrorist incidents, confidently trumpeted a decline of 36% in 1992, with 361 events compared to 567 in 1991. It labeled Iran as the most dangerous sponsor of terrorism in 1992 and cited the March 17, 1992, truck bombing of the Israeli Embassy in Buenos Aires, which killed 29 and wounded 242, as the year's most spectacular act. Only two U.S. citizens died at the hands of terrorists in 1992. By 1994 America boasted it was winning the war and cited a 23-year low of only 321 incidents.

The six countries then listed as sponsoring terrorism were Iran, North Korea, Syria, Cuba, Iraq, and Libya. The subsequent death of Kim Il Sung of North Korea and the efforts of Cuba and Syria to gain international respectability have tempered, fitfully, the activities of these nations in the use of terror or the subsidizing of insurgencies. The other three remain players in this deadly game.

Countries like Haiti have seen repeated resortings to awful acts of terrorism as factions battle for control of the nation. And at least one of the thuggish leaders was, in 1995, reported to have been an employee of the CIA.

Tensions can be reflected in the activities of exile groups in America, as the political turmoil gets expressed in our streets. Pro- and anti-Castro Cubans have clashed on New York and Florida streets and have escalated the violence; a Chilean exile was blown up in our capital, and a Spanish exile was plucked from the streets of Manhattan by a Latin American dictator in 1956.

Suicidal terrorists pose particularly deadly threats—much in the manner of the Japanese kamikazes who threatened the U.S. Navy in the Pacific in the 1940s. In France, Algerian Islamic fundamentalists had to be stormed and killed before take-off, on the day after Christmas in 1994, because they were going to blow the plane up, in flight, with 171 hostages board. A special team of French commandos killed the four hijackers and recovered 20 sticks of dynamite. Just six years earlier, this time four days before Christmas, Pan Am Flight 103 exploded over Lockerbie, Scotland, killing all aboard. As 1995 was ending, Algerian terrorists had France in fearful thrall as they exploded bombs, repeatedly, to change the nation's policy toward Algeria.

Charges flew of American contributions to terrorism elsewhere by allowing fundraising among émigré colonies in the states for such groups as the Irish Republican Army or the militant Islamic movement Hamas. A major irony lies in the transformation of such groups into respected political bodies, as their ends are achieved through the use of terror. It is easy to forget that violence can work.

The Palestine Liberation Organization, just like its Israeli enemies, discovered the need to reverse roles speedily as it assumed responsibility for its territory and now had to curb the extremists in its midst, who threatened the new peace. Another irony lies in the number of enemies the cause of peace can entertain, as dramatically illustrated by Prime Minister Yitzhak Rabin's assassination by a militant Israeli in late 1995.

Fanatics seeking independence for Puerto Rico from its popular status of Commonwealth of the United States—as verified in repeated elections—led to shootings in the hall of Congress, an assassination attempt on President Harry Truman, five bombings of government buildings in New York City in 1982, and other terrorist acts. Only the overwhelming unpopularity of the cause and the terrorist-ennervating effects of freedom, which keeps the majority from joining the effort, have led to the movement's declining activities. It remains a permanent potential threat, however.

NATIONAL TERRORISM

Internally, native terrorism has evolved with the issues seizing the nation's imagination at any given moment. Occasional echoes remind us of the rapidly shifting tides of political violence.

Katherine Ann Power surrendered, after a 23-year life as a fugitive, on September 15, 1993, to answer for a bank robbery and murder of a cop in 1970. Her crimes had been expressions of opposition to the Vietnam War—another example of legitimate dissent crossing the line into criminality. In a plea bargain, she admitted guilt to charges of manslaughter and bank robbery and received a sentence of 8–12 years. This result testified not only to cooled passions but also to how differently her actions were viewed from the perspective of a nation that had concluded that her views on the war were correct, even as her actions were reprehensible and unforgettable. A female associate in the bank robbery served eight years and ran a successful computer company from jail.

Still another associate served three years in prison for the 1970 bombing of the Army Math Center at the University of Wisconsin in Madison, in which a researcher was killed and four were injured. An associate in this act later apologized to the researcher's family, following a prison stint. A third suspect is still at large, and a fourth went to prison, emerged, and obtained a law degree, but was unable to gain admittance to the Oregon bar.

Some blew up power transmission lines, because of their supposed effects on livestock. Others were convicted of inciting to riot and even advocating anarchy. Black militants committed crimes and engaged in gun battles with the police at the height of the civil rights struggle. Urban riots surfaced whenever a serious grievance impacted the ghetto. The threat of such insurrections remains alive to this day, as the questionable acquittal of Los Angeles Police Department cops in the March 1991 beating of Rodney King made abundantly clear. It seems distinctly possible that a conviction of O.J. Simpson in 1995 would have set off similar disturbances.

A snapshot of some of the Black Panther[3] leaders is useful for what it tells us about the directions taken by some of the more volatile activists in the civil rights struggle of the 1960s. One converted to Islam and became a soft-spoken minister in Atlanta, another succumbed to drug addiction and was shot to death in 1989 in Oakland, and a third had drug charges against him dropped, registered as a Republican, and owns a recycling company. Their names were, in the struggle's heyday, bywords for militancy—H. Rap Brown, Huey Newton, and Elridge Cleaver. Stokely Carmichael changed his name to Kwane Teure and moved to Guinea.

The Weather Underground[4] employed violence in its antiwar protests in the 1960s—a sort of political oxymoron—and other protesters accidentally blew up a Greenwich Village townhouse while making bombs. It was clear that, by the early 1990s, there was a national sense that the violent, criminal aspect of the Vietnam War and nuclear arms protests needed to be laid to rest.

The shifting tides of activism had the left waxing in the 1960s and waning in the 1990s, as the right began to surge. The still-simmering bubbles of racism continued to froth, visibly and subtly. The derailment of a train on October 9, 1995, killing one, denoted shifting political tides. In this attack a note signed by "The Sons of Gestapo" claimed responsibility. The note was still another echo of the right's grievances against the government and its actions in Waco, Ruby Ridge, and elsewhere.

PERSONAL TERRORISM

While most terrorism swabs the large canvas of political ideas or religious movements, some of the more suggestive artisans learn to apply the strokes to their own tiny frames.

A man was charged with mailing a bomb to his wife, which exploded in her hands on July 10, 1995, in Raleigh, North Carolina. Most of her left hand was blown off. She had recently increased her life insurance. A coworker at the woman's phone company office was also injured.

A spurned lover mailed six bombs to his girlfriend's mother, sibling, and relatives, with four exploding, killing five within 90 minutes of each other, in late December 1993, in upstate New York. Only alertness and suspicion prevented the other two from taking additional lives. The suitor and a gullible, pathetic stooge—who'd inexplicably helped him—were charged with the crimes. The mastermind was described by neighbors as a weirdo.

But for the use of bombs and the elaborate preparations that betoken the acts of terrorists, these might be labeled simple murders. There is clearly aping behavior, but might not have these occurred anyway? Perhaps not.

A husband lured his estranged wife, their baby daughter, and the wife's two other children into his car to buy clothes for the kids. He blew himself and them up in a Maryland mall's lot on September 11, 1995.

An army paratrooper mailed a pipe bomb to the man he suspected of being his wife's boyfriend, but was thwarted by the wife's previous warning not to open any suspicious packages. The husband had also been able to secure a gullible buddy's aid, and both were charged, on September 29, 1994, with the crime.

A businessman sent his partner an inflatable doll rigged with enough dynamite to crack a nearby house's foundation when it exploded. It killed the target's 19-year-old son and maimed his nephew in the fall of 1993. The motive was insurance, as their joint business was experiencing financial problems.

Two teenagers were set on fire in a subway car in New York City on December 15, 1994. Thirteen were seriously burned in a similar subway incident just six days later, only this bomb went off while still held by the suspect, severely burning him. The devices were mayonnaise-type glass jars filled with a flammable liquid and wired to batteries. The suspect's house yielded evidence linking him to the devices, as well as notes indicating his intention to extort money—probably from the Transit Authority. He had a history of contentious relationships and slipping prosperity and was unemployed at the time of the explosions.

Accidental detonations that lead to the easy capture of the terrorists have long been one of the unaccountable boons of such awful crimes. This does little to ease the sense of vulnerability of the random targets of these acts. The 1994 incident seemed a macabre reprise of the Mad Bomber of the subway system in the 1950s.

But the individual personal acts that copycat terrorism at least possess a rationale. There is a motive, and the animus is aimed at a specific person or place: The bomb is mailed to an enemy, the poison is transmitted to the insured, the killing is of a now-despised former lover, and so on. This may, as we've seen, alert the possible victims and allow them to act to prevent injury.

Terrifying to contemplate is the employment of terror for no reason other than to inflict cruelty on the innocent by, for example, booby-trapping public areas.

One such frightening act occurred when a Chinese restaurant

chef, working long hours to support his family, tripped a wire across a sidewalk in Miami, setting off a pipe bomb that killed him instantly. The device was apparently intended for anyone walking that route.[5]

The usual acts of terrorists, however, are aimed at targets with symbolic or strategic value, and the persons frequenting those locations—whether as workers, visitors, tourists, passersby, or whatever—must rely on the random, fickle nature of such tragedies. Looking at some specific acts serves to illustrate the threat.

THE WORLD TRADE CENTER

Shortly after noon on Friday, February 26, 1993, a bomb exploded in the underground garage of the World Trade Center,[6] at Manhattan's southern tip, rocking the 107-floor edifice, killing six, injuring over a thousand, causing panic in the building and traffic snarls in the area, and sending a cold frisson of fear through the nation.

In the numbing aftermath of the shock, America's attention shifted from Balkan groups to Hezbollah—the pro-Iranian group credited with the 1983 suicide car-bombing of the U.S. Embassy in Beirut and the 1992 devastation of the Israeli Embassy in Buenos Aires—to the Irish Republican Army. No group claimed responsibility for the blast. A letter to the *New York Times*, received four days after the explosion, signed by "The Liberation Army Fifth Battalion," was believed to be authentic. Its contents criticized the United States for its support of Israel and for meddling in Middle Eastern affairs.

As the headlines shouted, a clearly panicked nation searched frantically for answers. The need for explanations drove both the media and officials into such unhelpful speculations as guessing as to the motives, the identity of the group responsible, or even the materials used. The pressure from the fearful public was intense. It got full voice in the media's hysterical demands for solutions.

Unnamed officials, speaking on condition of anonymity, fed the speculations in a kind of deadly guessing game to see who would be proved right. Serbian groups, the "suspects de jour," were thrown into the bubbling cauldron of suspicion, along with the usual targets.

And then, on March 4, 1993, an Islamic fundamentalist was arrested and charged. The unraveling of the mystery got into high gear. He had attempted to retrieve a $400 deposit on the van used to blow up the World Trade Center garage. The van had been identified through the meticulous collection of fragments in the rubble. The police had, years earlier, lobbied for the imprinting of identifying serial numbers on auto parts to solve such crimes as this, as well as to attack the cannibalization of autos for parts by thieves.

Now came the task of discovering coconspirators, searching suspect locations for clues, establishing motives, and calming the nation. The suspect was quickly linked to a sect of extremist Islamic fundamentalists that opposed the secular Egyptian regime and that had been tied to the assassination of Anwar el-Sadat in 1981. The group also had connections to the man accused of killing Rabbi Meir Kahane, who was acquitted of the murder but was convicted—and is now serving time—for gun possession and other crimes related to the event.

A second suspect, a chemical engineer, was arrested on March 10, 1993. The 1000-pound bomb was found to have been made from routine ingredients, such as those found in fertilizer, the cost of which probably didn't exceed $400. Ignition was by a blasting cap, such as those frequently used at construction sites. As would be clear in the Oklahoma City blast in April 1995, there was no mystery about building such a bomb. Libraries were full of accounts and descriptions, and the materials were and are ubiquitous and easy to buy. High school students were able to lend real weight to their threat to blow up their school, having gotten information on how to build a bomb on the Internet.

An outspoken enemy of the Egyptian regime, the blind cleric Sheik Omar Abdel Rahman, was quickly fingered as the inciter of the plot and as the leader who inspired the band of terrorists who carried out the attack. He vigorously denied the charges. He had been twice admitted into the United States despite his appearance on the State Department's list of suspected terrorists.

As the investigation ground on, the number of suspects widened, and the picture of a plot against Israel—in the killing of Meir Kahane—and America, as Egypt's ally, became clearer, as did the connections of the accused to the cleric and to Kahane's possible assassin.

Exactly one month after the explosion, the investigators had identified the six Middle Eastern terrorists believed to be responsible for the crime. The sixth was being sought and was captured later. The number involved would grow to 11 by July 1993.

On July 8, 1993, Egypt hanged seven militant followers of Sheik Omar Abdel Rahman for attacks on foreign tourists. Later that month another five were executed, bringing the total to 14 during those weeks.

In July 1993 the FBI revealed that it had had a paid informant within the terrorist group since November 1991.

Additional plots to blow up other sites—and one to assassinate Egyptian President Hosni Mubarak by a suicide mission during that official's visit to the United States in early April 1993—were uncovered. By August 1993 Sheik Omar Abdel Rahman and 14 others were indicted for seditious conspiracy—which meant that, while the authorities could not prove direct complicity in the World Trade Center attack, they would charge him and his associates with encouraging and abetting a campaign of urban terrorism against the United States.

Thus did the investigation and following prosecutions bifurcate into one against the bombers of the World Trade Center and the second against the bombers' associates in the general plot to attack American installations and persons who could not be linked directly to the February bombing, other than for exhorting such an act. For the seditious conspiracy case the government would have to rely first on their highly paid informant (well over $1 million and $2700 a month for expenses) and then on the taped statements of the Sheik, the literature in the case, and the discussions among the plotters. The bombing case would rely on physical evidence and the testimony of cooperating plotters—if they could be turned with the promise of a deal. The possibility of the death penalty—absent in this case—weakened the prosecutors' bargaining position.

The trial of the first four of the seven accused of the bombing began on September 14, 1993. The press followed the progress avidly. The trial unfolded along the predictable path of the event and the carnage, the van used to transport the explosives, and the recovery of chemicals and other evidence in the residences and other buildings used by the accused.

On February 14, 1994, the defense made closing arguments. On March 4, 1994—over a year after the explosion—the first four defendants charged were convicted of the attack. They were given sentences that would ensure their stay in prison for the rest of their lives.

Now the prosecutors would concentrate on the subtler conspiracy trial involving Sheik Omar Abdel Rahman and 11 associates. The trial, which began on January 9, 1995, was rocked by the defection of a principal, who would now be a government witness against his mentor and colleagues. He then reversed himself and declined to cooperate, having provided the government with useful information. Then he pleaded guilty, in February 1995, and testified against his associates. Another defendant turned on August 4, 1995, pleading guilty to a lesser charge.

Meanwhile, the alleged mastermind and ring leader of the World Trade Center blast was captured in Pakistan in February 1995, further ravaging the plotters' thinning ranks. He was indicted also on charges of plotting to blow up a number of flights in the Far East and had explosives in his suitcase at the time of his arrest.

This shadowy figure was linked, through fingerprints and other evidence, to terrorist plots all over the world that reflected his Islamic fundamentalism. His modus operandi was to plunge into the worlds of the politically disaffected—such as Sheik Abdel Rahman's circle of exiled militants—and recruit likely candidates for terrorist plots. A true catalyst, he represented a menace to the

Pope, presidents, political opponents, and the random targets that would publicize his cause.

WE ARE NOT EXEMPT

Such a combination of heinous acts requires a skilled, determined terrorist, a demagogue to inspire, and a group of the gullible to follow. Before we get too comfortable with the notion that these are, after all, exotic Middle Easterners pursuing esoteric ends in millennia-long grievances, we should remind ourselves of the replication within our borders of the genre.

Gathering the passion from the virus in the air and launched by the fervor of religious leaders, some of our citizens kill, burn, and bomb—in the name of saving life and serving God—in the field of abortion. Abortion—not generally included in our statistics on terrorism—is of a piece with the activities of those who employ violence for the purpose of achieving a political, religious, economic, or social end.[7–11]

The manhunt for the sixth suspect ended on August 1, 1995, with his capture in Jordan. His fingerprints had been found in the apartment used to assemble the World Trade Center bomb. He and the sheik would be tried together.

The World Trade Center explosion of February 26, 1993, had now been solved, two-and-a-half years after the event, with the arrests of the seven Middle Easterners who rented the van, prepared the explosives, and set off the blast. The governments or other official sponsors of the tragedy, if any, remained mysteries.

As the summer of 1995 was ending, the conspiracy trial of the sheik and what were, by then, nine other defendants, was in its seventh month. Its outcome would likely have a powerful influence on the course of terrorism in America. The accused were not likely to be dissuaded—and onlookers would either be encouraged by acquittals or discouraged by convictions.

The sheik and the nine associates were convicted on October 2, 1995, of plotting a day of horror against the United Nations, the Holland and Lincoln tunnels, the George Washington Bridge, and the Federal Building in Manhattan. The objective had been to coerce America into abandoning Israel and the loathed regime in Cairo.

There had been an abundance of intelligence pointing to the dangers posed by this group many months earlier, through the reports of the informer, the murder of a disaffected associate—Mustafa Shalabi—in 1992, the Rabbi Meir Kahane assassination and its link to El Sayyid A. Nossair, and the murder of another target in Cleveland. Yet the times had so shifted against political surveillance and infiltration as to prompt no action by the authorities.

At the multiple conspiracies' end, 14 had been convicted, four had pleaded guilty in several trials, and two had trials still waiting. One, Ramzid Ahmed Yousef, could be described as a world-class terrorist; another, Sheik Omar Abdel Rahman, could be held to be the religious and intellectual inspiration of the plotters. The rest constituted the malleable stuff of which exile life, and sometimes terror, is made.

The Aftermath

What, then, might we conclude about what was called, until the Oklahoma City explosion two years later, America's worst act of terrorism?

The most glaring result is the contrast between a brilliant and successful investigation—following the tragedy—and the flaccid, even indifferent, response to the hints of coming terrorism that preceded it. Murders in the Islamic fundamentalist exile group were treated as quotidian urban events. The assassination of a militant Zionist[12] was handled as an isolated, ad hoc expression of political animus, and the clues pointing to wider conspiracies—the making of bombs and other possible acts of terrorism—were largely ignored by the investigators encountering them.

The bombing of a gay bar on April 28, 1990, by Islamists opposed to homosexuality was treated as an act of urban vandalism.

Warnings by the Egyptian government were ignored.

Sheik Abdel Rahman was admitted to the United States twice,

while his name appeared on a list of terrorists to be denied entry. His preachings, incitements, and writings should have been enough to arouse the sleepiest intelligence agency. Although blind, he seemed to move with more assurance than his trackers.

Information relating to various targets for terrorist attacks, secured in 1990, was neglected. The sweeping conspiracy to spread terror in the United States was hatched in 1989 and included the November 1991 attempt by the sheik to convince the government informer to kill President Mubarak. This was treated as the typical ranting of a fanatic.

Can all of these be explained by attributing the cause to bureaucratic fecklessness? Not very likely, especially given the alacrity with which the actual event was met. The answer lies in the unspoken word omitted from even the most aggressive proposals for attacking terrorism—infiltration. This is the only really effective way of interdicting such conspiracies.

The abuses of Hoover's FBI, the Watergate scandal, the spying on innocent organizations committed to peace or nuclear disarmament, and the overwhelmingly persuasive rhetoric of the left about possible constitutional breaches in such actions have all combined to make infiltration anathema to law enforcers.

The World Trade Center plot would have been foreseen and forestalled by any law enforcement agency worthy of the name, but it would have had to be willing to undertake such actions as those being employed in drug deals and against organized crime. The nation's politics effectively forbade such an approach. There was also the reluctance to believe, and act on, the disclosures of the FBI's own informant, whose revelations tended to be pooh-poohed.

The event that would overshadow the World Trade Center explosion, just over two years later, suffered from a similarly disabling inhibition.

OKLAHOMA CITY

The World Trade Center's unwanted distinction as the worst act of terrorism to occur on American soil, ever, was to last a scant 26 months. The new record was set in an unlikely location by nondescript types whose kooky beliefs would not, save for the awful toll their ideas would take, ever receive anyone's serious attention.

The destruction of the Alfred P. Murrah building in Oklahoma City[13] by another car bomb, consisting of easily obtained fertilizer, and weighing almost 5000 pounds, a bit after 9 A.M. on Wednesday, April 19, 1995, took 168 lives, including 15 children; shattered the confidence of a complacent nation; and swept the World Trade Center off the charts. The toll came to include the leg of what was first described as a male drifter, later found to belong to an African-American female clad in military gear.

The horror of the event, magnified by the deaths of scores of babies and children, again galvanized the authorities into frenzies of activity that stood in stark contrast to the official somnolence preceding the assault. Within 48 hours the principal suspect, Timothy James McVeigh, would be arrested. By August another, Terry L. Nichols, would share the indictment with McVeigh, and a third participant—a marginal player—pleaded guilty to lesser charges and agreed to testify against his two former associates.

Thousands of FBI agents and other law enforcers combed the country for clues. As the figurative smoke of the inquiry cleared, it became obvious that this had been an entirely home-grown event.

While the Trade Center plot was redolent with international intrigue, the exotica of tangled Middle Eastern webs, and the incomprehensible ferocity of Islamic fundamentalism, the Oklahoma City blast had its roots in the long and sordid history of such terrorists as Klansmen, American Nazis, and gun nuts. Even the date would have its roots in the extreme rightists' angst over what it saw as fascistic government interference with the rights of the Branch Davidians to purchase and own as many firearms as they pleased. That it also proved the eve of Hitler's birthday was undoubtedly entirely ironic and unintendedly coincidental—yet worth noting, given the predilections of the plotters.

April 19 was the second anniversary of the climactic raid in Waco, Texas, by federal forces against the holed-up followers of David Koresh. The ensuing firestorm, following a tear gas attempt to roust and capture the occupants, took scores of lives, fanning the flames of hatred among those who saw the feds as "jack-booted fascists" bent on depriving Americans of a basic right. Confusion and controversy over the origin of the blaze enabled the right to go on demonizing the feds.

The climax had its origins in the ideological river of notions relating to racism, anti-Semitism, and rugged individualism that has been the heady stuff of white supremacist dreams.

While it was not a surprise that the extreme right would seize on the Ruby Ridge, Idaho, shoot-out with the FBI in 1992[14] as a sort of Götterdämmerung of their movement—justified and verified by a jury's siding with the accused criminals, not the cops—it was shockingly unexpected that they would be drawn to the cultish, sexually exploitative, and outright bizarre religious practices and beliefs of the Branch Davidians.[15,16] Extremism, like politics, makes for strange bedfellows indeed. The jury's verdict was a signal of waning citizen confidence in the government, just as the Simpson verdict proved a comment on race relations.

The Ruby Ridge incident had enough twists and turns to satisfy partisans on any side of the issue.

The feds were trying to arrest Randall C. Weaver for failing to appear in court to answer charges of having sold two illegal sawed-off shotguns to undercover agents in 1992. A shoot-out occurred at the Weaver cabin on August 21, 1992, in which a federal marshal and Mr. Weaver's 14-year-old son were killed. This skyrocketed the controversy. The response of the FBI hostage rescue team fed the flames of dissent when one of their snipers shot Mrs. Weaver dead as she held an infant.

The trial of Randall Weaver and Kevin Harris for the murder of the marshal ended in their acquittal, although Mr. Weaver was convicted of minor charges and sentenced to 18 months in prison. He sued the government for the death of his wife.

In 1995 details of an FBI cover-up, in connection with the identify of the official who authorized the sniper's shooting, ballooned into a full-blown scandal as charges of duplicity and destruction of records led to the demotion of the FBI's number two man and an obstruction of justice investigation by the Justice Department of a number of agents. In the end they concluded no crime had been committed.

More fuel was added to the mixture when the federal government agreed to pay the Weaver family $3.1 million, almost three years to the day of the tragedy, August 15, 1995, for the loss of mother and son.

Ruby Ridge would become a sort of latter-day Lexington in the fevered reckonings of the disaffected.

The drama at Oklahoma City, unlike the World Trade Center blast, in which the dead and injured were quickly removed and attended to and the building secured with repairs beginning almost immediately, played out over weeks of agonizing searches among the obscenely naked remnants of the once-proud structure. America's eyes were riveted on the exposed tangle of wires. The eviscerated building burned its image onto the national consciousness. While the nation had learned to live with a murder rate that replicated the 12-year carnage of the Vietnam War every 29 months, it hadn't gotten used to this form of danger.

As the inquiry accelerated, it began to center on militias—paramilitary organizations set up to resist such government intrusions as the levying of taxes or the confiscation of illegal guns. United States sovereignty was seen as forfeited to the United Nations, while myths of perfect personal autonomy were sustained as representing American freedoms.

Even the sending of American troops to keep the peace in Bosnia, under United Nations and NATO direction, fed the fevered imaginations of those who loved this country, yet hated its government. The refusal of a 22-year-old soldier to wear a United Nations beret or its shoulder patch led to his court martial and martyrdom on the radio talk show circuit of the right in early 1996. He was convicted and sentenced to a bad conduct discharge.[17]

These paramilitary groups, with their newsletters, radio programs, meetings, speeches, and such incendiary tracts as *The Turner Diaries* by Andrew MacDonald (a pseudonym) had, because of the central involvement of the Bureau of Alcohol, Tobacco, and Firearms agents in the February 1993 raid on the Branch Davidians, held Waco up as the most vivid example of big government's interference with the rights of Americans—especially the purported, if erroneous, right in the Second Amendment to bear arms without limit.

The presence of child sexual abuse and other morally inde-
fensible practices had to be sloughed over because of the convenient presence of their *bête noire*—the Bureau of Alcohol, Tobacco,
and Firearms—in the controversy. "Family values" and similar
rhetoric of the right had to be soft-pedalled, given Koresh's sexual
exploitation of children in his charge.

In another irony, those who used "law and order" as code
words for racist repression now painted the forces of law enforcement—no longer seen as allies since the reforms following
the Selmas of the 1960s—as the enemy.

All of this ideology inspired the bombing of the Oklahoma
City federal building—an act strikingly similar to fantasized attacks on the government enemy that was included in so much of
the literature of the extreme right. This included a reference to a
car-bombing explosion at the FBI building in Washington, D.C., in
one of the tracts. Conspiracy theories are as abundant as references to the patriots who practice "leaderless resistance" (small,
impenetrable cells of fighters) against the government. By the time
of the blast, such citizen militias existed in 30 states, concentrated
in rural areas and in the West.

As the evidence piled up and the indictments were issued, the
picture that emerged out of the flames, horror, and smoke of the
April 19 blast was of at least two persuaded acolytes of the extremist movements evolving—to suit the times—in American political life. The suspects stood as mute but dramatic testimony to the
power of ideas. The tsunami of publicity following the event
resulted in expanding membership rolls for these fringe groups.

The 11-count indictment, handed up on August 10, 1995,
charged Timothy J. McVeigh and Terry L. Nichols with robbing a
gun dealer to finance the plot, stealing dynamite and fuses from a
quarry, renting storage spaces for the materials, mixing a 4800-
pound brew of ammonium nitrate fertilizer and diesel fuel, transporting it in a rented van to the federal building, and setting it off,
resulting in the 168 deaths. The death penalty would be sought.

A third suspect, Michael J. Fortier, took a plea to lesser
charges and agreed to testify against McVeigh and Nichols. All
three had met in basic training as soldiers. McVeigh's sister—21

and believer in his theories of an oppressive government—was forced to testify against him at the grand jury hearing and emerged swathed in tears.

And so concluded the investigative and charging phase of a case that had begun less than four months earlier. Just like the Trade Center, the aftermath of the Oklahoma City terrorism had been characterized by remarkably energetic and effective investigative attention that, like the Trade Center tragedy, stood in stark contrast to the governmental indifference that preceded it. And, like the Trade Center, the trail led to those demonizing the American government as the Great Satan—only this time they were locals.

Again we have indications that cry out for investigative attention and follow-through. There were reports of an attempt by McVeigh to sell a rocket to a government agent that were largely ignored. There had been the robbery of a gun dealer and the taking of a vast array of weaponry, which was treated as a routine crime. The gun dealer had entertained well-founded suspicions as to the identity of the culprits. All of the information on the right-wing militants came from nonofficial bodies that, alarmed over the possibilities, at least monitored and collected intelligence on these groups. The private sector seemed able to track citizens' credit histories and to monitor suspect political activities, while civil libertarians fulminated over every potential governmental intrusion intended to provide a more peaceful nation.

The exhorters—whether commentators, writers, recruiters, exploiters, or whatever—bore no direct, legal responsibility for the deaths of the children and others, but they clearly bore a heavy moral responsibility for such grotesque rhetoric as that which, even today, attempts to paint the incident as a secret government plot on which to predicate further acts of repression. This was a reprise of the 1933 Nazi burning of the Reichstag in order to justify and accelerate the growth of that garrison state through an act of provocation that was blamed on the communists.

The demagogues play on commonly held concerns over a decaying society and appeal to survivalists with a mélange of options that attract those anxious to grow their own food as well as the troglodytes prepared to take to the hills and fire at the feds from the ramparts.

The event had been an attempt by the few to cover the many. It took place in the heartland and included many government employees among the victims. Particularly tragic was the awful toll of those taken in the dawn of life.

The FBI director sought congressional guidance as to how "proactive" to become—by which he probably meant, "Should we infiltrate or not?" Meanwhile and predictably, measures were being suggested for the expulsion of aliens, the erection of barricades, the hiring of additional agents, the adoption of ever-more restrictive security measures, and other mindless actions intended to expand the growing garrison state—and its mentality—without adding measurably to the ability to meet such challenges.

The extremists may not have been winning the gun battles, but they seemed to be making real headway in altering America's thinking. The simplistic, gun-crazy, paranoiac, mackinaw-clad and -minded romantics of the far right looked like naïfs—if deadly ones—when compared to the purposeful fanatics of the World Trade Center bombing or the loftier intellectual heft of a lone figure who terrorized the nation and made a menace of every innocent package arriving in the mail.

THE UNABOMBER

The Unabomber—so dubbed by the FBI because of his choosing universities and airlines as his early targets—first struck on May 25, 1978, when an unmailed parcel exploded at Northwestern University, injuring a security guard.[18,19]

The second also went off at Northwestern in 1979, injuring one. Another exploded in a flight from Chicago to Washington, D.C., later that year, injuring 12 through smoke inhalation. The Illinois connection continued in 1980, when the president of United Airlines was hurt after a package mailed to his home exploded. These early signals inspired the FBI to canvass Chicago area high schools in an attempt to identify the terrorist.

The geography expanded with a 1981 blast in a classroom of the University of Utah, with no injuries. The next year a bomb placed in a coffee lounge at the University of California at Berkeley exploded, injuring a professor. Three years later, in 1985, Berkeley experienced a blast in a computer terminal room, seriously wounding a student. Three days later Boeing employees in Washington state dismantled a bomb mailed to their fabrication section. In November a bomb mailed to a University of Michigan psychology professor's home exploded, injuring a research assistant, and, less than a month later, on December 11, 1985, a bomb left in a package in a computer rental store went off, killing the owner. This was the first fatality in the series.

It would be over a year before the Unabomber would strike again, with a return to Salt Lake City, as a bomb placed in a bag went off in the parking lot of a computer firm, maiming a worker.

Then came a baffling silence of over six years, until June 22, 1993, when a geneticist in California opened a package mailed to his home, injuring him when it went off. Just two days later a Yale University computer scientist was seriously wounded by a mail bomb sent to his office. On December 10, 1994, an executive at a public relations firm was killed when he opened a package mailed to his home in New Jersey, and, just over four months later, a timber industry lobbyist was killed by a bomb sent to his predecessor in California.

The bomber accompanied his missiles with warning missives to *The New York Times* and other media, in which he included an identifying code and which sometimes referred to explosions that would follow. The distinctive signature made it clear that the bomber and the writer were identical, but making certain of the identity, the bomber included "F.C." on the bombs—all of which reflected deep and growing complexity and technical competence—on parts that would survive the blast.

While his bombs killed one person and injured 22 over the first 16 years, the toll increased as the deadliness of the devices was enhanced. The explosions of December 1994 and April 1995 killed both recipients. By then there had been 16 bombs, three deaths, and 23 injuries.

A letter delivered April 24, 1995, to *The New York Times* and others listed the targets as "specialists in technical fields." The bomber sought the "destruction of the worldwide industrial system" and described his group (using "we" repeatedly) as anarchists. Although the image was not invoked—perhaps because of its lapse into memory's deeper recesses—Luddite seemed a more apt description of the Unabomber.

In a taunting letter postmarked April 20, 1995, to the Yale computer professor who had been seriously injured in a June 1993 blast, the Unabomber criticized the invasion of privacy threatened by computers, genetic engineering (to which computers contribute), and environmental degradation as a result of computer-assisted economic growth.

The Unabomber's manifesto to *The New York Times*, in June 1995, revealed a philosophical bent rooted in a solid education and reflected in an impressive ability to express complex ideas fluidly. It is hard to imagine the "limited-education" loner described in the early FBI profiles as being remotely representative of this intellectual terrorist.

In an example of entrepreneurial journalism, Bob Guccione, the publisher of *Penthouse* magazine, offered to publish the manifesto fully and sniffed at having been ignored as possibly not being a "nationally distributed periodical." His full-page ads thrust his magazine into the vortex of publicity and controversy surrounding the terrorist's document. And, in the style of "La Ronde," a Northwestern University fraternity, Chi Delta Chi, made shirts with the Unabomber's likeness over the caption, "I've got your package," in an attempt to recruit pledges in the fall of 1995.

The question was now whether "F.C." would remember the example of George P. Metesky, the Mad Bomber of the New York subway system who placed 47 pipe bombs in the 1940s and 1950s, injuring scores but miraculously killing none. Metesky was flushed by an open letter from the *Journal American*, which he felt compelled to answer. The response contained clues of former employment at Consolidated Edison that led to his arrest in 1957.

He was sent to an asylum until 1973, when he was released. Metesky died in May 1994, at age 90.

While the extremist Islamic fundamentalists and right-wing extremists cried out for infiltration—because of organizational need, funding requirements, recruitment imperatives, and other encompassing considerations—loners like Metesky, the Son of Sam serial killer, and the Unabomber could not be infiltrated.

The loner represents another sort of challenge—one that requires meticulous, ongoing gathering of facts and evidence (not rumors or resort to psychics or other unprofessional, desperate measures unworthy of law enforcers), and one that involves the public.

People see, hear, and know things, but they aren't always in a position to evaluate the significance of the information. In order to exploit this knowledge, investigators have to make the public partners in the inquiry by revealing as much as possible and by coaxing the public to participate in a sort of "Catch the Unabomber" game. A reward such as that offered in the case—$1 million—lends a real incentive to the contest.

For example, there is a sort of itinerary of the Unabomber and a distinctive, and very possibly recognizable, voice in the style (there is now an extensive array of writings); there was a recovered message to "call Nathan R Wed 7 p.m."; there is a sketch of the suspect from the one sighting and other connections—such as that some of the targets had been mentioned in *The New York Times*; there are the fictitious names and addresses used on the bomb packages; and there are such mistakes as sending a parcel to an executive who had retired a year earlier. However tenuous, these are connections. However bizarre, the Unabomber seems to have a clearly defined motivation. Surely someone knows something. The investigative challenge would be to find a way to get the public—perhaps only the segment of it that reads *The New York Times*—involved in the hunt, or to jog the consciousness of someone close to the bomber who has failed to add up the various elements.

The Unabomber's 35,000-word manifesto was published by

the *Washington Post* on September 19, 1995, with the costs shared by *The New York Times*. The sensible surrender to the extortion that he'd cease the killing received a predictably mixed response from the media.

Then, on April 4, 1996, the world was stunned by the revelation that the nation's biggest, longest manhunt was apparently over. The FBI announced the arrest of Theodore J. Kaczynski, a 53-year-old former mathematician who was living a hermit's life in a remote, primitive, tiny cabin in the Montana mountains. He was a Harvard graduate and a Ph.D.

When arraigned he was charged with possessing bomb-making implements. Instructional materials on the manufacture of explosives were recovered, as was the manual typewriter on which the manifesto was typed.

Now would come the laborious process of matching the materials traceable to the suspect to the carefully collected fragments and other evidence—such as unexploded bombs and other items—that were sent to the almost two dozen victims of the Unabomber. The DNA makeup of saliva on stamps and envelopes would also be matched.

With the arraignment began the meticulous gathering of evidence and preparation for trials that were likely to extend well into 1997 and beyond. It seemed very likely, however, that the FBI had, at long last, located the Unabomber.

Predictably, the lead came from someone close to the suspect—his brother—who matched the writings he knew had originated with Theodore to those attributed to the Unabomber. The issue of the $1-million reward was not a subject for early speculation, but it may have played a part in the discovery, as patriotism and decency might just as well have done. What is clear is that by revealing and publicizing a lot of the Unabomber's writings, the authorities were able to enlist the aid of a knowledgeable person close to the suspect who could point him out. It was a function of familial propinquity more than sleuthing skills.

The Unabomber—if this was indeed the culprit—would serve as a key player in the capital punishment debate. This was a calculated series of crimes, resulting in three deaths, and it seemed desirable to place death on the scale of calculation of anyone else contemplating such strikes against innocent humans. Guilt would have to be established beyond a shadow of a doubt, and the suspect would have to be proved criminally sane.

If the execution of Hauptmann proved an object lesson for would-be kidnappers, it seemed logical to assume that the execution of the Unabomber would prove a similar deterrent to would-be terrorists.

IMPACT

Still, it is statistically demonstrable that any of us is a lot likelier to be struck by lightning than by one of his bombs—or by that of any other terrorist, for that matter. So, why worry?

Besides the disquieting effects of the randomness of it all—that totally unanticipatable targets made up the casualty lists—there is another element that affects each of us.

The three New York metropolitan airports were closed down for more than an hour on August 28, 1995, confusing travelers all over the nation in a domino effect. Imagine being in charge of such a facility. A bomb threat arrives, as happened here; a decision must be made. The cost-benefit analysis pits the odds of a bomb against massive inconvenience, and worse, if paralysis is chosen. The decision-maker can assess the nature of the call—was it specific, knowledgeable, similar to others that preceded an actual explosion, or was it a psycho, a drunk, or a kid? Then comes an assessment of the facility—is it open to the public, vulnerable and a place where a bomb might have been left easily, or is it in an area restricted to known and cleared employees?

In the airport case, the area threatened was secure and available only to workers, so why did they evacuate? In normal circumstances they would have called the police, alerted the workers, undertaken a search, and carried on.

The shadows of the Unabomber, the World Trade Center, and Oklahoma City persuaded the executive to opt for the paralysis.

Absent these incidents and realities, the travelers would never have known of the incident. There was no bomb.

The existence of terrorism holds a society hostage, not just to fanatics practicing this violence, but also to every nut or idiot with a quarter.

Every society produces grievances and aggrieved individuals. Some tiny minority will dedicate their lives to vengeance or victory, and some have won, as is evidenced in the histories of many states. The causes shift and the players change, but the constant is the willingness to employ violence, spread terror, and achieve an identifiable objective.

We have had terror from the left and from the right; we have had terror employed by racists and those fighting racism. The terror can frequently be traced to a legitimate debate in the body politic, in which the rhetoric is taken to its extreme point and is used to justify the crimes committed in its name.

When leftist lawyers charge the government with fabricating evidence and plotting to destroy political dissenters, they play the equal, if converse, role of those who see the government as interfering with God-granted freedoms and rights.

And, for those who think that leftist terrorism was an artifact of the 1960s, there are the enviroterrorist attacks on power lines in Arizona and against logging interests, in the form of tree spikings in the Northwest, to temper misplaced optimism.

Society faces the intricate task of erasing terror without eradicating rights or undermining the Constitution.

The advent of nuclear weapons and deadly chemicals and gases geometrically increase the stakes in a nation that is a latticework of interdependencies dotted with essential and vulnerable targets.

While the United States continues to maintain a military establishment that still costs at least $300 billion a year (notwithstanding a defense budget that is about 10% to 20% lower and including secret funds), it largely ignores a number of threats within. This is as true of terrorism as it is of street crime—where political correctness requires calls for more cops, tougher laws, and more prisons, rather than any attempt to also get at the underlying causes.

The antiterrorism measures proposed by President Clinton very predictably followed the timeworn path of more agents, tougher penalties, using the military more extensively in such inquiries (in direct contravention of a policy adopted well over 100 years ago banning such dangerous activities), and expanding the authority to wiretap and widen the admissibility of evidence in court that was found to have been obtained "in good faith"—a thoughtless and extravagant gesture that assaults the Fourth Amendment's protections against unreasonable searches and seizures.

The proposed act contained a useful call for "tagging" explosives to facilitate their tracing and a broadening of the laws on chemicals and gases. The president carefully eschewed any initiative to broaden investigative authority to look into or infiltrate groups without solid evidence of a crime or plot. This was another serious flaw and mirrored, precisely, the prevailing reluctance to really debate the issues and develop a coherent approach. Fortunately, one of the aftermaths of the congressional hearing on Ruby Ridge was a loss of confidence in the FBI that got translated into a dramatic cooling of the political ardor for this flawed antiterrorism legislation. A diluted, less harmful version was being hurriedly passed to commemorate the first anniversary of the Oklahoma City bombing.

While survivors continued to lay flowers on victims of racism and a town in Indiana was shaken to its core by the discovery of a Ku Klux Klan membership list (1923–1926) linking families to this now-discredited organization, white supremacists and right wing militias bound by paranoia (about an intrusive government, taxes, communism, One Worldism, and other phantoms), perfervid religious views, anti-Semitism, racism, a passion for guns, and an unexpressed anarchical belief in the limitless freedom of the individual were commanding the national attention.[20–22]

Suspicion of government agencies by the far right in the 1990s was an eerie echo of the attacks of the far left on the FBI, CIA, and other government agencies in the 1960s. Central to this observation is the realization that extremism leads to crimes and that the government has a responsibility for safeguarding its citizens. And it cannot be ignored or forgotten that government agencies will abuse power if left unmonitored and uncontrolled.

So the challenge explodes in our faces and kills our children. The immediate impulse is to react, swiftly and violently, yet there is our nagging sense that we risk our democracy with precipitate responses.

Terrorism exists in our society—and always has. The threat is real and it is impossible to predict when a "tipping factor" that places foes of democracy in control of a group might occur.

What measures are needed? There must be a mix of toughness, concern for preserving the Constitution, and the need to control governmental excesses. A program to combat terrorism needs to include:

- A provision for the gathering of intelligence, the preparation of files, and the authority to infiltrate when an articulable possibility of crime is being explored.
- The use of court-authorized bugs, wiretaps, and search warrants: The need to justify such actions, to a judge, requires the collection and presentation of evidence—a very useful process. This should also guide the internal administrative authority to infiltrate.
- The use of "taggants" on explosives: We now take serial numbers on guns and auto parts for granted, but they've proved invaluable in the investigation of terrorism and other crimes. Obviously, some key ingredients, like fertilizer, would have to be exempt.
- National registration of all firearms: Handguns should be licensed only to those demonstrating a real need and proficiency in their use.
- Plea bargain arrangements to secure the cooperation of coconspirators and the death penalty in mass, premeditated killings: Mandated sentences paralyze the process.

- A RICO-type law that permits asset seizures, funds for a witness protection program, and a civil section that permits taking control of criminally led terrorist groups, which would either be disbanded or led to legitimate pursuits.
- A systematized process for incentives, bounties, and other rewards (such as a percentage of recovered assets from convicted criminals) to encourage informers.

We need to confront the reality that, in order to safeguard society in all areas of crime, whether white collar, organized, street, political, or terrorist, we need national, central files that contain reliable and useful criminal data. Imagine the filtration that could take place if licensed brokers, or others requiring official documents to function, could be checked against a central index. In order to be meaningful we would also have to adopt a national identity card based on the Social Security number.

There isn't much hope for such reforms, given the current antigovernment climate in America.

In the last presidential campaign of the twentieth century, only one candidate—Senator Richard Lugar—addressed the potential problem of nuclear terrorism and, judging from the reaction, wasn't heard. The advent of nuclear power and its increasing proliferation—totally consonant with the history of every new weapon—makes it certain that it will be obtained, and possibly used, by a rogue state or terrorist group, sometime ahead.

The time to control this potential problem is now—with laws, treaties, and the development and exchange of intelligence as well as with tight legal controls over production and the raw materials involved.

Nothing in this is inconsistent with the U.S. Constitution. It is essential that we remind ourselves that this central document was never intended to hamstring the operations of an honest government protecting its citizens.

The incidence of all this criminality has created an age of anxiety that might well produce overreactions that threaten our freedoms without furnishing the desired protections. The adopted Crime Bill and the orphaned terrorist proposal are both good examples of the useless genre. Any legislative steps need to be preceded by informed debate. Americans are going to have to learn the hard lesson that good responses require thought; that mindless, reflexive action taken in panic or to curry popular favor produce expensive problems, not solutions; and that demagogues stand ever-ready to furnish prescriptions.

7

Religion, Sects, Cults, and Other Searches

A people bombarded with evidence of moral disintegration and debased values everywhere will scurry for answers. Funks and malaises, such as we're now experiencing, produce mystical panaceas. If there is one thing certain, it is that self-seekers will arrive with nostrums.

When the world of politics is widely reviled as mendacious and corrupt—as evidenced by politicians running against Washington, the very site and symbol of our political life—when the world of commerce is seen as a moral abyss in which only the ruthless survive, when people rail about the decline of family values, and when every institution is made suspect by its strivings for secret advantage, the people are thrown into confusion.

Religions have long served as the transmitters of values and as the answers to mysteries—or as pointers of the way—to those lost.[1] They are the keepers of the flame of faith. It is in the temples that we utter our most solemn oaths—the places where lies cannot be told. Our moral compasses are set on the Sabbath.

Every major religion is based on love, peace, altruism, and salvation; yet there have been splinterings or temporal aberrations such as the Crusades and the Inquisition, the corruption of Rome, the excesses of Byzantium, the terror of Islamic extremists, Hindu massacres, the Salem witch trials, Jewish terrorism in Palestine, and, later, through such groups as The Jewish Defense League and the Ku Klux Klan. Instead of plenary indulgences, the Catholic Church was peddling annulments in the 1990s—reaching an estimated 50,000, versus a mere 450 in 1961. It looked like a new concession to the rich and powerful, but this action fed cynics who noted that some annulments were granted to persons who'd been divorced and who had remarried. What God had joined, the Church felt confident it could put asunder.

Every religion has known extremism that led to bloodshed, and every tyrant has invoked God as his sponsor. Nevertheless, there came reformations and corrections, and it could be asserted that mainstream religions hewed to the mainstream thoughts of benign founders and lasted because of the timeless worth embodied in virtue's message.

But the casual violation of sacred vows uttered in God's house has inevitably soaked into the social fabric, of which religion is such an essential part. Notwithstanding church attendance figures, the actions of Americans clearly show that religion's ties aren't very binding. And the children of such betrayals—so intimately affected—know, personally and instinctively, that they cannot trust the institutions their parents support with their lips.

But there is something in the human condition that determinedly refuses to accept the notion that this is all there is. There must be more. Where do we go from here? Simple extinction is an unacceptable idea.

The search is thus combined with human gullibility and the charlatan's high skills and ends with the conversion that leads to political, economic, or sexual exploitation. The advent of television, computers, and other vehicles for mass communication between the demagogue and the curiously lonely target make explosive growth possible.

As some came to see mainstream faiths as failing to answer the growing problems, a few moved to the edges, reluctant to abandon the faith altogether. Muslims shifted into fundamentalist tenets that justified the murder of enemies; Christians ambled to the paranoid excesses of racism and the troglodyte individualism of the Christian right; Jews fought for the ouster of Arabs—one went so far as to even massacre praying Muslims in Hebron; and the Balkans were aflame with "ethnic cleansings" and atrocities against women and children and the massive slaughter of men. All of the actions invoked the names of figures who had insisted humans should not kill, that they should love others and cherish justice and mercy.

The struggle between faith and science, vividly remembered from Galileo through Darwin, was heating to another boiling point over abortion, alternative inseminations, creationism, and the development of gene patents and animal experiments.

Extremists saw themselves as the true preservers of the message, but, for many others, the waters had been irremediably polluted, and they sought new answers.

Those lost and disaffected souls often sought, in such sports-related movements as the Jesus-loving Promise Keepers[2]—men who committed to spiritual renewal—The Way. Salvation lay in taking charge of the family and trying to ignore the statistical realities reflected in the lives of most of those praying and promising so fervently in these stadiums.

Although interracial, the message was masculinist—and it was a very safe bet that many of the converts had had their problems with relationships, substances, and life. Growing rapidly in 1995, the Promise Keepers had their roots in the techniques so tellingly perfected by the now discredited televangelists, except for the clear connection to America's real religion—sports.

THE TELEVANGELISTS

America has had historical affinities to preachers who spouted politics over instruments of mass communication.[3,4] Radio had its fascist, race-mongering fundamentalists, and television produces a slicker product. Among the early proselytizers for aberrant messages could be cited such household names as Billy Sunday (1916), Aimee Semple McPherson (in the 1920s), and Father Charles Coughlin (in the 1930s).

Reverend Jerry Falwell presides over a ministry that might be labeled broadcast. He founded the Moral Majority (now defunct) as a vehicle for furthering religious views in political life and promoted the most scurrilous attacks on President Clinton over his *Old Time Gospel House*, including charges that the president might have been implicated in murder.

Falwell's operation rankled many who believed that enjoying tax-exempt status precluded using the forum for political purposes. The Internal Revenue Service proved these skeptics right and forced the organization to pay taxes and to announce publicly the revocation of its tax-free status.

The 1980s were marked by the phenomenal success of preachers using television to reach mass audiences and raise incredible sums for sometimes suspect, or outright criminal, projects. The amazing thing was that these religious figures—onto a very good thing—were, just like the Wall Streeters, unable to evade the temptation to overplay their hands. It is nothing short of amazing how the human animal, having had prayers of prosperity more than answered, invariably overreaches.

Jim Bakker went to prison for mishandling contributions. Not content to sell the inexhaustible stock of salvation, he made the blunder of selling something finite. Just like the film *The Producers*—premised on the funny notion that the schemers would sell 150% of a deliberately created flop in order to pay debts and pocket the money, only to find they had inadvertently created a hit and wound up in jail—Bakker sold more spaces in a spa than could be accommodated. He emerged from prison at 53, after serving four years, in July 1994, to find himself divorced from Tammy Faye, who had married the chief builder of the theme park that started the trouble. Bakker was now contrite.

Jimmy Swaggart, another of the fabled televangelists, was linked to a tawdry tableau with prostitutes.

Oral Roberts raised money under the threat that God would kill him if the contributors failed to pony up the required amounts.

And Robert Tilton pulled his TV shows off the air amid charges that the checks were kept, but the accompanying requests for prayers were tossed in the trash basket.

Reverend Pat Robertson, sitting atop a huge media empire—the Christian Coalition—rode the vehicle to an attempt at the presidency and, failing, at least saw his ideas and followers dominate the 1992 Republican Convention.

Tony Alamo, whose roots were in a ministry for the homeless and drug abusers, nurtured that project into a business that, 20 years later, earned more than $9 million over four years. He married eight of his followers—some of them 15-year-old girls—under the threat of expelling the family from the church and threw out husbands who stood in the way. He was convicted, in 1994, for tax evasion and jailed.

The Traditional Values Coalition sent the Reverend Louis Sheldon, 60, to Washington, D.C., in 1994, to stress his organization's antigay message and opposition to homosexual rights.

These televangelists, having learned to use the media and mastering aspects of the political process, blurred the line between church and state. But the really scary thing about the religious right is their intractable belief that salvation is possible only through faith—in Jesus Christ, the Savior. The consequence of this tenet is to render any good work worthless, absent the investment of faith. The redemptive power of a good life is lost in the thicket of faith's unwavering requirement. In a real sense this subverts the civilizing ethical influence of religion.

The attempt to reach mass audiences with the invective of the far right struck pay dirt in talk radio, where hosts could pander to the listeners' paranoia and many callers could express their prejudice and anger; some even advised on how most effectively to shoot federal agents—aiming at body parts not protected by armor.

The Internet—America's computer bulletin board—became the vehicle for such notions as that the federal income tax is illegal and shouldn't be paid, that national citizenship is a Washington plot, that the federal government has no jurisdiction within the states, that the American Civil War had nothing to do with slavery and everything to do with economics, and that the U.S. Constitution was a plot to establish a totalitarian regime with Alexander Hamilton as the ringleader.

Libertarians announce that everyone is free to do whatever they please, with a resonant echo among the extreme right, who bitterly resent any intrusion on absolute freedom to the point of refusing to obtain licenses, register cars, vote, or pay taxes.

MAINSTREAM PROBLEMS

Adding to the growing skepticism were repeated disclosures of clerical wrongdoing.

In March 1995, a minister suspected of murdering a trusting couple crashed his car against an abutment, killing himself, having just bought a bookmark with the 23rd Psalm, "though I walk through the Valley of Death, I shall fear no evil." He had siphoned off about $45,000 from the account of the unworldly pair he'd brought together.

A rabbi whose wife was bludgeoned to death and who was suspected of extramarital affairs resigned his post the same month and year, citing "behavior I am not proud of."

A citizen in Marlboro Township, New Jersey, caused such traffic jams of people seeking to share his Sunday sightings of the Virgin Mary that his neighbors were forced to serve a court order to ease the congestions. The visions stopped in the spring of 1995, after three years of turmoil.

Another minister was, in a remarkable reprise of the suicide, charged with murdering a couple whose savings he was looting. Both parishioners, 90, had been beaten and strangled. At their funeral the accused minister had reported how proud he had been to call them Mom and Dad.

In early 1995 the Episcopal Church was shaken by a series of disclosures that included a bishop's suicide—following revelations of sexual improprieties and an attempt to bring a colleague to trial for ordaining a homosexual—and the charge that its treasurer may have misused as much as $2.2 million of church funds.

Catholic priests were regularly surfacing as suspects in cases involving the sexual abuse and exploitation of boys.[5,6] In a dramatic reversal, one, the accusation of sexual abuse against Joseph Cardinal Bernardin of Chicago, was dropped and the accuser apologized. In an extraordinary act of forgiveness, the cardinal sought out his accuser and prayed with him and anointed him, despite the pain and humiliation the charges had caused. The accuser died of AIDS but was unburdened of the guilt of his false charges. The Church, no doubt, fervently wished the scandal that had rocked Covenant House and its famous founder had ended as satisfyingly. It didn't.

In modern America, martyrdom came in unanticipated ways, as Reverend Samual Nathaniel Booth of the Pentecostal Christian Faith Tabernacle Church—a humble outpost in the ghetto—was robbed and stabbed to death on Christmas Eve, 1994, by a suspect who was arrested. Black churches were again being torched in the south in 1996.

Hasidic students were shot as they crossed the Brooklyn Bridge on March 1, 1994, killing one and wounding three. Their crime had been that they were Jewish. Their assailant, convicted, was a Lebanese immigrant. An Australian rabbinical student was murdered in the wake of racial tensions following an accident, in which a part of a famous rabbi's motorcade struck and killed a black child. And a rabbi who'd pleaded guilt to taking a $50,000 bribe to void the marriage of a prisoner he was ministering to faced resentencing when it was discovered that the payments had been in two checks, for $5000 and $45,000, rather than one payment of $50,000. He'd attempted to walk on the technicality that it had been two payments, not one, as alleged in the formal charge. The conviction, however, stood.

An Episcopal priest in the Bronx was ordered into a mentoring program that would help him understand his role because he'd allowed a layperson to celebrate Mass and used the sanctuary to bless same-sex relations. The congregation was outraged and protested the discipline.

Buddhists and New Age believers also saw spiritual leaders charged with sexual improprieties in Massachusetts and California.

And the malling of mainstream religion accelerated as marketers offered a menu of jazzy services to suit every taste at these latter-day meccas of American suburban life. Their very names conveyed the zeitgeist, with such labels as the Community Church of Joy. Not to be outdone by Phoenix, a Houston church dubbed itself The Fellowship of Excitement. The services offered by these entrepreneurial bodies rivaled the organizational complexities of mighty industrial empires.

The Catholic Church in New Mexico was shocked by the resignation of the first Hispanic Archbishop, on charges of sexual relations with several women in the 1970s and 1980s and on the accusations that 14 priests had been sexually molesting children over the past 20 years. The same charge was leveled against a priest in upstate New York in 1993. That priest was the third removed from a Hudson Valley parish, on similar charges, during that same year. And two parishioners were legally barred from Catholic services because of their rosary chanting, which disrupted services. They spent six hours in jail for refusing to desist in what they held were the legitimate expressions of true piety.

At the same time, the National Conference of Catholic Bishops fought for moral renewal—attacking poverty and violence and promoting a broad, if largely ignored, agenda of social, economic, and racial justice. In the mixed bag was included opposition to abortion, euthanasia, and, surprisingly, the death penalty.

Antipathy toward Islam led to the burning of five American mosques in 1994–95. A total of 222 individual attacks (spitting, death threats, shots at mosques) were directed against Muslims following the April 1995 bombing in Oklahoma City.

This was both an ironic and an eerie echo of the lynching of a Jew, Leo Frank, in Marietta, Georgia, in 1915, for a crime he did not commit. The public reaction to the outrage in Oklahoma City needed a focus and found a convenient scapegoat in Muslim fundamentalism. And, as with most such precipitate actions, it proved dead wrong. It appeared as if Islam had replaced communism as The Evil Empire.

The World Trade Center explosion, following the agonizingly extended captivity of American hostages by Iranian revolutionaries and the suicide bombing of over 200 marines in Lebanon, flowed naturally into the killings in Oklahoma and fed the flames of prejudice. The vitriol in the pronouncements of the Nation of Islam's Louis Farrakhan added to the fuel.

There could be little doubt that the mainstream religions were suffering bombardments of criticisms and disclosures sufficient to shake the sturdiest believer. Yet, the question could be raised whether this presaged an alarming growth in inner decay or was merely the more extensive reporting of a more open and less hypocritical and, perhaps, even more introspective, society. If the latter proved true, we would have nothing to fear.

Such anecdotes feed subjectivity, but they don't help develop objective answers. The disclosures of corrupt or criminal acts indicate a serious problem—whether recent and growing or long-standing and covered-up. Since institutions reflect the outer society pretty faithfully, it seems fair to deduce a sharp increase in moral rot.

Where would the gullible—and now disillusioned—millions following such hucksters as the televangelists go?

THE CHRISTIAN RIGHT

Labeling the Christian right[7] is unfortunate, because it either attempts to carry too much philosophy or drifts into the arms of the amorphous. But labels have their uses—otherwise they wouldn't be employed so freely—and the antidote to ambiguousness is definition.

Conspiratorialists

The true believers share a rough outline of theories that encompass (1) an internationalist plot (e.g., the United Nations, the Trilateral Commission—a fevered concoction relating to secret plots of world domination by a cabal of internationalists, Freemasons, or the Vatican) that undermines patriotic nationalism; (2)

the use of all materials—discredited or absurd, and however old—as supporting literature (e.g., "The Protocols of the Elders of Zion"—a psychobabble of anti-Semitism, long since proved to be a forgery); (3) a conspiracy theory that has the international bankers in secret pacts with our enemies—communists, Islamic extremists, or whoever is the demon of the day; (4) a world takeover by a godless government; and (5) the use of the Bible as the source for these beliefs, which requires expansive interpretations that have not proved inhibitors to the febrile souls pushing the agenda.

As the Waco hearings ended, the fax machines in Congress spewed forth the sulfurous venom of Jew-hating, gun-loving, homophobic, racist enemies of the American government, faithfully pursuing the desiccated outline that reflects their belief system.

Concocted incidents of children allegedly punished for a religious act in a school, for example, form a staple of the diet fed the gullible and frightened searchers inhabiting these groups. Apocryphal tales of kids suspended for crossing themselves form staples of their imaginings. The attempt to ban books considered sexually or politically subversive has resulted in the exclusion of masterpieces from many libraries.

The Christian Coalition's audience of over 4000 was treated to the wooings of every Republican presidential aspirant, save one, in Washington, D.C., in September 1995. The Coalition represented about 1.7 million members who favored cutting taxes and putting prayer in the schools and opposed abortion. The pariah was the abortion rights supporter Senator Arlen Specter. Another proabortion candidate, Governor Pete Wilson of California, was invited but declined to attend, citing a scheduling problem. Soon thereafter, he withdrew from the race, having been blemished by several key reversals of policy and having betrayed his promise, on running for governor, that he'd not seek the presidency. Wilson served as an excellent paradigm of the age.

The Christian Right—at its extreme—harbors views of white Christian supremacy, anti-Semitism, and conspiratorial theories that demonize international forces (particularly, but not exclusively, the United Nations) and is antiabortion, progun, and racially separatist. Even its views on taxes can be seen as a subliminal attack on the mostly black underclass.

A healthy majority has been able to tolerate such extremists at its flanks, both left and right, but, as the majority's health falters, these splinters grow into dominant themes and often carry the day—and the society—to its destruction.

Outerfringe believers are attracted to such places as Idaho, with its remote mountain fastnesses and homogeneous population (only 3400 blacks in a state population of about one million). The Aryan Nation, whose doctrine is called Christian Identity, has its headquarters there. The tenets of Christian Identity are that Europeans are the lost tribe of Israel, that Jews are satanic and blacks are subhuman, and that the federal government is illegal.

Randy Weaver, the central figure in the Ruby Ridge shootout on August 21 and 22, 1992, in which his wife and son as well as a federal marshal were killed and who surrendered following a 10-day siege, subscribes to the Christian Identity philosophy.

The confusion and possible FBI cover-up of the approach to Ruby Ridge fed into the sympathy felt for Mr. Weaver by his neighbors and confirmed the sick musings of his allies. His acquittal and the $3.1 million settlement sealed the deal. It was a great example of governmental maladroitness feeding the rumor mills of its enemies.

The event at Ruby Ridge segued seamlessly into the Branch Davidian disaster in Waco, Texas, in early 1993. Both became defining moments in Christian Right mythology. And, of course, the resentment bred by these "federal intrusions into the lives of Americans exercising God-given rights" led directly to the second-anniversary bombing in Oklahoma City, on April 19, 1995. There were three deaths at Ruby Ridge, over 80 in Waco, and 168 in Oklahoma City.

The Oklahoma City plotters were influenced by such figures as retired Lieutenant Colonel James (Bo) Gritz, who was building a compound in the remotest area of Idaho, called "Almost Heaven," in which to preach self-defense and opposition to international bankers and the government. He had written, in his newsletter, that the "tyrants" who had ordered the Ruby Ridge and Waco assaults "should be tried and executed as traitors." The bombing, a year later, was a response to this exhortation.

The Aryan World Congress of July 1995 was held in the Church of Jesus Christ Christian Aryan Nations, at Hayden Lake, Idaho, and was presided over by Richard G. Butler, the church's 78-year-old pastor. It drew a few hundred believers. The vestigial remains of the Ku Klux Klan are fixtures at such events, and David Duke remains a central player in this pool.

Mark Thomas operates a ministry for racists in Pennsylvania, where he teaches shooting skills. He publishes a monthly newsletter attacking Jews and hosted a weekend Hitler Youth Festival attended by 200 neo-Nazi skinheads in April 1994. Thomas came to public attention when two brothers—neo-Nazi skinheads[8] who were said to have visited the compound many times—were accused of a grisly triple murder. They were charged with the brutal killings of their parents and brother in March 1995. Both had tattoos across their foreheads—one "Berzerker," the other "Sieg Heil." Their mother had complained her sons were getting out of control before she was stabbed and bludgeoned to death. The boys had had problems with drugs and alcohol. They represent the danger in such preachings to the gullible and confused.

The neo-Nazi skinhead movement was estimated to have quadrupled nationally, from 1000 hard-core members in 1987. The Internet has enabled the groups to interconnect across the country and to spread their message of white supremacy. *Resistance* magazine and Rahowa ("Racial Holy War" condensed), a rock group, spread the word. One irony, among many, is that Nazi artifacts and reproductions are illegal in Germany, so they get sent there by an American manufacturer in Lincoln, Nebraska.

The neo-Nazi skinhead movement is growing, globally, in 33 countries, with about 70,000 members.

As malaise and funk spread in America, the search for demons would take predictable turns and wind up aiming at the anticipated scapegoats.

This fringe cannot be said to be numerous, but its influence leeches naturally into the conservative elements of the Christian Right, who profess antipathy for these extremists, but who, in many areas, draw energies from these fanatics. Just as the left draws philosophical energy from its extreme—leavening and moving it rightward toward more acceptable, and reasonable, centrism, the right is in reaction to its militant elements and shifts leftward, to the broader field of general consensus. And, out there, there are the malleable, gullible, half-psychotic characters picking up the messages as magnets attracting iron filaments in the air.

One event set a ghastly incident in motion.

Wacogate

In the hagiography of the right, it is easy to understand the appeal of David Duke (who, after all, managed to entice over half the white voters in Louisiana to vote for him for governor and who was packaged carefully to soft-pedal the darker hues of the message), Randy Weaver, or even such latter-day radio prophets as G. Gordon Liddy. But David Koresh? That is a stretch—yet one made, with fateful consequences.

The skeletal facts are, as they usually are, pretty simple and straightforward.

David Koresh, born in 1959 in Houston, to a single mother, exhibited a remarkable capacity to cite the Bible in an otherwise unremarkable life and drifted to southern California—the incubus of strange creeds. He proselytized for a renegade offshoot of the Seventh-Day Adventists—the Branch Davidians. Koresh landed in a pastoral compound of the Davidians (named for the Biblical House of David) in Waco and emerged as the leader after a bloody struggle.

Koresh—he was born Vernon Wayne Howell, but took David for obvious reasons, his surname a Hebrew transliteration of Cyrus, the benefactor of Israelites—evolved into claiming he was Jesus Christ and preached an apocalyptic salvation that included his planting his seed in virgins as young as ten. Members were drawn from England, Australia, California, and Texas, and some held off-compound jobs to support the enterprise.

The Manichaean denouement he preached would require

weaponry, and the Davidians stockpiled a huge armament. Some of these would be used in early, internecine struggles for control of the sect. Many of the guns were illegal, even in Texas.

The Bureau of Alcohol, Tobacco and Firearms (BATF) investigated and conducted a raid, with 100 agents, on Sunday, February 28, 1993. A violent gun battle erupted, leaving four agents and an unknown number of Davidians dead. The element of surprise had been blown, but the BATF stubbornly insisted on going through with the attack.

Thus began the stand-off that culminated, 51 days later, with the burning of the compound to the ground and the loss of approximately 86 members of the cult and their children. The flashpoint was triggered by a second raid, this time by the FBI, using tear gas and armored vehicles.

Behind the facts lay complexities in the governmental ranks that mirrored the bizarre realities within the compound.

The beleaguered BATF had barely survived a National Rifle Association (NRA)-inspired legislative effort, before Congress, to abolish the agency altogether, in the mid-1980s. Only a carefully orchestrated intervention by the nation's police chiefs saved BATF from almost certain extinction. It left the agency shaken and hungry for victories it might exploit, with publicity, into a more secure future. A society of police chiefs was, once again, preparing a defense of BATF before the determined congressional assaults that would begin with House of Representatives hearings on the Waco raid in July 1995. This would probably be followed by NRA-framed legislation against the hated agency.

Returning to the raid, the FBI, which gradually took control of operations at Waco, was then led by William S. Sessions, who had been the subject of a scathingly critical report by his boss, the U.S. Attorney General, as he departed with the Bush administration. As a result of Sessions' egregious abuses of office, in terms of perks, travel, and other emoluments, he was ultimately ousted by President Clinton, midway through the director's ten-year term. It was a measure of the weight of the evidence against him—much of it compiled by the Republican administration that appointed him—that he could be forced out, despite his determination to stay and the requirement of Congress' approval of his dismissal. This was not an ordinary presidential appointee who served at the whim of the chief executive.

So the nascent Clinton administration was advised by a discredited FBI director on one of the touchiest issues of the time— and there wasn't a day's experience as a cop among the dramatis personae, including the attorney general, making up this *opera buffa*.

At the scene were cops who were tired, bored, and fed up. Where was it to end? Were we men or mice? Are we going to let these scumbags get away with killing our brothers? Something very close to hysteria seizes cops over a cop-killing.

Cool and experienced heads were needed, to say contain, negotiate, and wear them out. They're not going anywhere. Surround them with concertina wire and call it the Waco Federal Detention Center. There is no need to precipitate action when nothing dramatically bad is happening at the moment. If they start killing people and throwing bodies out, then we need to have a plan of action and follow it, but not otherwise. Every urban police department had mastered negotiating and containment techniques in the ghetto violence of the 1970s. In this case the government became the embodiment of the cult leader's apocalyptic prophecy by attacking.

There was no one to counsel the new president, they didn't know where to turn for such advice, and they wound up listening to Sessions—and then firing him for reasons they knew only too well many months earlier.

The chickens would come home to roost on the second anniversary of this avoidable tragedy.

Might Koresh have, in Jim Jones' Guyana style, led his group in a mass suicide anyway? Perhaps yes, but then, as with Jones, it would be easy to lay the blame for the act. As it happened, gullible conspiracy theorists had been granted the boon of a believable scenario launched by an oppressive government.

In both Waco and Ruby Ridge unwise police tactics fed into the appetite of the crazies, anxious to believe the worst. And such lapses tragically lead to more disasters. At the 1996 FBI siege of the

Freemen in Montana, the feds had learned the bitter lessons of the past as well as the value of patience and containment.

Further along the thought chain can be found even slimmer splinters.

AUM SHINRIKYO

Ignoring the hostility to society, the paranoia, and the stock-piling of weapons, citizens could hold that the Joneses and Ko-reshes engaged in practices that victimized a few malleable souls and that the violence was, in the main, inner-directed. Such asser-tions would ignore the death of four BATF agents, the sexual abuse of children, and the inspiring of the holocaust in Oklahoma City, but the deeper impression was of the danger of death to the converts, rather than to the rest of us.

On March 20, 1995, an attack, using Sarin nerve gas, killed 12 and injured more than 5000 in the Tokyo subway. The Japanese police began a huge and tortured investigation that led to the discovery of caches of chemicals and arms and evidence of re-search into biological weapons. During the inquiry, on March 30, the director of the National Police Agency was shot and seriously wounded by a suspected cult member. The sect's chief scientist was himself stabbed and killed by an angry citizen, on April 23, as a large number of television crews filmed the incident. Toxic gas was released in a Yokohama train station on April 19, sending 560 to the hospital. It was the very day of the Oklahoma City tragedy.

Shoko Asabara, the cult's leader, was arrested on May 16, along with a clutch of followers. Consistent with the imagery, he and others were discovered in a secret chamber that had been overlooked in earlier raids.

Initiation into the sect involved isolation, disorientation, loss of sleep, repetitive video messages, chanting mantras, singing Aum songs, and practicing yoga. It was, ostensibly, a mix of Tibetan Buddhism and a touch of Hinduism, with Shiva, the Hindu God of destruction and reproduction, as the chief symbol.

Cult members contributed their possessions and the guru exacted obedience and submission, in all things.

When the cult leader allegedly confessed, there were hints of the Japanese police using sleep deprivation and disorientation to induce the admissions. If this was turnabout, was it fair play?

The cult came to be seen as a nation within the nation, at war with society.[9] There had been hints and incidents, but the semiotic factors were ignored by authorities nervous over possible charges of curbing religious freedom. It made one want to ask whether they would tolerate human sacrifice as well.

Previous gas incidents, kidnappings, murders, and suspicious gas emissions were treated as individual and ad hoc episodes and forgotten. As the inquiry unfolded, a host of crimes surfaced that should have served as goads to official action, but they were ignored, with fatal, and fateful, consequences to the anonymous innocents who trusted the authorities to protect them from such nameless dangers, at least to the point possible and rational. Those who were unlucky enough to run afoul of the sect, whether through obduracy in consenting to extortions or other "interferences," suffered more direct reprisals. The sect was able to operate with relative impunity for years.

This was war, and Japan now mobilized 60,000 cops to meet the threat, but, in the ashes of the disaster lay such questions as what the factors in the society were that enabled such groups to thrive, why the authorities had turned a blind eye to previous telltale crimes, and how to meet future threats.

By using the criminal weapons of outlaw nations, Aum Shinrikyio raised the awful specter of mass destruction for the millions of Japanese pursuing quotidian interests in the midst of "peace and prosperity." The people's adamant search for some form of salvation, however, seemed to ensure the cult's success even after all of the foregoing revelations. As 1995 ended Aum Shinrikyio was reported to be thriving.

Earlier, another secretive religious sect captured, albeit briefly, the world's attention, with an awful and still uncomprehended act.

THE ORDER OF THE SOLAR TEMPLE

On October 5, 1994, 48 members of the Order of the Solar Temple[10] were found dead in burned-out Swiss chalets in Cheiry, Switzerland. Five other members were found dead in Quebec. The bodies were clad in ceremonial robes and had been shot or had plastic bags over their heads.

The founder, Luc Jouret, was a 46-year-old, secretive, charismatic, Belgian-born physician who had been charged in Canada with illegal weapons possession. Jouret preached a coming apocalypse and lectured on heightened consciousness, personal auras, and a looming Armageddon. Fire was seen as a purifying force. It was a reprise on the cartoonish "The End of the World Is Near" buffoonery—only with the exotic turn of fatal consequences.

The four documents sent at the time of the deaths spoke of an escape from a corrupt world, toward salvation. The sincerity of Jouret was questioned, however, until his body was found among those burned in one of the Swiss chalets.

As with the mass suicide deaths of the Reverend Jim Jones and 914 of his followers in Guyana in 1978, the extinction of this group meant the end of public interest, as headlines led elsewhere and only the believers had suffered. But the organization's obituary proved, as said Mark Twain, premature, as another 16 members were found dead around the remains of a campfire in the Vercors region of southeastern France in December 1995. They had launched their voyage on the winter solstice to "see another world." Three small children accompanied the gullible, if not mentally unstable, travelers.

For those not apocalyptically inclined—yet hungering for answers in an increasingly confusing and troublesome world— there was the offer of escape into magic, the wisdom of psychics, the glories of seances, the exotic appearances of ghosts and visions, or the stubborn belief in extraterrestrial experiences.

While life and death had never been sufficient to still the egotistical demand for importance beyond the temporal, the advent of moral decay—even in the midst of prosperity and peace— accelerated the flight into cults, sects, satanic covens, or other escape routes that offered simple, understandable solutions to the eager believers.

As with most insights, this thirst for escape is mirrored in the arts. Movies, literature, music, and other forms offer a cornucopia of creations based on magic. A scan of popular titles quickly reveals this trend—whether it's *Lorenzo's Oil* or *Millroy the Magician*.

Hoodoo—a cross between Haitian voodoo and Christianity—worries about possession by evil spirits. Most tales of satanic ritualism were debunked by a study by the National Center on Child Abuse and Neglect in 1994, but the number believing the charges of such acts continues to grow, and some police officers and even psychologists fed the superstition with dark tales of sacrifice.

THE UNIFICATION CHURCH

The Reverend Sun Myung Moon preached that Jesus Christ appeared to him on a mountaintop in Korea when Moon was 16 and told him that God had chosen him to finish Christ's failed mission on Earth.

Thus were the Moonies born,[11–13] and with them an impressive empire that includes a major newspaper, a university, real estate holdings, and a suspected large treasury. Temporal matters sent the reverend to prison on tax charges in 1982.

The virtual death of communism—the sect's *bête noire*—dissipated a lot of the energy building in a group that allegedly brainwashed and exploited thousands of our youth.

By 1995 the Reverend Moon received an honorary degree from the University of Bridgeport, which he had rescued from bankruptcy 3 years earlier. In accepting the "honor" before almost 1000 students and faculty, he claimed credit for the collapse of communism and promised to resolve conflicts in the Middle East and Korea.

Another grasp at respectability came from the hiring of former President George Bush, by Hak Ja Han Moon, the reverend's wife, to deliver several speeches for the Women's Federation for

World Peace, in several cities in Japan in September 1995. While the fee remained a closely guarded secret, *The New York Times* described it as being "in the millions." The thesis was "family values," and Mr. Bush's spokesman insisted there were no ties to the Unification Church.

Another political-religious leader who found himself in trouble with the tax authorities emerged from five years in prison early in 1994. Spouting apocalyptic predictions and conspiracy theories of truly bizarre proportions, he has run for president in every election since 1976.

The shadowy Church of Scientology[14] listed assets of $400 million and annual income of $300 million for counseling fees, book sales, investments, and contributions in 1993. Scientology claimed 8 million members, but knowledgeable former insiders and other observers put the figure at 700,000 and perhaps as low as 50,000. Founded in 1954, the religion is based on the writings of L. Ron Hubbard, a one-time writer of science fiction who died in 1986. Scientology preaches following scriptural precepts, including evaluation ("auditing") sessions geared to raising spiritual consciousness and exorcising painful experiences. Stars of the entertainment world are avidly recruited, and a good deal of attention centers on public relations efforts to popularize the sect.

A German member of Parliament sought to ban the group as not a religion, but a conspiratorial movement with global political aims. The scientologists responded with full-page ads in *The New York Times* in 1994, alleging discrimination (the expulsion of children of scientology members from schools) and likening their treatment to that of the Jews in the Nazi era. Some former members, who share information on the group through a computer network, have alleged abuses by the Church of Scientology. Factnet, an anti-scientology bulletin board on the Internet, disseminated information critical of the church, resulting in raids and seizure of materials that were, in September 1995, ordered returned to the critics by the courts.

And so, the landscape is dotted with signs whose portents cannot be easily deciphered. The millions attracted to the televangelists and Promise Keepers are out there, gullible and needy—a kinetic force to be reckoned with if a person comes along to marshal and channel that energy.

Americans are disturbed by a decline in values but have not fixed on a cure. They traverse roiling waters and sense that a safe shore exists, somewhere, but where? The search for simple answers is likely to produce demagogues. The hard answers require stilling paranoia and buckling-down to the basics of sharing and caring that characterize the ages' old search for racial, economic, and social justice that form the only solid foundations for social harmony.

8

The Custodians

"Who shall have custody over the custodians?"

The Romans worried about the overseers, and humankind has been haunted by the question ever since.

How can a people protect themselves from the moral erosions that appear to be the inevitable concomitants of power? Hasn't every successful society exhibited ethical vigor and communal thrust, only to see the temptations of prosperity convert these energies into corrupt self-seekings? It is the subtle shift from a sense of common destiny, embodied in tribal ambitions, to the consensus that the society exists to gratify individual desires that spells the doom of a people. Even expansionist or imperialist ambitions convey a shared destiny, toward which all strive together. As America enters its third century as a republic, it becomes more critical than ever that the question of decline into self-absorption be debated if a reversal, or even a slowing of the descent, is to be started.

There are at least three things that serve as repositories of our confidence—humans, institutions, and processes. In examining the depredations of white collar and organized criminals and politicians, we see how flawed and corrupt humans are twisting processes such as elections, corporate governance, the provision of services, or the functionings of government into instruments of private profit and public loss. The outcome is a deep and yawning chasm of trust between the people and the individual sent to rule and between the processes by which they are selected and kept in office and a questioning of the trustworthiness of methods we rely on for the control of our economic lives.

The sense that good systems produce good people who do useful things has given way to cynicism, under a barrage of disclosures depicting endless betrayals.

Americans also depend on institutions. We've been reared to believe in God, country, and family. We rely on the decencies of religion, the rightness of the nation's path, and the indissolubility of the family.

While the Central Intelligence Agency fights the silent struggle against foreign foes and safeguards our shores, the Federal Bureau of Investigation keeps us safe at home.

Or do they?

The CIA, the sort of undemocratic institution that the nation had always resisted creating, emerged from the romantic and successful exploits of the innocently named Office of Strategic Services of World War II and has been rocked by scandals involving corrupted agents who betrayed their country and sold out to the enemy for money. The agency has also done a lot of dirty business to achieve secret national objectives that the great majority of us didn't even know we had. Most Americans embrace the myths behind Old Glory. It proved a rude awakening indeed to discover that we've engaged in a lot of shabby tricks, just like the other guys, and that such secrets, unmonitored, lead to monstrous abuses that have nothing to do with protecting the nation, like the use of psychics to divine the nefarious intentions of our enemies and the mystical reliance on such pseudoscience as polygraphs.

THE CENTRAL INTELLIGENCE AGENCY

Even the Central Intelligence Agency's rumored successes came back to haunt it in the mid-1990s.[1,2] Our engagement in a life-and-death struggle with communism led us to authorize crimes, beyond our borders, that would have been unthinkable within. Or so we came to hope.

The overthrow of an Iranian nationalist in the early 1950s to reverse the move to nationalize the oil in that nation resulted in the restoration of a compliant Shah. This monarch's secret police spearheaded excesses that ironically led to a violent reaction that placed Islamic fundamentalists at the helm. Their byword was, to our shock, that "America is the Great Satan." Thus did the chickens come home to roost, even if the trip took three decades.

The overthrow and murder of a leftist president of Guatemala led to over four decades of deadly assaults on Mayan peasants disaffected with an oligarchy that kept their feet firmly planted on the necks of the poor. We had been happy to support such oppressions because we could count on their votes against the Evil Empire. This drama continued on the boards through 1995, as the new CIA director cleaned house.

The purported suicide of Chile's elected president led to a military dictatorship that lasted, in different guises, for decades and that led to a political assassination that took the life of an American, as well as a Chilean exile, within sight of the White House.

In December 1995 the CIA admitted that Haiti's most notorious thug had been on its payroll from 1991 to 1994. The killing of Patrice Lumumba by Africans reportedly doing the work of the West, about 40 years ago, contributed to unrest that wracks the African continent to this day.

And, throughout, we were happy to work with such tyrants as Trujillo in the Dominican Republic, Batista in Cuba, Duvalier in Haiti, Stroessner in Paraguay, and countless others in the tumultuous continent of South America and elsewhere. The bywords by which they earned our favor centered on anticommunism and, frequently and for good measure, antigay policies.

Some of these shadowy events—the full and official record of our participation may never be known—clearly involved the CIA, which periodically feels the need to leak some information to counter criticisms, as it did, in 1995, when it revealed it had—many years earlier—broken the Soviet code that provided proof of Ethel and Julius Rosenberg's espionage activities. Thus was the simmering controversy surrounding their guilt or innocence finally resolved—40 years after their executions.

Where the FBI was the personal instrument of a leader bent on spreading and deepening his grip on national power, the CIA developed into an aggressive instrument of national policy that was not bound by the niceties of law needing to be observed within our borders. As such it was able to give vent to the secret ambitions of men who had the assurance of permanently shrouded actions and no fear of being held accountable. And it was all done in the name of God and country. No one bothered to assess the toll on our national soul or conscience. We'd emerge with the chastening knowledge that we really weren't a much better people than the other guys.

The worst blemish on the CIA's escutcheon in the Cold War is very likely the Aldrich Hazen Ames case. Ames was the agency's most awful nightmare come to life—a mole who had burrowed to the core to betray America's secrets to the Soviet Union purely for money. Perhaps 12 American agents behind the Iron Curtain met death because of him, and perhaps twice that number were betrayed. Scores of operations were scuttled as Ames delivered reams of material and information to the KGB.

Yet Ames could have been assessed as a security risk, with a failed marriage, a drinking problem, an affair with a foreign national, and enough ostentatious consumption and unexplained cash flows to alert the sleepiest detectors. He profited to the tune of over $2 million from Moscow and, in his final deal, confessed and was sentenced to life—in exchange for leniency for the woman he'd married and who had worked with him in his treason. She served a short prison term. Ames served as a Soviet agent from 1985 to 1994.

Huge purchases for cash, the transfer of hundreds of thousands of dollars into his bank account, poor evaluations, and incredible sloppiness never—until the FBI stormed into the case in 1993—aroused his bosses' suspicions. The CIA had relied on polygraphs—those instruments of modern technological witch-craft—to ensure Ames' integrity. He'd been coached, by his Soviet handlers, to be rested and calm before the tests and to be very courteous to the examiner. Ames passed three tests handily. So much for the scientific detection of lies.

Then the CIA revealed that about $20 million was spent over a 20-year period, mostly by the Pentagon, on psychics who tried developing military intelligence by channeling the thoughts of others and using "paranormal powers" and processes to locate tunnels that the North Koreans were suspected of digging under the demilitarized zone. This revelation, in late 1995, of the government's secret "Stargate" program, demonstrated the outlandish notions driving covert, unmonitored actions. It was a short step behind the mystical reliance on lie detectors.

Late in 1994, the CIA came under withering scrutiny for concealing—from Congress—the construction of a $350 million new spy satellite headquarters near Dulles Airport. The appropriation had been buried among the agency's amorphous budget.

The culture of this secretive agency defeated President Clinton's choice as its head, who was forced to leave after just over two years, in December 1994, under the scathing criticism of his congressional "overseers."

The CIA was driven to the extremity of having its operators lobby friends in Congress to refurbish the agency's image and secure more favorable treatment of its budget and programs. The retired Air Force general first chosen as the replacement withdrew under a hail of charges involving possible violations of immigration law in connection with favors he extended to household help he had brought to America.

On top of all this, the descriptions of entourages and servants being flown to and fro at huge expense was beginning to resemble Imperial Rome.

As noted earlier, in 1995 revelations were surfacing that a Guatemalan colonel on the CIA's payroll had ordered the killings of an American citizen and a guerrilla leader who had married an

American lawyer. She had made a nuisance of herself by going on highly publicized hunger strikes to get the truth out. The House of Representatives came close to removing the congressman courageous enough to announce these atrocities from the House's Committee on Intelligence. It was another example of an obstreperous citizen fighting to get the facts out and an American government working to keep them hidden.

Twenty years earlier, the publication of the *Pentagon Papers* had been treated as an act of subversion during the Vietnam War, only to be judged, in historical retrospect, as a cathartic and necessary act of public disclosure, debate, and cleansing. In 1995 it was obvious that the moral lessons had not been fully learned.

The CIA's acting director was forced to admit his agency had failed to advise Congress, three years earlier, that it knew of these deaths in Guatemala and of their agent's implication in the disaster. It had, he said, "slipped under the carpet."

Some carpet. Some slip.

Finally, in 1995, the new CIA director dismissed two senior officials and disciplined several for their connections with the Guatemalan military responsible for this, and other, tragedies.

How was it that the mistakes never involved overinforming the elected representatives charged with monitoring the CIA's actions? How was it that, despite the patent use of secrecy to cover up terrible errors and crimes, the CIA's invariable posture was to call for longer lists of matters that ought to be shielded from the American people's view? On April 17, 1995, President Clinton signed an executive order lifting the shroud of secrecy over mounds of documents over 25 years old. This important reform was undertaken in the face of determined bureaucratic opposition.

How were these actions, and the actions of others such as those in the FBI, to reinforce the confidence of the American people in cherished institutions?

The president finally plucked a reluctant dragon from the Pentagon to clean up the mess. His appointments and response to the Guatemalan challenge hinted at the possibility that the agency might—just might—be brought under control. It was another testament for the importance of the selection process, a lesson too often lost on presidents more anxious to repay political debts than to make the right choices.

The Aldrich Ames case had shaken the CIA to its foundations. The new director was feared to be hesitant to do too much, lest he injure his chances to head his alma mater; nevertheless, he began major personnel changes, undertook reviews of policies and actions, and began shaking the organizational culture that had so many observers cringing over the years.

John Deutch, appointed in 1995, began as anything but the caretaker some obviously hoped for, as he undertook actions that were different from those needed by its sister intelligence agency across town. Where the FBI had been twisted to the private impulses of its ruler, whatever the needs or commands of the government, the CIA had never been anything but an instrument of governmental policies; only now were those secret programs being called into question.

Simultaneous with the travail of the CIA came a drumbeat of awful disclosures centering on the FBI, following the death of its long-time director and the publication of reports and biographies revealing a sordid abuse of power that lasted for a large chunk of this century.

THE FBI

The Federal Bureau of Investigation was the embodiment of its leader—J. Edgar Hoover—from 1924 to his death on May 2, 1972. No one in this nation's history approached him as the avatar of law and order.[3-5]

Since Hoover's death we have been exposed to revelations of the corrupt use of that agency as an instrument of his personal power. Files were compiled to threaten reprisal and secure compliance with Hoover's goals. Enemies were punished, friends rewarded.

Hoover's was a delicately wrought, single-minded, 24-hour-a-day approach to employing his agency for his private agendas—

never mind talk of enforcing drug laws or admitting the existence of organized crime. The agency was turned into an instrument that committed crimes in its desire to attack those it suspected of political wrongs, even as it avoided more serious perils. It was Hoover's biases that mattered, and he was a superpatriot.

The FBI, under Hoover, would be shaped into an uncorrupted and incorruptible institution—the better to pursue the grotesque personal bidding of its master. The anomaly was that Hoover—able to devote all his time and energy to his creation—kept it clean through an efficient apparatus of administrative control, careful recruiting of the right sort of white males, high educational requirements, large salaries, and terror. The result was a smooth-running, responsive, and honest organization bent to the single-minded, and twisted, purposes of its leader.

Hoover, single and without family or other outside claims on his interest—except a well-known predilection for horse racing, which he somehow managed to meld into his official life, and other, much darker interests that are only just beginning to surface—was able to devote his life, like some obsessed sculptor, to the shaping of the nation's premier law enforcers.

Political enemies were targeted, whatever their potential for wrongdoing. The point would be to secure damaging information, rather than focusing on breaches of law. This dirt would be used to coerce the targets into compliance or to discredit those who were getting too big for their britches and whose views didn't coincide with the director's.

Thus the Reverend Martin Luther King, Jr., was subjected to surveillance that may well titillate future generations, as the presidentially imposed veil of secrecy is lifted from the file well after the twenty-first century gets under way. John Lennon, the murdered ex-Beatle, had been tailed in connection with his anti-Vietnam War activities and the paranoia of the Nixon administration.

The actions of composer Leonard Bernstein received more than 30 years' worth of interest and documentation. Walt Disney served as an informer from 1940 until his death in 1966, passing on names of Hollywood figures who might be Communists or subversives. A huge dossier was compiled on Pablo Picasso, and the activities of Charlie Chaplin were minutely scrutinized, finally forcing him to seek exile in Switzerland.

Even the president had good reason to suspect that Hoover had something on him, as he shared a woman with one of the Mafia's top leaders.

Of particular interest to future Americans will be the disclosures sure to come out about the specific abuses Hoover engaged in over his interminable reign, as the veil of secrecy gets lifted by the Freedom of Information Act or by executive order. Allegations of racial bias in hiring and harassment of minority employees added to the FBI's woes, mostly self-inflicted. How could the nation's foremost instrument of justice practice such injustice and be so unjustly constituted itself? It seemed another example of inherited organizational hubris.

Over the almost quarter-century since Hoover's death, the FBI has been led by men who have been accused of tampering with evidence in the Watergate case, others who were little more than colorless caretakers, and at least two who had been jurists. The second, William Sessions, may well have been chosen because the first, William Webster, was thought to have performed well in the post. Webster went on to become CIA director. The temptation to reach into the judicial ranks produced, as we have seen, Waco.

Sessions, brought in to refurbish the image and substance of the agency in 1987, was driven from office midway through his ten-year term, in 1993, amid allegations of abuse of the perquisites of office, detailed in a Justice Department report to the president. That he had been out of his depth in trying to manage the complex agency was the subject of widespread gossip within. The ouster of Sessions had been a hideously painful public twisting in the wind, for many months, as he stubbornly clung to office.

The disastrous mishandling of the Branch Davidian flaming holocaust in April 1993 in Waco, Texas, which took about 86 lives (the actual number has never been established), might be laid to the total inexperience in police operations of a director more interested in jets, limos, and trips to exotica than in the real-world life of sieges and negotiations. Another stand-off, in the mountains of

Idaho, also ended in tragedy as two suspects in the shooting death of a U.S. marshall were acquitted. The suspects were linked to a white-supremacy sect and had been the targets of an 11-day siege in the summer of 1992. It should have served as an object lesson to be employed in Waco, but its teachings were ignored by an official more concerned with the emoluments of office than with its law enforcement possibilities. The lesson would finally be learned, by his successor and in Montana in 1996, as the siege of the Freemen—a bunch of criminals seeking to evade justice behind the screen of political activism—ended without violence.

The acquittals, and the 1984 finding of innocence in the John Z. DeLorean trial for possession of $24 million worth of cocaine, fed the ravenous appetites of those seeing the government as an evil, aggressive, and possibly maladroit force.[6,7]

The newly appointed director, Louis J. Freeh, himself a former agent and judge, reprimanded 12 employees, including his own choice for the number two job, for their handling of the Idaho stand-off, following receipt of a critical report in early 1995. As with the CIA director's appointment, President Clinton seemed to have finally gotten it almost right.

Notwithstanding its brilliant successes against the Mafia, the FBI reeled under the impact of severe criticism over its handling of the April 1993 Waco raid, the disaster at Ruby Ridge, in 1992, and the subsequent attempt to cover up headquarters errors, which forced Director Freeh to oust the man he had chosen as his principal aide.

The revealed attendance of FBI, BATF, and other federals at a law enforcement three-day seminar from May 18 to May 20, 1995, at which racist signs, symbols, and messages had surfaced in past years, proved another blow to an organization seeking to emerge from the dark shadows of a chiaroscuro past. And the possible overreaction in questioning 50,000 federal employees as to whether they'd attended "The Good Ol' Boys Round Up" brought the American Civil Liberties Union to the defense of the agents. As the inquiry unfolded, it was revealed that the federal government had been set up by a disaffected participant who was denied access to the latest round-up.

The indisputably successful (whatever the final trial's outcome, following two major, successful trials and several guilty pleas) investigation into the bombing of the World Trade Center burnished the FBI's reputation, but it also demonstrated its reliance on lavishly paid informers for critical information. The agency still hadn't learned the superiority of using its own agents to infiltrate criminal conspiracies, rather than having to use frequently discredited informers. The 1995 prosecution of Qbillah Shabbaz for the plot to kill the Nation of Islam's Louis Farrakhan relied on an informer whose background was more an embarrassment than a help to his employers. That Ms. Shabbaz had been present at the assassination of her father (Malcolm X) in February 1965 garnered her some well-earned sympathy. Not the least of the FBI's problems was that the informer could be seen as an agent provocateur or entrapper. They finally worked out a deal, and the case was mercifully closed.

In 1996, Farrakhan then went from the glory of an enormously successful "Million Man March" in 1995 to the ignominy of savage criticism of the United States, while visiting America's enemies in such places as Libya and the Sudan, as he received their promises of financial support.

Reliances on tainted sources were not as evident in the political stings and organized crime penetrations the FBI pulled off with such brilliance in the 1980s and 1990s. Even when it used easy-to-discredit mafiosi, the FBI buttressed its cases with bugs, wiretaps, surveillances, and other evidence. It would be impossible to credit the agency sufficiently for its assault on organized crime, as we have seen. After two-thirds of a century's somnolence, the FBI got a wake-up call from Bobby Kennedy and went at its task with enormous energy, initiative, inventiveness, and effectiveness. The result was an offensive that delivered one body blow after another at a swaying Mafia.

Still, the reaction to Hoover's abuses led to an almost total abandonment of spying techniques called infiltrations and intelligence gatherings. Revulsion at the awful excesses of Hoover and his minions led to a paralysis that kept the agency from penetrating the Branch Davidians and the World Trade Center plotters and their associates (save through an enormously well-paid defector), from monitoring the activities of the plotters of the ghastly bombing of the Federal Building in Oklahoma City on the second anniversary of the raid on the Branch Davidians, or from gathering solid information on such dangerous groups as those that caused a train derailment in Hyder, Arizona, on October 9, 1995.[8] The FBI could, however, avoid criticism for having failed to prevent such events because spying, by this time, was in such foul odor as to be unacceptable to almost anyone, whatever the legal ramifications. Thrown out with the bath water of abuse of power was the baby of prevention.

THE RESULT

Few institutions enjoyed the misty-eyed trust of the American people more unquestioningly and unswervingly than the FBI. The CIA was regarded as a group of patriotic silent warriors battling for the nation in the murky depths of international intrigue. Many were drawn from the cloisters of the Ivy League and worked hard at the macho image they felt appropriate to new and unfamiliar tasks. The curtain's peeling back revealed very flawed institutions, often led by feckless officials, or worse.

In what or whom could anyone trust?

A free people was making the painful discovery of the value of openness, the need for debate and discussion, the absolute centrality of citizen involvement, and the painful fact that most government secrecy is simply an attempt to secure protection from the disclosure of human fallibility or cupidity.

There can be no doubt that some operations and activities must be secret, but that requires informing the people's elected representatives. There are intelligence committees in Congress to oversee these operations and they have demonstrated their ability to keep secrets. This is what accountability and civilian control are all about. Colonel Oliver North simply didn't get it when his suspicions of the reliability and integrity of Congress grew to such proportions as to encourage him, and others in the Iran-Contra inquiry, to mislead our rulers deliberately. It is in this trust, or lack of it, that the mettle of the democracy is really tested.

If the FBI and CIA proved anything, it was that unaccounted power will be abused. And yet, it was indisputable that a dangerous world and a complex and delicately interconnected domestic society cried out for the protection promised by focused and responsible intelligence-gathering and law-enforcing agencies. There clearly was nothing in the Constitution impeding the effective pursuit of intelligence or the timely gathering of evidence. The point was to get these investigative agencies to enforce the law without breaking it. Our Founding Parents never intended that we should lie naked and helpless before our enemies.

Balancing the need for public protection with the requirement that the custodians be guarded and directed effectively continued to be one of the great challenges facing a people determined to stay free. In the final analysis it was up to the people to ensure their own freedom and safety.

After a really faltering start, President Clinton appeared to have made amends with the promising appointments of John Deutch to head the CIA and Louis J. Freeh to direct the FBI. They seemed to constitute, perhaps, a last chance of openness, accountability, and reform of two agencies that, in separate ways, strayed dangerously from democracy's path.

9

Street Crime

No account of national decline is free to exclude its most visible symbol—street crime.

America's visible drama—and threat—is the violence that terrifies each of us. Contained within the carnage are the symbols that define our society: a struggle between classes and races, an oppressive police, escape into addictions, and other massive shifts and movements that betoken disintegration. Within many of these individual tragedies lie the signs that capture the angst and spirit of the age. Violence on our streets becomes the visible product of the decay of a body politic that, in the other forms of decline, remain largely—except for the occasional surfacings in headlines—invisible.

What is spooking America are not the incomprehensibly slick depredations of white collar criminals, the subtle terrors of organized crime, or the random assaults of terrorists, but rather, the grim visages on the nightly news.

Every night we see the scary totems of our culture—whirring, dazzling lights; ear-splitting sirens; blood-curdling explosions; fleshy blobs; manacled suspects; and tears. Rape, murder, muggings, burglaries, carjackings, and batterings are the nightly fare; guns and drugs, the invariable companions. It is at once a tiresome and a gripping scene.

The general breakdown can be seen in the disintegration and abandonment of both our cities and families, two institutions that, however hard we try, we cannot live without. Anecdotes impress, but data persuade.

Forced to choose the tipping moment at which America's descent began, 1960 would serve as well as any other year. It was then that, fueled by television and accelerated by the beginning of triplings in divorce, murder, illegitimacy, imprisonment, and related indices of decay, we turned the corner downward.

Although there is no reliable national gauge of our crime rate—since the two main ones are flawed, one by gross (as much as 50%) nonreporting and the other by the failure of respondents to remember crime victimization in their households[1]—we know that about one-fourth of U.S. households were victimized by violence or theft every year of the 1990s. It is hard for Americans to escape street crime, but we're trying. In fact, Americans only had to be asked what was the nation's most important problem to answer "crime;" it was clear that no one had to specify "street" to refine the definition.

The decay in the cities sparked panic fights, of whites, to the suburbs. Detroit, with its massive abandonment and creation of an impenetrable iron ring of segregated suburbs, became a paradigm. Swiftly and slowly, every urban center followed the lead until 1992 became the first time in the nation's history that more suburbanites voted for president than urbanites. There had been a massive shift in political, as well as economic, power. While ghetto residents escaped through drugs and alcohol, suburbanites lapsed into less dangerous distractions.

Sports replaced Judeo-Christian observances as our national religion. Materialism and consumerism became the motivating impulses. Children lost their way in the confusing tangle of shifting relationships. Would every kid wind up with multiple sets of parents and no family? Would the male ever show up in ghetto kitchens again?

Murders have risen from 8464 in 1960 and 9850 in 1965 to around 24,000 in the 1990s. Principal trends are the increasing involvement of younger victims and perpetrators; the high incidence of blacks—as victims and as killers; the frightening decline of solutions, and the accompanying factor that more murders are stranger-to-stranger crimes, increasing the difficulty of solving them. In 1965, 90% of murders were solved, versus 65% in 1992—meaning that one-third of all killers were getting away with murder.

The leading cause of death for black males in the prime of life (age 19–45) became murder; the percentage of those under 18 charged with murder went from around 10% in 1970 to 14% in 1992, with the majority being black males.

The overall trend of street crime has climbed dramatically upward, despite a tripling of the prison population to over 1 million in 1995 and the fact that one in three black male adults was, by then, under some form of criminal justice system control. Huge new expenditures for more cops, tougher judges, and bigger prisons had not begun to stem the tide.

The least safe places were still the home and workplace, but the explosion of crack cocaine use in 1985 sped up the casualty totals among "mushrooms" (innocent bystanders struck by flying bullets) and killings for other than passion or drunkenness. It also accelerated the flight of mothers from the nurturing role that had become the only protection for otherwise helpless kids, as they too lapsed into addiction.

Comparisons with other industrialized countries invariably had America in the lead. The availability of guns facilitated the mayhem.[2] Two exceptions are countries emerging from eons of oppression: Russia, with about twice our rate, and South Africa, with the astonishing total of ten times ours.

The violence principally revolves around 15- to 24-year-old males in the "at-risk" population.[3] It is most effectively demonstrated by the disparities of income that characterize the overclass and the underclasses, especially in the cities.

The gross characterization could be made that increasing the underclass increases the population of street criminals—however many bromides might be uttered that the "overwhelming majority of the poor are law-abiding" (which happens to be both true and, ultimately, cold comfort). Of the ten largest cities in the United States, the top 20% of the population earned, in 1990, from a low of just over $63,000 to a high of just over $123,000, while the poorest 20% earned from a low of $3109 to a high of over $8600. The disparity produces the class warfare that is so large a part of what we call street crime. It is small wonder that many commentators called the Los Angeles riots of 1992 "rebellions."

The profile of the street criminal is well known: male; age 15–24; born to a teenaged mother; no positive male role model present, at birth or later; school drop-out; unemployable; user of tobacco, alcohol, or illegal drugs, or a gambler; ghetto dweller; welfare client; himself an absent father; and otherwise precluded from meaningful participation in society.

So, he is easy to demonize.

No one cares to ask how he was shaped, why he wasn't salvaged, why social welfare policies weren't structured to preserve his family, why he wasn't educated or employed, and why we insist on returning him, from prison, to the conditions that produced his crimes.

Instead we use his image to feed our racist inclinations and strike at the programs that might have helped.

Was the war on poverty lost?

Is the war on drugs lost?

The fact is that people drank less during Prohibition,[4] gambled less when it was mostly illegal, and smoke less when the age limit on the purchase of tobacco products is raised—but each can, and has, been pointed to as a futile effort to regulate the unregulatable.

A community that doesn't want to produce social, economic, or racial justice will reap the harvest of criminality that is our current fate—whether that be white collar, organized, political terrorist, or street crime. Each person will, in his way, see to it that he gets his—when the order of the day is to take what you can, while you can.

But when all else is stripped away and the euphoria over this or that year's minor decline vaporizes—usually following a welter of police chiefs' analyses of how their programs are working—the terrifying fact is that, following a decline in the population of the dangerous male cohort, there will be large increases over the next 15 years. The resulting tsunami of street crime will then be followed by police chiefs' analyses of societal factors, as they continue their consistent plea to hire more cops.

The impact of *Roe v. Wade* in facilitating the abortion of millions of "at-risk" males over the past almost quarter-century is never discussed in criminal justice system circles. But criminologists hint at their awareness of this by pointing at the swelling cohort of 15- to 24-year-old "at-risk" males in our immediate future. The silence surrounding this fact attests to the hypersensitivity of the subject matter. But even the trough in births provided by the 1973 Supreme Court ruling is destined to end, as the inexorable climb leads to a great increase in "at risk" teenagers up to 2015.

MEDEA

A society may be understood through the knowledge of one crime. Some events reveal the forces at work shaping tragedies. The account of a family's murder often contains casual references to abandonments, divorces, and other signs of disintegration.

On October 23, 1989, Charles K. Stuart, wounded in the stomach by a bullet, told police that his pregnant wife had been shot and killed by a black robber. A frantic manhunt followed, in which blacks were stopped, searched, questioned, and otherwise violated in their civil rights. The popular angst justified any measure. It seemed a reprise of the novel *Native Son* a half-century earlier. One black male was fingered and identified as the suspect. Several months later Mr. Stuart committed suicide after his brother implicated him in the wife's killing.

An eerie reprise followed, almost exactly five years later, when, on October 25, 1994, a white mother reported her auto carjacked, with her two sons, Alexander, 14 months, and Michael, three, strapped in the back seat. The suspect was described by the mother as a black male 20–30 years old, 5'9"–6' tall. The nation joined, as a chorus, in her prayers and in public appeals for her babies' safety. Hundreds of volunteers combed the area. Roads were scanned for hundreds of miles, searching for her 1990 burgundy Mazda.[5]

The smiling, trusting faces looked out from the nation's papers. Susan Smith's estranged husband, David, joined in fervent public appeals for the return of their boys. A sense of dread pervaded and spread as days passed without a trace of the victims. Susan Smith, 23, became the symbol of anguished motherhood in a dangerous age. Her televised image became an icon.

Then, on November 4, 1994, the bodies of the boys were found entombed in the wet grave of the missing car at the bottom of nearby John D. Long Lake. That day Susan Smith was charged with rolling the car into the lake, drowning her boys.

Anguished neighbors now reviled the unhappy woman, who had apparently rid herself of two impediments to an ambitious romance in what looked a lot like Theodore Dreiser's *An American Tragedy*. Upward mobility was certainly a subtext of the plot unfolding in Union, South Carolina.

Despite the unbelievable pressure of a nation's intense determination to resolve the mystery—and the microscopic examination that goes with it—Susan Smith steadfastly clung to her role of victim. A shrewd and knowing sheriff, who had patiently resisted a hare and hounds chase after the "black suspect," coaxed a confession from Ms. Smith while they prayed together on November 3.

As a person vilified as a monster, Susan Smith faced the death penalty for her crime. As the trial unfolded, however, the facts emerging began to paint a more understanding portrait of this Medea. Susan Smith, it came out, had had a troubled past. She'd been molested by her stepfather when she was 15 (her father committed suicide when she was 7), had herself attempted suicide twice as a teenager, and, in what seemed a pathetic attempt at using any favor to curry approval, had slept with the boyfriend she'd sought to marry—and who had spurned her—his father, her stepfather, and her estranged husband in the month before she murdered her sons.

In a wrongheaded attempt at justice, the prosecutor adamantly—and inappropriately—sought the death penalty. Her defense was predicated on soliciting sufficient jury sympathy to result in a rejection of killing Ms. Smith. Her lawyer succeeded, and she was sentenced to life imprisonment, making her eligible for parole after serving 30 years.

In a nation imprinted with the image of black murderers, neither Mr. Stuart nor Ms. Smith had much trouble having their concoctions embraced. Smith's was a case straight out of Greek— or American—tragedy. Sex, race, infanticide, virtual incest, and suicide attempts—all within the context of unrooted relationships and unexpected betrayals—became the foundation on which the safety of two little boys rested. They never had much chance. Their fate held the nation in thrall. What of the less dramatic fates of the millions destroyed more silently and routinely?

Notwithstanding the contrast between the eager racism of the Boston police and the political patience of the South Carolina sheriff, the same frisson of fear swept through the black community, as their silent prayer of, "God, don't let it be a black suspect who committed this crime" soared heavenward.

While this Medea played out, another arena featured, this time, the Shakespearean tragedy of Othello.

CRI DE COEUR

The crime—or trial—of the century. What event aspires to such lofty eminence?

The entries would surely include the murder of Stanford White by Harry K. Thaw in 1906, the kidnapping of Charles Lindbergh's son in 1932, the 1920 hold-up and murder attributed to Nicola Sacco and Bartolomeo Vanzetti, or the 1950 spy trial of Julius and Ethel Rosenberg. Another entry, the Lizzie Borden case, belongs to the previous century.

Certain to join this pantheon is the 1995 trial of O. J. Simpson.[6]

The case, a relatively quotidian—albeit certainly tragic—event, contained symbolic, iconographic elements that coursed deeply through America's soul. Sex, race, sports, celebrity, beauty, and glamour. The mighty brought low, only to rise, Phoenix-like, as he'd done from the grasp of mighty pursuers on the gridiron. Public theater of the highest order. America's own games, shifted from the coliseum to the magical box of television.

The facts were deceptively simple—the case's fascination lay in the subtexts.

A little after midnight on Monday, June 13, 1994, the bodies of Nicole Brown Simpson and Ronald Lyle Goldman were found, hideously slashed and stabbed, outside her condominium in Los Angeles—another perfect example of the horrible street violence terrifying nightly viewers of the news. The two had been murdered late on the night of Sunday, June 12. Her children had been inside, sleeping.

Nicole was the beautiful, white, 35-year-old former wife of football superstar O.J. Simpson, 47, black and rather beautiful himself. They'd been married 9 years and divorced in 1992, having produced two children, Sydney, a girl, nine, and Justin, a boy, seven.

Theirs had been the obsessive romance of Othello and Desdemona, punctuated by violence. O.J. had pleaded guilty to an assault on Nicole on January 1, 1989, there had been a 911 call in October 1993 of a domestic incident, and testimony by Nicole's sister Denise described incidents of abuse. The relationship was underlined by the growing terror experienced by the stalked woman. Nicole's fear was described by a social worker.

In reconstructing the final day, it became impossible to evaluate the significance of possibly fateful events. Sydney had been in a dance recital at a school, which was attended by Nicole and her family. No seat was reserved for O.J., who arrived and made no display of umbrage at the studied slight. The family then went for dinner at a chic Italian restaurant near Nicole's condo, Mezzaluna, where Ronald Goldman, 25, was a waiter. Nicole, a regular and familiar to the staff, apparently left her glasses there and, in returning them later, Mr. Goldman met his cruel fate.

O.J. had taken a late flight to Chicago on June 12 and was notified in a hotel room there. He vanished briefly, only to turn up on Friday, June 17, 1994, in a slow, 60-mile pursuit with his friend Al Cowlings at the wheel of Simpson's now famous white Bronco, ending at 8 P.M. at his home. A note from O.J., strongly hinting at suicide and claiming innocence in Nicole's murder, had been read at 5 P.M. that day, by a friend, to reporters.

O.J.'s arrest ended the street theater and shifted the drama to the more orderly stage of the courtroom. O.J. Simpson was arraigned, brought before a judge, and charged for the two murders, on Monday, June 20. He pleaded not guilty.

Now began the pretrial phase, as O.J. gathered his "Dream Team" of defense lawyers and they began sparring over what would be admitted or excluded in the trial and over the critical process of jury selection.

In retrospect the selection of jurors, now elevated to a science that involved the hiring of Jo Ellan Dimitrius of Pasadena, California, and the preparation of a 294-question form that would permit the selection of candidates fitting the profile of those most likely to be sympathetic to the defendant, proved to be the key to the entire drama. It was no accident that Johnny Cochran, the successful defense lawyer, first thanked Ms. Dimitrius, sitting just beside him, at the triumphant press conference following acquittal.

On January 4, 1995, Judge Lance A. Ito announced that the jury would be sequestered. Their virtual imprisonment would last exactly the term of human gestation. So many were dropped along the way that it became an achievement to retain a full panel at the end.

The prosecution had previously decided against seeking the death penalty.

As the trial developed, it became clear that Judge Ito was seeking to avoid a reversal on appeal and granted a lot of the prosecution's requests for admission of evidence that the defense had sought to exclude. It often looked as if the lawyers had been given altogether too much latitude, as they seemed to be directing the proceedings.

Bickerings and clashes became the order of the day, with the lone television camera, on which much of the nation was glued, picking up every tic save those of the protected jurors.

The defense used hand-picked expert lawyers to attack the prosecution's witnesses. DNA analysis, matching the victims' blood on a glove found in Simpson's driveway, became crucial, as did blood evidence. The defense cleverly attacked the sloppy handling of the blood and successfully assailed the chain of custody of the evidence, planting in the jurors' minds the suspicion of police corruption, at worst, and laboratory sloppiness at best.

The trial's denouement, however, came with the 6 days of testimony of Los Angeles Police Department Detective Mark Fuhrman, who was widely reported, on leaving the stand, as "unscathed"—having "held his own" against the withering assaults of F. Lee Bailey.

But had he?

The key question had been if Detective Fuhrman was as sure of his discovering the glove linking O.J. to the murders in the suspect's driveway as he was that he hadn't used the pejorative "nigger" over the past 10 years. Fuhrman had, firmly and even a bit defiantly, answered yes. Then, many weeks later, the ticking "N" bomb was detonated, as the defense came up with Professor Laura Hart McKinny, a would-be screen writer, who had taped a number of interviews with Mark Fuhrman between 1985 and 1994.

Judge Ito ruled that the jury could hear only two of the 41 references to "niggers" on the tape. And Fuhrman, sealing his destruction, retired from the force and took the Fifth Amendment's protection against self-incrimination for perjury when the prospect of his retestifying arose.

To illustrate the wide range of views surrounding this case, an organization called the National Association of Chiefs of Police (NACOP) sent out a mailing to 15,000 households in April 1995 that called Fuhrman "a genuine American police hero." The effort raised less than $10,000 and the letter was pulled when the McKinny tapes were revealed, but the fact remained that the charges of racism had been leveled as early as July 1994. And the letter seemed to indicate that funds contributed would go to Fuhrman. They actually went to the NACOP, which was not a major, recognized, national organization of police executives, but the product of an entrepreneur cashing in on our fears.

Was Mark Fuhrman a rotten apple in an otherwise healthy barrel, as police chiefs hastened to explain?

Was the LAPD uniquely flawed among the nation's agencies?

The answer to both questions had to be an unequivocal no.

Every police department in the nation suffers, in spades, the racism pervading the outer society, which is exacerbated by their assignment, by the overclass, to keep the underclass in its place. And every police department has its 1–2% share of thumpers—the hamfisted dispensers of street justice, Dirty Harrys, and meat eaters, the few who lead the herd by setting the tone and defining the illegalities that the culture will, nevertheless, tolerate—who if unaddressed, create an illicit and unspoken, but pervasive, climate within which the rest work.

It was typical police mendacity to state that O.J. had not been a suspect, in the early hours of the inquiry, when a clutch of detectives was dispatched to his home. The hypocrisy was not lost on jurors, who'd likely had more than passing negative experiences with the police, directly or through family histories.

The thin blue line is a closed fraternity in which loyalty predominates and the blue code of silence rules. And, with police unions and civil service regulations frustrating any attempts at management reforms, virtually every police chief found it a lot more convenient to slip into bed with his cops—apologizing for or winking at abuses—and not have to face the political muscle of activist unions. Mark Fuhrman is, in actuality, a paradigm of a small, but influential, element in the ranks.

The trial ended on September 29, when the judge began his instructions to the jury. It was, by then, composed of eight black females (three married, three single, two divorced); two white females (one divorced, one single); one black male (married); and one Hispanic male (single, with a son).

Amazingly, the jury reached a unanimous verdict within four

hours of starting deliberations on October 2, 1995. The nation froze in anticipation of the next day's announcement. With the nation's eye fixed compulsively on O.J.'s seemingly tutored face, the clerk intoned the "not guilty" verdict on all counts.

O.J. was a free man.

Whites greeted the result in stunned silence; blacks exploded in a celebration that shocked white America. While the winners might have rioted had they lost, it seemed safe to guess that the actual losers would, over ensuing months and years, subtly but insistently make the blacks pay for their victory.

Thus, the only serious racial debate in decades ended sourly.

It would be hard to imagine a judge permitting television cameras in the courtroom after the microscopic scrutiny given this case—yet the camera had precluded the sort of sidewalk-trial-by-camera that characterized many other cases, as wily defense attorneys learned the uses of on-the-street press commentaries as a way of influencing the outcome.

The issue of domestic abuse was firmly tabled by a juror who stoutly maintained that wasn't what the trial had been about. Yet it was a classic case of woman-battering, with the escalating violence that characterizes such cases and that often results in homicide. The least safe places in America were the home and the workplace, for reasons this case underlined.

Simpson's mother was a presence throughout the trial—her face at once the tortured map of black suffering and the inspiring hope of faith. The victims' families anguished in unassuaged grief. The one consolation available had been denied them.

The cost was estimated by experts as a rich person's net worth. They'd take it all. At the start O.J. had a net worth of $10.8 million. Nevertheless, as Harry K. Thaw and Loeb and Leopold had proved before him, the availability of huge resources proves an inestimable aid to the flimsiest defense. The prosecution was estimated to have cost taxpayers $9 million.

There had been no eyewitnesses, the weapon used had not been recovered, the undoubtedly bloody clothes of the killer were never found. Still, it was undeniable that any experienced observer would have bet heavily on conviction, except for two factors—resources and race.

In the end there was a scurrying for agents as the principals cashed in on a celebrity that, in contemporary society, was indistinguishable from notoriety, and highly perishable, to boot.

O.J. had written his *I Want To Tell You* with the aid of Lawrence Schiller early on, and it rose to the *New York Times'* best seller list's top position on February 12, 1995. Little, Brown dubbed it the fastest-selling book in its history. The timing—midway—was impeccable.

Even earlier in October 1994, Nicole's one-time tenant, Faye D. Resnick (with Mike Walker) had weighed in with *Nicole Brown Simpson: The Private Diary of a Life Interrupted*. The initial printing was a gaudy 750,000 copies.

The weekly newspaper tracking media coverage, *Advertising Age*, gave the "Cover Story Crown" to this case for 1994. It would be even bigger in 1995.

O.J. emerged repeating his determination to search for the "real killers," which he'd first uttered on July 20, 1994, when he offered a half-million-dollar reward. A wag, noting O.J.'s frequent appearance on the links, jibed that "O.J. must think a caddy did it."

There would now be a "wrongful death" civil suit by Ronald Goldman's family, in which a preponderance of evidence would prevail, rather than guilt beyond a reasonable doubt, as is required in a criminal case. Nicole's parents would have to decide whether to fight for custody of their grandchildren or return them to the man they believed murdered the children's mother.

Frequently, these cases evolve into defense prosecutions of the victim, but, since this wouldn't fly here, they settled for a successful prosecution of the LAPD. The defense mantra—"rush to justice"—flowed nicely into subliminal messages of "racism." It seemed a cunning use of onomatopoeia.

A much-heralded interview with NBC was canceled by Simpson's lawyers (always the convenient—and lavishly paid—fall guys when the star missteps) on October 11, 1995. There were many reports of his attempting to cash in on his desirability as a celebrity—but this was proving to be a moral dilemma to O.J.'s potential employers and a tactical burden to his lawyer defending the civil suit. He'd sign sports memorabilia at a show in Atlantic City in February 1996, but would not autograph photos of the white Bronco. A helmet, autographed, would go for $185.

And so, the case had not been about guilt or innocence, but about race. The cry from the heart erupting in a joyous, triumphant roar from black throats offered a flashing glimpse of the yawning, widening chasm between the races. Yet no whites seemed tempted to ask what the daily lives of blacks must be like in America to provoke such an outburst.

It looked as if the drama would play out over coming months and years, as a rapt audience fixed an inner gaze on the arena below.

THE BACKDROP

There, a full complement of actors worked feverishly to create the climate in which these spectacular acts were performed. Street crime was clearly the most visible and dramatic of our depredations. Whites were set afire and murdered in black neighborhoods, and blacks got chased, beaten, and killed in white ones.

From One Crime You May Know a Nation

Just as Jack the Ripper came to be seen as the avatar of Victorian England's unmentionable suppressions and Bluebeard as the embodiment of the darker fantasies of medieval central Europe, so does a brief scan of America's contemporary police blotter yield images that define the underbelly of our civilization.

Here, a crime has to possess the sensationalism of the multiple murder of mother and infants and the ripping out of a sought-after fetus in the womb—to satisfy another woman's craving for a child—to capture the nation's distracted attentions. Thus, the casual trail of mutilated bodies left behind by a glib, personable thrill-killer in California who had created a long record of documented atrocities that had been ignored by an overworked and underperforming criminal justice system.

In Brooklyn, subway robbers sprayed a booth and incinerated the token clerk in a failed effort to steal the money. And the killers of women continued to surface as proof of the dangers lurking for women in a society where restraints vanished and officialdom failed.

No one better illustrated the fate of the vulnerable and helpless more dramatically than Elisa Izquierdo, the six-year-old whose death was a cautionary tale of urban life and its burdens.[7] Her father had died, leaving the child to the tender mercies of an addicted and distracted mother who'd borne six children and had been stabbed repeatedly by the man she was currently trying to please. She was ultimately charged with the child's murder.

The case captured general attention because a princely patron had offered to pay the child's tuition at a Montessori school. The bureaucratic landscape was replete with warning signs of abuse that had been ignored. Elisa was a paradigm for the age.

A judge was shocked when confronted with an incestuous grandfather and granddaughter, 71 and 32, who'd produced two children and who plotted to kill the woman's husband for insurance. Several attempts failed.

In Detroit a mother sold her teenage son to drug dealers to settle a $1000 debt for crack. He became addicted and was used as a cocaine delivery boy and as a plaything for the thugs around him. Although the boy absolved his mother of some blame, this was modern America's version of indentured servitude.

None of these events, all occurring in late 1995, could be seen as other than harbingers of the destruction that the decline of family and city were producing.

The overall trend—in what might be called the *negative indices* (street crime, illegitimacy, divorce, murder, imprisonment)— had been marching steadily upward over the past 35 years. Most negatives had tripled, some merely doubled. Minor, temporary declines were trumpeted as the long-awaited turnabout. The key index became not the number of cops, but the size of the "at-risk" male cohort between the ages of 15 and 24. And a bulge was coming.

An international tremor erupted with the killing of visiting tourists in Florida. All but 1% of Americans thought crime a serious problem in 1994. The trend was for more violence by younger offenders. Whites fled to the suburbs to escape the onslaught. Young mothers took their teenage sons from Gary and Chicago to Minneapolis. Detroit, a cesspool of urban violence and decay, became the future dreaded by everyone, yet it pointed the direction every city was taking.

Even bank robberies—a crime with a very high solution rate (75%) because of security cameras and other measures—soared in the 1990s, rising over 40%, attesting to the desperation of many on the street.

Cities with tough gun laws[8] tended to have somewhat less violence than those with loose ones, and the availability of drugs added to the bloodshed. Alcohol was a permanent fixture attending violence, and gambling looked like it would become the addiction of the twenty-first century, adding to the crime totals.

Some mothers had lost three sons, in different episodes, to street mayhem. Gangs took their tolls in Los Angeles and Chicago, but individuals created just as much carnage in Detroit and D.C. Stranger-to-stranger crimes frightened more than the predictable variety between familiars. Folks remained cooler when it was just "them doing it to them." Some victims were more important than others, and the treatment of the suspects, by the criminal justice system, proved it. Recidivism and the problems of predicting behavior or treating violent, sexual, or criminal disorders made criminology little more than a deadly guessing game.

The slaughter of innocents lost the power to shock, as numbed citizens angrily called for ever-tougher measures. Thrill-killers on weekend sprees became common fare relegated to inside pages. Those with nothing to lose had little to fear.

No justice, no peace.

Carjacking, child abuse, and the experiences reported by young women unlucky enough to be on the streets testified to the true jungle urban centers had become. There were street gangs, motorcycle gangs, and dangers lurking in the ghetto. Novels centered on one wrong turn in a bad neighborhood—every suburbanite's nightmare. The decline of civility was bringing days when citizens averted their gaze at outrages. Politicians delivered more cops and bigger prisons, while enlarging the swamp of poverty and racism breeding deadly mosquitos.

With the killing of good samaritans, the message of decline spread through neighborhoods. Aggressive police tactics—stings, decoys, and stake-outs—that wound up snaring black males were softpedaled or avoided altogether as a sop to rising black political power in the cities. Tough drug enforcement continued to be politically acceptable with all power centers.

The issues not only failed to get addressed, but a lot of politicians also pointed with pride at the regenerations in Detroit, Cleveland, and the Bronx, ignoring the spreading blight and decay and playing into the hands of those content with the status quo.

Mothers were killing their sons' molesters, neighborhoods banded together to promote safety, other mothers hired killers to secure cheerleaders' celebrity for their daughters, a woman sexually maimed her abusive husband, a teenager shot her lover's wife, and sons killed parents and blamed it on sexual exploitation. The privatization of security was so far along that private cops now outnumbered public cops by much more than two to one. Residential communities hired security firms, malls had their own cops, commercial groups created forces to protect their interests, and hardly anyone thought of renting a city apartment that came without a doorman and other security features. The overclass was finding ways of purchasing its own protection.

Still the frightening images paraded along.

In March 1994 in Los Angeles, two gang members were charged with shooting two Japanese students, both 19-year-olds, in the head, killing both. They wanted the 1994 Honda Civic the victims drove.

Japanese tourists were reported to be shunning California.

In Florida the National Guard patrolled a highway where scores of incidents of violence had been reported in the early

1990s. The winter season of 1992–93 saw nine tourists murdered in Florida. A wrong turn could lead to a deadly snare. Cars bumped tourist autos, crammed with luggage, and robbed and murdered the occupants when they pulled over. German newspapers shrieked "Florida Again" and called it a jungle. This was serious mainly because it impacted the hugely lucrative tourist industry.

Even the arrests of the suspects engendered hostility as aggressive, and perhaps overzealous, police tactics angered black communities. Two white men kidnapped a black tourist and set him aflame in a racial assault in Florida in 1993. The burning of homeless vagrants became a nameless urban pastime for sadistic kids.

Elsewhere in the urban jungle innocent bystanders were being struck at such a rate as to inspire metaphors of battlefields. They were standing passively about, in the dark, and getting picked off.

And headlines blared the comforting news that, for the third straight year, the number of killings declined, from 25,470 in 1993 to 23,730 in 1994. Ignored was the trend that saw the total triple over the past quarter-century or the coming tide of teenagers sure to surpass these totals in the years just ahead.

Swimming like giant sharks among the piranhas of urban life are serial killers, who simply murder compulsively until stopped. These mostly white, almost invariably male hunters are driven by sexual, misogynistic, misanthropic impulses. Their names are familiar and made more so by the sick commercialization of their exploits in collectors' cards—David Berkowitz (the Son of Sam killer); Theodore Bundy (the boy next door); John Wayne Gacy (a killer of children, executed, like Bundy); Jeffrey Dahmer (a sexual fantasist, sadist, and practitioner of cannibalism who preyed mainly on minorities and was murdered by an inmate in a Wisconsin prison), Joel Rifkin (a killer of prostitutes); and Nathaniel White (who killed six women).

Frequently, these killers' profiles included histories of early and prolonged physical and sexual abuse that kindled a ferocious rage that exploded, later, in acts of symbolic revenge.[9] Serial killers differ from rampage killers in that the latter usually suffer one explosive episode—a firing, jilting, or slight, often involving drugs and alcohol, and invariably facilitated by the ready availability of firearms, kill a number of people, and often follow it with their own suicide. These can be particularly dangerous for those unlucky enough to be in the wrong place at the moment of devastation. The workplace is a particularly dangerous place in these episodes.

The victims of serial killers tend to reflect the predators' predilections. Hannibal Lecter of *The Silence of the Lambs* served as literature's creation of the prototypical male serialist. There are, of course, exceptions that prove the rule, such as Aileen Wuornos, who admitted she killed seven men she had picked up on a Florida highway in the late 1980s and 1990. She had been working as a prostitute and the victims were mainly johns. Adding a touch of mockery, Ms. Wuornos was a lesbian. She received six life sentences.

A dysfunctional society was spawning monsters.

Gangs

Fitting snugly into its role of avatar and advance guard for the nation—at least in the areas labeled weird—Los Angeles produced wild and violent gangs and one leader who, fittingly, bared all in a book accurately titled *Monster: The Autobiography of an L.A. Gang Member.* In its pages Sanyika Shakur, a.k.a. Kody Scott, depicted his life as a leader of the Crips from the reflective confines of a San Quentin prison solitary confinement section.

The gang became the key social structure in Shakur's life after he was recruited at age 11. Escalating violence gradually inured him to its effects. The few fragile institutions were gradually obliterated, leaving a ghetto moonscape. He learned it felt better to hit than to be hit and rapidly overcame whatever inhibitions civilization had instilled. Overhead, the Orwellian nightmare of dazzling helicopter searchlights cast a ghostly, intrusive prison camp glow onto the eerie battlefield below. Shakur's account is really just that, a battlefield report, only the action takes place in the heart of a nation "at peace."

A father of three who spent most of his life in prison, having robbed, shot, and killed casually, the transformation of this gifted youth wound from gangbanger to political revolutionary. The anger merely shifted; he was still at war, now with the overclass. Now 29, this fatherless, furious, frustrated, and excluded man will be loosed on a hostile and oppressive society.

Across the continent another monster was held in isolated fastness in the deepest recesses of the state's sequestrations. Not a gang member but regarded as the most dangerous criminal in New York State's history, Willie Bosket,[10] 33 in 1996, has been in lock-ups since the age of 9, with short periods of freedom during which he mugged, stabbed, and murdered—committing about 2,000 crimes. Regarded as so menacing as to require his separation from other inmates and guards, he is our African-American Hannibal Lecter.

His father, whom Willie never met, was a double murderer who killed himself in a shoot-out with the police. The younger Bosket described himself as a product of the system. Both Willie and his father registered at the highest levels of I.Q. tests. Reviled, loathed, and feared, Bosket is perfectly illustrative of the system's effect on ghetto youth. The society, content to put him away, made no effort to understand this man, labeling him a monster. What are his chances? Ours?

Juvenile Delinquents

The progression is trackable—a dysfunctional family with absent positive male models, dangerous friends, indifferent schools, television, drugs, unemployability, fatherhood, violence, and anomie. The first serious crime predictably occurs around 15; imprisonment, addiction, and oblivion induce disappearance around 30.[11,12]

Battered, sexually abused, shaken kids become acculturated

to violence. The prevalence and availability of drugs spread the decay. The ubiquitousness of weaponry lends efficacy to every vagrant whim or fear.

Despite *Roe v. Wade*, the rate of births to teenage mothers increased 27% from 1986 to 1991. Suicides of adolescents rose 120% from 1980 to 1992, from 0.8 per 100,000 to 1.7. Arrests of juveniles ages, 10–17 for violent crimes went from 288 per 100,000 in 1973 to 488 per 100,000 in 1993. By 1995 one in three black males in their twenties was in prison or on parole or probation. Just over half the prisoners in our vast and exploding system are black males, although they comprise only about 6% of the general population.

In 1992 white babies could anticipate being greeted by a father about 70% of the time, black babies about 30%.[13]

The rate of murder victims under age 19 was 12% in 1983 and 17% in 1992. A young man in Rhode Island killed two women and two girls (ages eight and ten) and served five years because he was only 16 at the time of the crime. He was released in October 1994, and his criminal record was expunged. In the Bronx, desperate parents chained a girl to a radiator to keep her off the streets and free of the drugs threatening her life. They narrowly escaped prosecution.

Kids were found to be, increasingly, abandoned by adults and subjected to depression, experiencing problems with drugs and alcohol, engaging in fights, and suffering from other behavioral disorders and both behavioral and mental problems. The availability of a handgun escalated the danger posed by a traumatic event, such as a break-up with a girlfriend, an arrest, trouble in school, stress over a test, or a move or other uprooting.

In this dysfunctional atmosphere the missing child became a symbol of the struggle, with 800,000 reported in 1992 versus 100,000 in 1982. Of these 450,000 ran away from intolerable situations at home, 350,000 were taken by a family member in ugly family tugs of war, and about 3200–4600 were lured away by sex perverts. A total of 200–300 are actually kidnapped and about 150 of these are murdered. Uncounted are 127,000 thrown out by parents.

Kids are the true casualties in a disintegrating society. Two studies revealed the trends. One, by SUNY Albany, found that there was a higher percentage of crimes by those who were abused or neglected as children, with 26% delinquency among those who were and 16.8% among those who were not. The figures were narrower for adult criminality, with 23.6% having been abused and 21.1% not, but, in violent crimes, the differences were starker, with 11.2% having been abused and 7.9% not. A second study revealed family risks, with 52% of prisoners found to have criminal relatives.

The problems of adolescents 7–16 years old were centering on such symptoms as withdrawal or social problems, attention or thinking problems leading to failure in school, delinquency or aggression, or anxiety and depression. A feeling of loneliness and of being unloved were also pervasive. Suicide had risen to become the second- or third-leading cause of death among 15- to 24-year-olds, rising from 7.5 per 100,000 in 1933 to 13 per 100,000 in 1989. As of December 1993 there were almost 37 million Americans living in poverty—i.e., a family of four with a total income of $14,279 or less.

Proposals to meet the surging threat of adolescent criminality centered on building juvenile detection facilities; hiring more probation officers, judges, and public defenders; treating 14- to 17-year-olds as adults in serious crimes; mandated stiffer sentences, keeping criminal records up to age 23; and extending the jurisdiction over juveniles to additional infractions. In the meanwhile, summer jobs were cut, national service programs were slashed, and recreational programs were derided as "midnight basketball."

A very few isolated facilities served as "points of light" in an otherwise darkening landscape. Milton Hershey School provided residential education—much in the way of orphanages—to 1100 youngsters in kindergarten through twelfth grade, spending about $35,000 per student from a fund provided by the founder. Girard College hosted 550 from the first through twelfth grades. The unlucky rest dodged bullets and faced the grim realities of street life.

Observers who regularly visited America's prisons reported growing segregation and a furious anger among the burgeoning number of blacks in confinement.[14] And all of these were being returned to the very conditions that triggered their murderous assaults, as well as to our midst.

Among the 10–17 age group, arrests for violent crimes rose from 215.9 per 100,000 in 1970 to 430.6 in 1990; arrests for murder went from 6.0 to 12.1 in that period. Curiously, high school dropout rates declined slightly for whites and dramatically for blacks, from 27.9 in 1970 to 13.2 in 1990. The percentage of families in poverty went from 15% in 1970 to 23% in 1991. And, while sexual activity increased among 15-year-old girls, the rate of live births declined for black, unmarried, teenage girls, from 1970 to 1990, attesting to the influence of *Roe v. Wade*. A surprising number of pregnancies were found to have been caused by males four to seven years older, suggesting an epidemic of statutory rape.

It would be hard to imagine circumstances in which the prospects for success among America's impoverished youth could possibly be bleaker—and the trend was inexorably downward.

The Family

Salvaging the family is a tall order,[15] but a program must include refighting the war on poverty—with government involvement in health, housing, welfare, education, jobs, and related social programs—but this time insisting on performance by the recipients. Lives must be structured, orderly, and disciplined. There must be accountability, individual responsibility, and consequence.

Money should be rerouted from programs now trying to react downstream to problems originating upstream. The internal threat is far more serious than any external one, and we should be doing more things, internationally, through partnerships such as those including the United Nations. All should share the costs of worldwide peacekeeping. This would enable us to pare the defense budget to meet the internal threat. Expenditures on cops, prisons, and other repressive programs need to be reconsidered. We're making the same mistake here we made with the defense budget, reflexively assuming that this was one area not subject to discussion and a concern that no party can afford to surrender to the other. Politicians are going to have to be willing to risk being soft on crime, just as they should have been willing to risk being labeled soft on Communism when attempting to address the hideous complexities of the Cold War. That they didn't then doesn't augur well for their courage now.

We can limit the number of children we help to those that can be safely managed through welfare incentives and reductions in payments; we can insist on clean and orderly—drug free—homes; society can demand that those helped secure educations and look for jobs and otherwise undertake those tasks once associated with respectability.

Who would take a job if it meant losing health coverage for their children in an atmosphere in which childcare is all but unobtainable? The liberal notion of "entitlements" subverted the process of performance. The conservative idea of bootstrappism consigned the underclass to permanent fetters and widened the chasm with the overclass.

Reinstituting family values will be even more difficult in a society in which even our leaders and models are divorced (almost invariably for reasons that imply the search for a better deal of more pleasure, rather than to escape abuse or intolerable pain); avoided military service; philandered; engaged in tawdry, suspect, or outright criminal acts; and for whom concepts of ethics and honor are charming, irrelevant anachronisms. What must begin—if any progress is to be made—is a tough, candid, public discussion of what "family values" actually entail and how this might be translated into virtuous behavior.

The Cities

While the family—extended and nuclear—faded into the panicked search for fulfillment, the city[16,17] suffered abandonment as the rich, energetic, and talented mostly white middle class escaped into the safety, sterility, and isolation of suburban life.

Could America live without the principal cornerstones of its social edifice—cities and families? Whatever the answer, the nation was clearly trying.

As cities were scorned—save as places in which to make money—they were turned over to caretakers, often black, who would preside over an orderly slide.

Riots would be avoided or, more likely, postponed or diminished, by placing compliant African Americans in highly visible posts. They would get theirs and ensure that the police treaded more lightly on black necks. There would be no such aggressiveness as was characterized by the LAPD under Daryl Gates. There would be no stakeouts, sting operations, decoys, or other tactics that netted mostly black males. The sop would be to allow aggressiveness in drug busts. Every once in a while whites wrested control back into their hands, if only to reinforce the message of whose interests the caretakers were there to preserve.

On Halloween 1995, Detroit had to enlist 35,000 citizens to patrol the city and prevent the Devil's Night arsons that spread the stain on the city's blemished reputation. It was labeled a success.

Gary, Indiana, Washington, D.C., and others used National Guard troops to patrol urban ghettos. Los Angeles used klieg lights from above to monitor activities in the 'hood.

Harlem and the South Bronx developed into faithful metaphors for the urban dilemma. Graffiti became, for some, a cry for help and, for others, the act of vandals—and, for a few, art.[18]

Urban renewal evolved into an oxymoron that mocked its half-hearted intentions, except in the glitzy downtowns.

Every mayoral race became a spitting contest in which candidates had to decide how many more cops they could credibly promise.

A political solution to the decaying or urban areas is to suck the prosperous and able encircling towns into the struggle through some form of metropolitan government. In areas where the county line encompasses suburbs and where an infrastructure of county government already exists, transferring municipal duties to the county makes economic, political, and moral sense and invites the ringing communities to share their energies, wealth, and talents with the core urban centers. It is not an idea whose appeal can be assured, since suburbanites are certain to oppose it.

ARTIFACTS

It is a measure of the alienation of blacks that so many of them believe that whites make alcohol, drugs, and other addictives freely available in the core cities to perpetuate their bondage. We do, as a society, indirectly provide ready supplies of substances that keep what would otherwise certainly be restive ghetto dwellers reasonably pacified.

Social decay is, as we so painfully observed in the short life of Elisa Izquierdo, accelerated by deadly addictions to crack cocaine or heroin. Marijuana frequently acts as a stepping stone between tobacco, alcohol, and hard drugs, and even gambling enters into the deadly equation as it spreads wildly.

It is not too hyperbolic an assertion to guess that 90% of our street criminals are addicted to something or were under a substance's influence at the time of their crimes. Despite reports of declines here and there, drug use among teenagers began climbing in 1992, and *Reader's Digest* was carrying an article titled "Drugs Are Back—Big Time" in 1996.

Facilitating the carnage is an arsenal of weaponry unequaled in the world. It is reliably and fairly universally estimated—by those on both sides of the issue—that there is more than one firearm out there for every man, woman, and child in America. No other advanced nation tolerates the profusion of firearms Americans have learned to live—and die—with. Many states currently have higher numbers of firearms deaths than those occurring through auto accidents. It seems distinctly possible that we may have more gun deaths through murder, suicide, and accident in the near future than automobile fatalities, which currently run around 45,000 a year nationally. The only possible impediment is the lifting of a 55-mile-per-hour speed limit by President Clinton and Congress in November 1995, which is likely to raise highway deaths, notwithstanding the additional safety afforded by seat belts, air bags, better-made cars, and safer roads. The fallible, and sometimes drunk, human behind the wheel has not been similarly upgraded.

We can see the need for punishments, but we can't see the virtues of prevention or the costs of cruel social, economic, and racial policies.

Money matters in America.

Race matters.

The sum of these totals means that we are not that concerned that white collar and organized crime extract many billions more from our pockets than do muggers and burglars. And it doesn't really matter to us that the urban dwellers mainly stab, shoot, rob, and kill each other. What matters to us is when their actions spill over into our sandboxes.

Street crime is mainly the province of the underclass—poor, urban and mostly black—but it is the overclass that makes street crime the inevitable outcome of intolerable conditions. Punishment works, but sole reliance upon it is both morally wrong and intellectually bankrupt. It must be allied with hope. Real crime prevention lies in adopting programs such as Project for Pride in Living, in Minnesota, which houses and employs the underclass and holds them to stiff standards of accountability and performance.

The models, not many, are out there—scattered, scorned, and ignored. There are none so blind as those who will not see.

10

The System's Response

The criminal justice system is mostly centered on meeting the challenge of the street criminal. That's where the numbers are. While white collar, organized, political, and terrorist crime are pervasive and enormously costly, they are also both relatively rare—in comparison to the millions touched by drugs, guns, burglars, thieves, and muggers—and highly specialized. They are also largely the provinces of federal authorities. The comparison is made easier when we see that prisoners in federal facilities constitute 10% or less of America's prosecutions and jailed population.

Blacks constituted 54.2% of the prison population in 1992, and they had a rate of 1,432 imprisonments per 100,000, while whites were imprisoned at the rate of 203 per 100,000, or one-seventh of the black total.[1]

The criminal justice system is a conglomerate of human institutions—police, courts, probation, prisons, defense, and others—and, as such, is fallible. Its imperfections are greatly heightened by the terror of a public insistent on protections but not willing to look upstream for the cure and begging for simple answers.

Contrary to widely held belief, the U.S. Constitution had proved anything but an impediment to police—or criminal justice system—effectiveness. The 30 years since the much-criticized decisions of the Earl Warren Supreme Court have seen enormous strides in police innovations and aggressiveness, which produced a wildly burgeoning prison population. It is absurd to hold that our founders intended the document to serve as an obstacle to public protections—and it has not served as such a handicap.

It would be relatively easy to upgrade greatly the professionalism of the police, for example, by raising minimum entrance standards to include at least a bachelor's degree. Advanced degrees at the higher levels are easily achievable. Similarly, selection, training, and physical plant and equipment levels can be raised dramatically.

The military has shown what can be done to integrate the races and afford opportunities for advancement to blacks, and the labor market is such as to offer a surfeit of qualified candidates of all races, genders, and backgrounds. Policing offers the psychic income once associated with the Peace Corps and can be easily marketed to appeal to the most altruistic. What stands in the way of such reforms is the ownership of the policing profession by a blue collar class that is reluctant to part with this unquestioned ladder into the middle class. The current background investigation of all applicants filters out the unfit very effectively.

Criminal and missing persons records need to be revamped and reformed, nationally. Their current state is a confused scandal of non- or disinformation.

Standing in the way of reforms are such political realities as civil service regulations, unions, the ambitions of chiefs, the turf jealousies all over the criminal justice systems, and similarly petty, provincial concerns—not the United States Constitution.

Positive change is both possible and necessary. Judges need to be selected more carefully—especially at the local level. Jury selection should encompass broader pools, and majority verdicts should be considered. There must be funding for meaningful defenses. Appeals can be screened and limited. The grand jury, like parole, has a role to play—as examiner of wrongdoing, as the people's voice in controversial cases, and as accuser.

The entire process—from arrest to final disposition—needs to be streamlined, through computerization; booking efficiencies; scheduling discipline; night—as well as day—trials; better collection, control, analysis, and presentation of evidence; and more training for all personnel in the system.

The criminal justice system is driven by the public pressures that result in legislative fiat. The president's hailed 1994 Crime Bill—in which Democrats sought to claim the tough ground on crime and not be labeled soft, as they had been on Communism—was nothing more than an intellectually bankrupt attempt to gain public favor. The possible appointment of a President's Crime Commission to inform its contents was dismissed as a bad idea, and a potpourri of palliatives was eagerly collected and fulsomely offered instead.

The Crime Bill, to be sure, contained some useful ideas—such as the ban on assault weapons—but it also included some horrid ones, from the addition of 100,000 cops, whose need was never established by study or plan and the funding for which would prove very troublesome, to lots of more and bigger jails, tougher judges, more prosecutors, and a host of additional actions calling for the death penalty. The Democrats wouldn't be soft on crime; they'd be soft-headed instead.

The Crime Bill of 1994 stands to fin de siècle America as the bloated defense budget did at midcentury. The defense budget burden ultimately crushed the Soviet Union. We were lucky to escape with mere tons of debt and waste.

Bail—set to guarantee the presumed innocent's appearance in court and to prevent further damage—has been distorted into a form of pretrial detention. And the use of the military in law enforcement operations, forbidden since the passage of the Posse Comitatus Act in 1870 and a role for which they are demonstrably unsuited, was greatly expanded. Clearly they needed a raison d'être, but it has always been dangerous to widen the powers of armed forces everywhere.

Mandated sentences placed unpopular crimes ahead of the rest of the criminal pack, often forcing the incarceration of non-violent offenders and affording no room for dangerous recidivists. Nowhere has this been more tellingly illustrated than in the heralded war on drugs, which exalted enforcement over prevention, education, and treatment programs. We've now had this draconian-only approach in place since Governor Rockefeller's 1973 tough drug laws, and it has produced hordes of prisoners, but no solutions.[2] Such proposals as "three strikes and you're out" (life imprisonment after the third felony conviction) became the leitmotifs of political campaigns and legislative initiatives. It is one of the unintended ironies of such proposals that they invariably flow from "tough-on-crime" legislators who turn pathetically flaccid when called on to punish their fellow members who have been convicted of crimes and other serious wrongdoings.

The problem of violent crime centers on the small percentage of repeaters among the general population of criminals. The criminal justice system has proved itself inept at establishing and acting on the menace factor presented by the recidivist.[3,4]

Not only has the system failed to separate the true menace from the quotidian, casual offender, but it has also neglected to evaluate and measure the menace factor (the threat posed to future victims) even when it has the population available for continuous and microscopic study—as it does when exercising control such as probation, incarceration, or parole.

Programs are labeled failures—recall the 1988 Willie Horton scandal—without regard to statistical realities that must attend every human enterprise. It is distinctly possible that Horton was the failure in an otherwise statistically successful operation, but no one had the political courage to find out or say so. Scared Straight was criticized because it failed to deter *all* of the kids exposed to the horrors of prison life from committing their own crimes.

This tendency to demonstrate anecdotally the failure of approaches such as military-style detention centers, Scared Straight and related programs—which expose youth to the awfulness of prison life, country club (low-security) prisons, plea bargaining (without which the criminal justice system couldn't function at all and which has served it better than any political figure could safely claim), and other programs not only ignores statistically acceptable and accepted realities but also totally overlooks the fact that criminals are released into the fetid environment from whence they sprang. What hope can there be for straightening out one's life in such circumstances? How can any meaningful discussion take place in such a highly charged, politically correct atmosphere of denial?

PRISONS

The total number of inmates in state and federal prisons went over the 1 million mark in 1994. There were under 200,000 as recently as 1970. Prison construction spending by states rose over 600% between 1979 and 1990. Notwithstanding the general view that we are soft on crime, America jails more people, per capita, than any other industrialized nation—by a very wide margin, and for longer periods.

There are a number of visible trends.

Prison construction is expensive and maintenance is costly. There has been a move to privatization as a way to cut costs, evade bureaucratic confusions, and circumvent civil service and union restrictions. On the other scale is the growing political heft of corrections officers' unions. The intractability of the unions, the smothering tangle of civil service protections, and the difficult-to-measure outcomes seem to have dealt a near-fatal blow to school privatization efforts, an object lesson to reformers.[5]

The corrections industry is also rapidly replacing the military–industrial complex as a center of power and influence and as a source of government funds. The debate surrounding the efficacy of imprisonment includes calls for treatment programs; chain gangs; educational, employment, and restitution efforts; and the elimination of sports, TV and related "frills." Prisoners have begun commercial enterprises such as selling inscribed t-shirts, and similarly kitschy souvenirs spawned the rebirth of *Prison Life* magazine and inspired the creation of Inmate-Corrections Television Cable programming in Florida.

Punishment

Does punishment work?

This is very like asking whether human behavior can be influenced or controlled, and, if so, how?

The empirical answer clearly suggests that human acts can be channeled, or influenced—if not controlled—by a carefully and relevantly doled issuance of rewards or punishments. This seems so obvious as to require no elaboration, yet human experience demonstrates the folly of assuming the inevitability of anything.

Criminals basically do not commit crimes in prison, and society is made safer by the sequestration of dangerous predators. If this is true—and it probably is—then why does crime keep rising even as the prison population soars? The answer lies in society's creating a swamp of poverty and desperation in which criminals are formed.

The imprisonment of nonviolent drug offenders—under mandated sentencing legislation—precludes the confinement of some violent ones. And longer and longer sentences ensure the aging of the population into toothless—and harmless—wonders, which is likely to turn prisons into expensive nursing homes in the near future.[6]

Racial disparities in drug sentencing is really a canard that obfuscates the confusing and unmentionable point that any net cast against any street crime factor will always bring in disproportionate numbers of black males. What white America wants to ignore is that it has created conditions so horrible as to make escape into crime, drugs, and violence the inevitable concomitant of modern life in the ghetto. Returning the freed inmates to the very swamps that produced them ensures a reversion to criminal form, very quickly. Small wonder rehabilitation doesn't work.

All of these factors speak against the success of a prison

system devoutly believed in by the people, ardently defended by the politicians, and powerfully supported by the industry it nurtures.

The craze to imprison has undermined public confidence in promising alternatives to incarceration, such as electronic bracelets or other tough monitoring measures, e.g., reporting to a machine periodically, intensive probation, or parole supervision. Expanding case loads to save dollars ensures the defeat of these useful measures, as does the publicity surrounding occasional and inevitable failures.

Capital Punishment

Punishment of any sort must be relevant and proportionate to be a useful deterrent. It must "fit the crime," or it becomes the sort of irrelevancy that attracted pickpockets to practice their trade at public hangings in medieval England, where all crimes were punishable by death.

The only persuasive scientific argument to be made for the death penalty is that executed criminals don't recidivate. The death penalty[7-11] has been a political rouser in contemporary America, and a real danger is to overapply its reach—as is done in Clinton's unfortunate Crime Bill.

It could be argued that the execution of Bruno Richard Hauptmann in 1936, for the Lindbergh kidnapping, served as a deterrent to childtakings for many decades.[12] Other arguments pro and con have been bruited about and about, with little persuasion at either extreme. Clearly, the vast majority of the American public supports it. Equally clearly, most of the rest of the world is moving away from it. We are re-embracing it enthusiastically, reaching a current peak of 37 executions in 1993. There are currently about 2500 prisoners, overwhelmingly male and almost half of them black, on death row. Executions should accelerate with the passage of antiterrorism legislation in 1996, which limits—and expedites—appeals.

Death must be dealt judiciously and realistically if whatever efficacy it has is to be preserved. It needs to be limited to murder—

and of a particularly egregious sort at that. It is silly to think that the broad majority of murders—mostly crimes of some passion among people who know each other—would be affected. Deterrence is only possible among the small minority of killings that involve a weighing of the gains and losses involved. Calculation, premeditation, and preparation should be considered with the circumstances—the cruelty involved, the identity of the victim(s), serial killings, professional murders, public assassinations, mass murders, and both the retribution and deterrent factors.

Those under 18 at the time of the crime, the mentally deficient or insane, or pregnant females should not be executed. Adoption of such strict distinctions would greatly reduce the numbers of those condemned to die in America and focus our energies on the very few killers who should be put to death. In an excess of enthusiasm for toughness, the president and congress greatly diluted the deterrent effect when they expanded capital punishment provisions irresponsibly in 1994.

Will errors occur? Can any human enterprise be cleansed of the possibility of error?

The answer is obviously that mistakes are possible. But humans have also learned to reduce their possibility through painstaking measures. Insisting on proof of guilt beyond the shadow of a doubt (as opposed to the lower standard of a reasonable doubt in criminal cases) before a sentence of death could be imposed—arrived at in a separate judicial process than the trial itself—would help reduce the prospect of a mistake.

Limiting appeals to one professionally prepared request for review, and execution within one year of sentencing, would reduce costs and make the process more credible, effective, and efficient. It is clearly constitutional since that document explicitly speaks of the possibility of being deprived of life, liberty, and property.

Is it fair?

Is life fair?

Really no more and no less than any other aspect of life in a society that hearkens to wealth and power and in which the weak suffer, whatever their merit. We are not going to make our courtrooms appreciably more impervious to the influence of wealth or power than we do other places.

Are some victims more important than others?

Victims are people—as are murderers—and, of course, the richer, abler, and stronger and those with greater resources tend to fare better—even in exacting vengeance in death—than those without. While actual victims get some mention in the debate, potential or possible future victims tend never to be considered. Yet it is a fact that serial killers often have convictions for previous killings in their backgrounds. It would seem that considering possible future victims would be an essential part of the government's role of protecting society.

In the final analysis the question might best be answered with a question.

If one believes that the killing of mass murderers such as John Wayne Gacy and Ted Bundy makes society safer, then that person is for—and if he or she doesn't think so, then that person is against. It is in the specific that we might find the justification for such generalizations as which murderers to execute.

The high moral and intellectual ground is with the abolitionists. The practical grasp of human affairs is with its advocates. Reluctantly, my experience as a cop places me firmly in the latter camp.

SUGGESTIONS

There are no simple solutions to the challenge represented by the street criminal, despite the temptations of the politicians to offer some. Upstream we must think of social programs that afford viability, such as the presence of a father at birth, a stable home life, education, health, housing, and employment opportunities[13]—in short, a social contract in which society, mostly through the government, but including nonprofits, corporations, and community groups, extends the hope of rescue while demanding performance.

Familial cohesion can be encouraged through tax policies that reward intact families and also through divorce laws that insist on substantive reasons for the granting of a decree, especially when children are involved.

Failure must include consequences. Individual responsibility, accountability, and penalties are central to the partnership. Prevention must be the focus, but outright failures cannot be ignored. One troublesome family can unhinge an entire neighborhood, one bucket-of-blood bar can be the focus of a lot of community violence. We must do a better job of identifying recidivists and targeting them for special treatment.

Downstream there must be punishments. These include the full panoply of possibilities, from incarceration to restitution, controls, house arrest, treatment, educational programs, and even death.

Society has not only a right to protect itself but also an obligation to its members to do the best it can in this connection. There are dangerous predators out there and they must be addressed. The fragile interconnections and interdependability of modern societies require the protections that allow continuous functioning.

11

The Culture

Despite figures that may, at any given time, show dramatic increases in church membership or attendance, America's real religion is diversion—from the fears, threats, or presentiments about our fate, variously described as funks or as a general malaise. We've seen how the search for answers leads many into cultish paths; even the devout are troubled in their wanderings. If God is dead, as Nietzsche held He was, we must either find a replacement or resign ourselves to the mostly unacceptable notion that this is all there is.

On what basis can we assert that escape into entertainment is the true American zeitgeist? Societies, especially ones in which choices can be freely expressed, methodically sort out their values through systems of rewards. Ours rewards mainly with cash. It is easy to establish our hierarchies through a simple analysis of the reward system.

Who are our most exalted and best-rewarded, among whom we shower treasure, celebrity, and status? Who are scorned and laid aside? Our icons are our sports and entertainment heroes, and our discarded are the transmitters of values—clergy, teachers, sages.

SPORTS

Where Rome had its circuses, America has its sports, both taking place on a wide and vivid canvas.[1,2] It is impossible to understand the nation's culture without a grasp of its principal diversion—athletic competitions. Our athletes are the idols on which we lavish every attention.

Unfortunately the exaltation has resulted in a climate in which economics rules—leading to loss of loyalty and identification—either with a team or with a community. Stars auction off their talents to the highest bidders and teams, which were once rooted in a community in which a sense of identification became critical to the affection flowing in both directions, have become little more than blackmailers holding towns hostage against the blandishments of other eager communities. Advertisers on the January 1995 Super Bowl paid an average of $1 million for each of the sixty 30-second commercials on television.

These facts, though, were—however troubling—abstractions that vanished into the fog of economic theories and business decisions. The icons were, however, concrete as individuals and comprehensible as role models.

A nation's faith in its heroes was encapsulated in the exchange between Shoeless Joe Jackson and a very young fan who, confronted with the unthinkable prospect of a World Series fix, plaintively pleaded, "Say it ain't so, Joe."

It was 1919 and America still believed.

The arrest of 22 for allegedly fixing harness races in Yonkers, New York, in 1995 indicated that the attempt to control outcomes likely survived.

In 1995 America's brightest baseball stars were tarnished with defrauding their government by not reporting income from signing cards for fans. This was now a highly lucrative enterprise—cashing in on what were once innocent reinforcers of fan enthusiasm and visions of innocent fan–star encounters on the playing fields. Hall of Famers shamefacedly admitted they had succumbed to the temptation to steal. The corrupting and commercialization of this once-innocent activity went unremarked.

Ingenious entrepreneurs parodied the practice with "Cardtoons" that made fun of such player foibles as egotism and greed. The Baseball Players Association helped their promotion by unsuccessfully suing to keep these jibes off the market. Other hustlers offered counterfeit memorabilia for sale.

Mickey Mantle, one of the accused tax evaders, had his bronze bust stolen from Yankee Stadium in 1976. Not to be outdone by the icon memorialized in the 8-by-10-inch bust, a fan offered the pilfered item for sale over the Internet on August 23, 1995. A former security guard at Yankee Stadium was arrested and charged with transporting stolen property. Ironically, Mantle might have made his greatest, and bravest, contribution when he begged kids not to emulate his own abuse of alcohol in the final weeks of his life.

The O. J. Simpson case was certainly about race, but it was also about domestic abuse—another of the lapses now attributed to our sports deities. Still, big-time college football programs found it economically inadvisable to exclude domestic batterers from competition. Too much was at stake.

Leagues wrestled torturously with drug policies that threatened the deprivation of services vital to a team's professional and economic progress. In the name of rehabilitation and second chances, addicts were employed to produce victories. When exposed, they were suspended briefly, ushered into treatment, and restored.

Heavyweight champions were imprisoned for rape and their associates were accused of fraud.[3] Politicians, performers, and even ministers arranged a welcome-home celebration in Harlem's storied Apollo Theater for Mike Tyson's return from prison. The community's outrage prompted a cancellation of the event.

In our contemporary Olympus, ambitious teenage swimmers use anabolic steroids to lend heft to their strokes. And exhibitors fight for the right to promote extreme or ultimate fighting—in which bare knuckled contestants punch, kick, and brawl their way to a bloody result.

Dogfighting and cock fights continue, with only animal rights activists occasionally casting light on the clandestine diversions.

Such are the activities and the idols our sons and daughters are to consider as heroes worthy of emulation. Showered with wealth, fame, and sexual opportunities, it isn't hard to see why the memoirs of these idols contain extravagant descriptions of sexual marathons involving casts of thousands.

Tobacco and alcohol were in essence, paying for it all, while their effects were glamorized. Former athletes are today revealing the underside of this idealized world. Their accounts often include descriptions of out-of-control excesses, homelessness, batterings, imprisonment, and disgrace.

Gambling by athletes had to be directly related to events in which the athlete participated to register official opposition. Where once sports figures were suspended for betting on any activity, in recent years much more egregious circumstances would have to be proved. Signs of slipping standards abounded.

Every season brought accounts of devoted outdoors folks' and sports enthusiasts' participation in activities they normally spoke of in hushed, reverential tones. Decoy metal deer get regularly peppered by hunters illegally shooting from vehicles or roadside. Ardent supporters of wildlife preservation are routinely found to have exceeded catch limits and used illegal decoys and other circumventions. And it is hard to see any disgrace or opprobrium attaching to these hypocrisies, invariably engaged in by pious "naturalists and outdoors folks."

Ethics in sports fared no better, even as lip service got fervently paid to the inculcation of values. Athletes who admitted fault or expressed contrition were treated as pariahs by teammates focused on winning. Assurances meant nothing as both performer and owner were expected to lie to protect their interests. The absence of a sense of outrage proved mute testimony to the grudging acceptance of such behavior.

Owners cynically uprooted historic franchises as cities bid obscenely high sums for the privilege of having big-league status conferred on their communities. Fan loyalty was simply assumed. Player unions understandably, and to great effect, demanded their share of this inflating pie. The teams were glittering toys for the superrich who had everything—except the cachet of a major league franchise and a lot of celebrity that went with it.

Certain to happen, the only question was what form the corrupting influence of sports would take, as the tawdry morals of professional sports got woven into the fabric of national life.

Fans used the excuse of a championship to celebrate riotously. They failed utterly to understand that society demanded that violence be confined to inside the ropes or between the markers. Athletes served as evidence of their activity's importance when they were set upon by assailants determined to advance a rival's progress, as happened in figure skating and tennis.

Institutions of learning bribed athletes to attend; any hope of an education was forfeited as the athletes were exploited for their market value. Disillusioned competitors frequently emerged from as much as 16 years of "education" as functional illiterates—with neither skills nor credentials to show for their service.

Newspapers are dotted with reports of the arrests of former athletes for crimes involving drugs, theft, and such. The obituary columns reflect the tortured ends of many once-promising youngsters or prominent pros. A basketball star dies of a heart attack and the tragedy swirls in controversy as survivors jockey for economic advantage against those alleging drug abuse.[4]

Wary of the consequences, professional teams ignored superathletes who'd repeatedly failed drug tests in drafting talent. One might wish for a loftier motive than the desire to avoid hassles in these decisions. No sport was exempt from the allure of drugs, the availability of sexual adventures, or the taint of scandal—whether it was as pristine as figure skating or swimming or as commercial as football or as violent as boxing.

Security, both in the stands and for the players, became a large and growing industry, as hooliganism spread in the stands, on the field, and, in the form of threats, behind the scenes. Sports pages now seemed as likely to include scandalous accounts of criminal wrongdoings by famous athletes as of box scores and scuttlebutt.

Athletics are a metaphor for life. World War I was said to have been won "on the playing fields of Eton," where gallant Britons learned to be brave, honorable, and true to their duty. Contemporary athletics have come a great distance from these heroic Olympian traditions.

While sports address our hopes for virtue and its triumph, entertainment seeks to do nothing more than to amuse and to divert our attention from life's grimmer realities. We are, increasingly, willing to pay kingly ransoms for this amusement. And we have become a nation of watchers, not doers, as the invention of the "couch potato" flowed from this reality.

THE WORLD OF ENTERTAINMENT

It is said that democracies must learn to live without heroes, but we need exemplars and models to help shape the roles we must play in life.

Artists both reflect and shape the culture.[5] They capture the signals in the air and deliver them to us—on canvas, on film, in rap lyrics, on the printed page, on television,[6,7] and, yes, even on talk radio. Artists can be prophets, but they can also be failed ones who have emphasized the wrong harbinger and ignored the right one. The great ones hold up societal mirrors in which we can, by seeing clearly who and what we are, predict what we are becoming. So it is critical to evaluations of our future that we approach our films, books, songs, and such both semiotically and hedonistically. Looking back on various epochs it is easy to see how some captured the zeitgeist. The roles played by Jimmy Stewart and Henry Fonda in 1930s films would very likely strike this cynical age as hopelessly naive or charmingly innocent, but irrelevant.

We reward our artists lavishly, not because they enlighten, but because they entertain.

The mysoginistic, violent, drug-immersed, sexually exploitative lyrics of rappers[8] alarm the overclass but never tempt it to evaluate the misery inspiring these cries. The words are raw and brutal, tempting the listeners to shoot the messenger and ignore the message. Ice-T's "Cop Killer" spread a storm of outrage, but it prompted no one to examine police response to and treatment of blacks in society. The Rodney King case inspired rap lyrics that predicted not just the Los Angeles riots, but that its targets would be Korean shopkeepers. It isn't easy—and perhaps not even possible—to distinguish prophecy from incitement.

Virulent racism can spark reactions such as the one that occurred in December 1995, when a black man shot, burned, and killed himself and seven others in an incident everyone was anxious to deny as being racially motivated. It was, in fact, inspired by anti-Semitic rhetoric surrounding a controversy between a black subtenant and a Jewish storeowner. The dispute had been marked by tense picketings and demonstrations and finally ignited an explosion in one of the more suggestible participants. The tragedy was followed with attempts at papering-over the racial element, thereby precluding the hope of getting at the underlying problems. Thus did blacks cooperate with whites in the conspiracy of silence attending race relations in America.

As if to reflect our angst in other mirrors, the singer Sinead O'Connor shocked the woman who produced the album *Erotica* and the book *Sex*, Madonna, with her attacks on the Pope and the Catholic Church. And a songwriter created a hit, in describing the sadness of a homeless woman amid the affluence of our indifferent paradise, without markedly affecting either our attitudes or behavior. "Another Day in Paradise" seemed to have been enjoyed and sung, but not really heard.

Meanwhile, rappers were walking the walk with actual murders, rapes, shootings, and early deaths. Michael Jackson stunned the nation when he was charged with molesting a boy, resulting in a settlement that cloaked the event in a secret mantle.[9]

Our artists have been raised high enough to prompt the

febrile plottings of assassins. John Lennon and Selena became martyrs to celebrity, and Ronald Reagan almost did in 1981.

In the midst of the sweaty sex, race cries, and gang violence stood a genre that might have been suspected of serving as advance guard to such pillagings but that was proving an innocent model of decorum—comics. The quintessential American obsession remained faithful to adolescent fantasies, cloaked in the search for, and triumph of, virtue.

The theater, except for one-person shows like those of Anna Deavere Smith—who bore witness to urban riots, race tensions, and social injustice—was proving curiously irrelevant to the turmoil enveloping the nation. Yes, there were plays like *The Day the Bronx Died* by Michael Henry Brown and *Night and Her Stars* by Richard Greenberg—a look at the TV quiz show scandals of the 1950s—but these served more to illustrate the paucity of commentary than they did to highlight the problems of moral decay.

The world of art staged its own attempts at celebrity and prophecy with the shocking works of Robert Mapplethorpe and the more public and insistent cries of graffiti artists in urban America.

Literature continued to force light under the rocks of every social problem, but sometimes blinded itself through questionable bidding wars for lurid disclosures. The occasional imputation of buying influence through hefty advances; the offering of self-serving platforms to monsters and pariahs, the occasional publication of a web of lies; the invention of violent, pornographic "transgressive fiction;" and the very valuable tradition of pushing the censorship envelope beyond the narrow confines of authority's baleful view all served to keep books a lively source of information and insight. But who reads?

Newspapers are all over the lot—from sensational tabloids printing incredible sagas (and paying handsomely for the privilege, while assaulting privacy and defying litigators) to somber analyses of foreign policy or domestic economics. The emulation of tabloids by TV programs extended the genre into America's living rooms, where latter-day Christians, in the form of guileless and exploited minorities, were thrown to the lions in the audience and served up to us as the modern equivalent of our Colosseum games.

The New York Times reported, on August 19, 1992, that *Soldier of Fortune* magazine had lost its appeal of $4.3-million damage award for running an ad in which a professional mercenary offered his gun for hire. The response led to the murder of a business associate and to the conviction of the three principals. The *Times* noted that, in the last ten years, the magazine had been linked to more than a half-dozen contract killings. The case was heading for the Supreme Court as the conflict between the first Amendment Freedom of the press and the responsibility of the publication to avoid harm waxed hot.

Parents were forced to cope with mind-boggling violence in the video games absorbing their children's attention, while Congress agonized over freedoms and exposure to licentiousness on the newly loosed genie of the computer Internet. How much more wouldn't they rather deal with such patently absurd, ersatz issues like flag burning?

The impact of radio could be summarized by the shock-jock antics of Howard Stern, who crossed media lines with a best-selling book, *Private Parts*, that in its title conveyed the center of this host's concerns. The shock comes from scathing references to "patently offensive" commentaries about masturbation, racial stereotypes, sadistic sex, defecation, and sexual fantasies with celebrities. The Federal Communications Commission fined Stern's employer $600,000 in December 1992, and his fame spread. By 1995, the dispute resulted in Stern's bosses agreeing to pay $1,715,000 to settle the controversy—labeling it a "voluntary contribution to the U.S. Treasury." The issue centered on the definition of the evanescent word "indecency," but what was really at stake was the small price to pay for the right to enunciate the musings of the darkest recesses of the human soul.

Stern's second best-seller, *Miss America*, followed, with Stern wearing eyeliner, lipstick, a gown, and falsies on the cover. Camp didn't quite describe this vision from outer space. Stern seemed a fitting avatar of the age and its decline.

The violence, sex, and declining moral standards on television had the nation on the verge of hysteria. The pain was encapsulated in Senator Paul Simon's comment, on July 5, 1993, that "the evidence is overwhelming that television adds to the violence in our society." In 1982 the National Institute of Mental Health reported that "violence on television does lead to aggressive behavior by children and teenagers." Our young, exposed to countless murders and sexual acts over the years, were clearly influenced by what was arguably the most important single influence in their lives. The factors driving adolescent addicts to drugs were dysfunctional families, poor choices of friends, uncaring schools, and exposure to television.

Between the programs came the Sistine Chapel Ceiling of American creative thought—the 30-second television commercial. There our most brilliant artists held forth in ingenious portrayals of scenes that would make each of us into committed, fervent consumers and materialists.

But it was in the preeminent artistic creation of our culture—the movie—that the message was most graphically, effectively, and creatively conveyed. Here movies like *Pulp Fiction* depicted a nihilistic society in which the only uniformed authority figure—whose arrival produces a palpable sigh of relief—turns out to be the most evil of a rotten lot.

Movies could now acceptably end with central characters having gotten away with murder. Evil could triumph. Exit laughing. The movie *The Player* was a wonderful, even lighthearted, example of this seduction.

In *Kids*, the blasted culture of youth lacks any adult figure to whom its lost souls might turn for help or guidance. Spike Lee's brilliant commentaries on life in the 'hood failed to ignite even curiosity about the bacillus nurtured in the steamy stew of the ghetto. *Leaving Las Vegas* was another illustration of the hopelessness of the age and the need for escape—even if that meant dying. Its author committed suicide two weeks after learning his book would become a movie. Life imitating art.

Ratings served as guides to titillation, as the borders between pornography and art were successively and successfully blurred. Politicians whose lives could not be held up as paradigms of virtue sensed the harvest to be reaped from the growing disquiet of the populace and attacked Hollywood for undermining our value system.

We were not shocked when Calvin Klein withdrew advertising that critics labeled "child pornography," but who gained predictable commercial advantage in the wake of all that free publicity?

Genuine American heroes committed suicide when the 15-minute glare of fame went out and they discovered they couldn't return to the humdrum lives from which their exploits had briefly lifted them, as happened to the rescuer of the little girl trapped in a well in Texas.

The American Family Association was outraged by the bombardment of these messages aimed at America's youth.

RESPONSE

Typically, the response was for censorship[10,11]—ignoring America's centuries' old battle with the definition of pornography and its halting attempts at banning such masterpieces as James Joyce's *Ulysses*, perhaps the century's finest novel. After a lengthy struggle, the Supreme Court seemed to have settled on material (1) lacking all artistic merit, (2) appealing exclusively to prurient interest, and (3) below acceptable community standards of morality as a working definition of obscenity. The temptation to legislate was leavened with fervent, if futile, appeals for self-correction.

This hope for restraint flies defiantly in the teeth of human experience and artistic truth. Certainly artists can also desensitize, seduce, and corrupt us. Theirs is the potential dual role of prophet and sinner. At their best, artists must express the inner truths gleaned from intense and informed observation. The message is painful, but humanity has learned the importance of deciphering it as well as the folly of shooting the messenger. Artists are the receptors and transmitters of society's signals.

12

The End?

Central to the debate on the direction of our nation is the need to take a balanced view; our need to conform, not intrude, should not deflect us from a tough, candid appraisal of painful issues. We can't afford to become a country that no longer searches for hard truths.

Confronting the effects of racism is painful, but confronting its products—violence, inequality, and misery—is worse. No one wants to believe they've injured their children through divorce, but how can we get our children to believe in anything if they can't believe in us?

Still, balance requires the inclusion of certain facts. Ours is a prosperous nation, at peace, with a long history of altruism. Millions of us are smoking and drinking less and jogging more. The existence of a vigorous press may be revealing scandals formerly papered over, and the rise of social dissolution may be nothing more than the end of hypocrisies in which such disintegration got routinely ignored. It is characteristic of Jeremiahs to launch jeremiads, as every generation feels its successor to be feckless.

The abandonment of cities is not an evil act; it is a flight that is often fraught with pangs of conscience, as Americans seek safety, order, comfort, and convenience.

It is a source of pride that we have the world's finest educational and medical systems, but it is also a costly disgrace that we have the worst—and the jingoists point to the former, while the few scattered and currently defeated liberals decry the latter.

We've won the Cold War, proved our system to be the best, and stand astride the planet as the unchallenged colossus. Our foreign policy is animated not by thoughts of empire or conquest; rather, it flows from a genuine desire to stop genocide, ethnic cleansings, mass rapes and murders, and other atrocities, and to, incidentally, make the world safe for capitalism. We are, as a people, probably the best champions peace and justice have ever had, but it would be a mistake to see ourselves as perfect.

Domestically, however, we've chosen to avert our gaze from the growing divisions between races and classes. We've opted for Draco over Socrates. Our fate is mirrored in the decline of the most important societal institutions—family and city.

FAMILY

Statistics reflect trends with the bland accuracy of abstractions; mere numbers can never reveal the toll of suffering behind the data. The plight of Dust Bowl farmers received scant concern until John Steinbeck gave us the chronicle of the Joad family in *Grapes of Wrath*. And the ghastly decimation of European Jews was breathed to life by the saga of a teenage girl caught up in the maws of Nazi Germany. Nevertheless, an anecdote is just that, unless it is emblematic of a much broader problem that rightly merits a colossus' attention.

Divorce

The divorce rate[1] for women went from about 10 per 1,000 in the 1920s and remained under 25 for over 40 years—starting a sharp climb in the late 1960s and early 1970s and leveling off at about 37 per 1,000 in 1990.

It is cold comfort that the trends toward unwed motherhood, rising divorce rates, smaller households, and the feminization of poverty are rising in Canada, Europe, and Japan as well. Our divorce rate is still much higher than in Europe, with Italy being low (perhaps as a consequence of Vatican-influenced policies that produce the same result, without formal divorce) and Denmark being high, but not as high as us, with about 45 per every 100 marriages, versus our rate of about 55.

Northern Europe leads in number of unwed mothers with babies, with about 35% out-of-wedlock births for all births; the United States has an overall total of 30%, but the figures are much higher for African Americans.

Parenting

It seems silly to hold that the socialization of humans mainly occurs in a family setting,[2,3] but this fact must be asserted even as hedonists and sybarites twist the argument to accommodate their personal search for happiness.

In an article in the April 1993 *Atlantic Monthly*, Barbara Dafoe Whitehead demonstrates, with ample statistics, the enormous impact of divorce on children and the likelihood of their developing into criminals, being impoverished, and perpetuating the cycle of illegitimate births. It is imperative that we return to the restrictions on divorce that once required specific justification, such as extreme cruelty, desertion, involuntary confinement, or adultery, in relationships involving dependent children. The state should move to create incentives for families to remain intact. Couples without children could retain the current features of our facile "no-fault" divorce proceedings.

Deadbeat dads become the images behind abandoned families, as almost half the fathers required to pay for the support of their children failed to meet such obligations in 1991. Women had custody in just over 86% of cases involving children under 21 in 1992. Being a parent imposes responsibilities, whether the union was sanctioned by a contract or not.

The problems of illegitimacy, absent fathers, and growing impoverishment are greatest in the ghetto, where over two-thirds of African-American babies have no father present at birth and have a less than 1 in 12 chance of living with their biological father through age 18. The dangers lurking behind these abandoning fathers cannot be ignored because of their threat to social safety and because they are, themselves, the very babies once abandoned in precisely the fashion they now abandon theirs.

From the brouhahas over situation comedies—such as occurred when former Vice President Dan Quayle criticized a television character, Murphy Brown, for being a single mother—to the stark realities on our streets, something closely resembling a fatherless America is surfacing.

The absent father also exacerbates other issues, such as crime, poverty, drug use, failure in schools or job, and likelihood to end up on welfare. The incalculable importance of the mother was brought forcefully to our attention when thousands of them fled their kids for crack, at the height of that epidemic, in 1985.

Fathers are often central to family crises, such as a wrecked car, an emergency such as a fire or a dispute, or an event threatening the family's safety. They are significant role models, especially to their own sons. The rise of feminism has both entailed healthy questioning of roles and provided a much-needed look at equality, but any such struggle contains the risk of imbalance, overemphasis, or skewing. It may sometimes include attacks on what is seen as the controlling or oppressing element—in this case men—but it also needs to be added that a return to authoritarian fathering and husbanding such as that advocated in the Promise

Keepers movement discussed earlier is an example of the opposite imbalance.

Sex education, abortion, and the wide availability of contraception have been found to reduce sharply the number of births among teenagers, but puritanical pedagogic views among Americans have stood in the way of many such reforms. And, of course, many young women want to escape their homes or have a baby who loves them.

Furthermore, what is the societal obligation, in the form of government intervention, to provide money, goods, and services to create a protective net beneath which no family falls?

WELFARE

A prosperous modern state must provide minimal standards of health, housing, food, and education. This can be defined as meeting the minimum economic levels that define living at what is officially described as the poverty line.

A society that values order, discipline, and structure must also add accountability, consequence, and the need for individual responsibility to the equation for social, economic, and racial justice.

The world has learned, to its sorrow, that handouts don't work. They discourage initiative and encourage sloth and irresponsible behaviors. Sanctions are needed, and negative behaviors must be punished—through reductions in benefits or however else is legally appropriate.

The numbers prove stark reminders of who constitutes the underclass. More than 72% of black children born between 1967 and 1969 spent time on welfare,[4] compared to 16% of other children. Of all families receiving Aid to Families with Dependent Children in 1990, 39.7% were black, 38.1% were white, 16.6% were Hispanic, and 5.6% were of other ethnic origin. Clearly, the plight of blacks, from birth to early death, is more stark and bleak than that of whites.

Births to teenagers particularly reflected both social and economic status and racism, as blacks went from 100 births per 1000 unmarried 15- to 19-year-old girls in 1970 to under 85 in 1985, very likely due to Roe v. Wade; the rate resumed a sharp upward climb to over 100 in 1989. White, unmarried teenagers went from 10 per 1000 in 1970 to over 25 in 1989.

The total recipients of Aid to Families with Dependent Children spurted dramatically upward, from about 4 million in 1965 to 13.5 million in 1990. There had been a drop, from almost 11 million in 1975, following the war on poverty, but a sharp upward climb started again in 1990. The average stay on the rolls is about six-and-a-half years.

The nation's states constitute a patchwork quilt in which southern states tend to give welfare recipients less than 60% of poverty level income; northwestern, midwestern, and some northeastern states give more than 80% of poverty income; and the majority fall in between, at 60% to 80% of poverty level income. This strongly suggests the variability bound to be produced by the revolution decreasing federal involvement with welfare.

Although Democrats love to point to studies revealing little welfare fraud, Republicans counter with examples of rampant food stamp thefts, sales, and counterfeitings and egregious visions of "welfare queenism" such as the woman who, at the peak of her activities in 1991, was using eight false names and claiming 46 children; she collected $450,000 in benefits in New York between 1987 and 1993. So many fraudulent claims for food stamps followed the California earthquake that federal officials shut down the program granting on-the-spot relief in January 1994.

As America dismantles the already thin and fraying economic safety net, which had taken 60 years to develop, the consequences for the underclass will be disastrous. Rebellion, in the form of riots and individual street crimes, is bound to follow.

Republicans seem determined to wreck welfare schemes that, to them, smack of socialism, while they extend benefits to corporations and individuals with access, power, and money.

Democrats refuse to surrender the notion that there ain't no free lunch and to admit that the fractious human animal doesn't do well with handouts.

No one seems to understand that a dialectically eclectic approach—combining the responsibility demanded by Republicans with the altruism insisted upon by the Democrats—is probably the only way out.

In Europe, which had long served as the Utopia of welfarism that liberals envied, one government after another was forced to retrench and face the chaos of general strikes, as budgets spun out of control and the newly emerging European community demanded fiscal restraint. The American deficit, which rightly appalled our citizens, was half to less than half, in proportionate terms, to what was routinely experienced in western Europe in the 1980s and early 1990s. Europe was, however, retreating to still-secure safety nets that would have been the envy of the most passionate welfare-statist here.

Altruism is clearly in flight—sparked by Ronald Reagan's revolution and Margaret Thatcher's mostly successful partial emulation—but the English were fleeing from an extreme level of coverage and protection, and we from a thin veneer of social justice.

As the economic chasm widens, tensions between the overclass and the underclass become exacerbated. And, as so often happens in such divisions, the separations are geographic as well as social, economic, and racial.

CITIES

Everywhere in America more prosperous whites fled to the suburbs ringing core cities[5–8] while they preserved and strengthened the commercial hubs of those same cities in order to protect the source of their prosperity. They'd need sanitary corridors to ensure safe comings and goings between their work places and homes.

The poor—comprising excluded blacks, whites, and the addicted, mentally disturbed, broke, and discarded homeless population—were herded into ghettos.

Street crime became an urban problem, mostly centering on the underclass—as both victims and perpetrators—but spilling over into the overclass turf often enough to create a perpetual state of agitation. The hysteria was fed by the images on the nightly news.

Notwithstanding that a quick peek outside would reveal, to whoever occupied the White House, the scene of the best-policed—yet least safe—city in the nation, our leaders never lost faith in the magic of more cops, tougher sentences, and bigger prisons.

Even cities like San Francisco are littered with bodies huddled on sidewalks, within easy view of City Hall. Its filthy streets communicate a sense of social decay, as the beggars on corners make pathetic efforts at amusing motorists as they cadge coins. The homeless represent both an underappreciated menace and a challenge to the society to care for those in need of food, shelter, and a lot of services.

Surfacing sporadically—often in the form of a berserk and deadly assault on unsuspecting and vulnerable persons—casualties of homelessness are seen by Americans as well within tolerable limits.

Only the roughest estimates are possible, but their visibility makes the problem stark. About one-fourth alcoholics or addicts, an equal number broke and alone or abandoned, another fourth mentally disturbed, and the rest suffering an agglomeration of disabilities rendering them incapable of coping, the homeless constitute a daily reminder of our neglect and indifference.

Harboring within their population a large percentage of males with serious criminal records, as well as delusional souls who often strike out in "self-defense" against imagined dangers, the homeless represent problems that are often more immediate than the social dissolution their presence advertises. Emptying mental institutions—as a result of the development of drugs to maintain a semblance of normal life—was typical of the unthinking generosity of liberals anxious to right social wrongs. The consequences, however, were ignored: How to ensure that the ill will take their medicine?

This is another example of the need to build accountability into reform measures. Those who pose a menace and refuse to take their medication must be confronted with such consequences as reinstitutionalization. Without the viable threat of commitment we will continue to have our children menaced by the neighborhood psychos wandering threateningly on our streets. Those publicly drunk and creating such nuisances as aggressive panhandling, public defecation, or urination should be taken to a detoxification center for sobering up, washing, medical evaluation, and the offer of treatment, and then released.

Detroit, perhaps the farthest gone of America's rapidly disintegrating, once-proud urban centers, suffered a massive exodus of whites in the 1960s and 1970s, who now ring the city with the most segregated communities in the nation.

While a huge citizen turnout made 1995 a peaceful experience, the night before Halloween—Devil's Night—saw hundreds of fires set in Detroit and its suburbs in 1994. Ten years earlier the city had earned the title "Arson Capital of the World," with 297 blazes.

All cities share the same loss of talent, energy, and wealth. All are asked to serve as camps for the underclass. And the cops are assigned to keep them under control and, if possible, out of sight, too. But we have forgotten that humans created cities for a reason and neglect to ask whether viable alternatives have been fashioned. We've lost faith in the two key institutions of our civilization—family and city—without developing alternatives or bothering to measure the cost.

Where should we center our educational, cultural, medical, and economic energies?

The American economy is rapidly expanding in the suburbs and contracting in the ghettos, with no easy way for the underclass to reach the jobs in the rings surrounding their cities. The result is huge unemployment among blacks, while jobs in suburbs inaccessible to inner-city kids went begging in areas that did not welcome ghetto residents. Even suburban malls hired security forces to control the ghetto kids attracted to those glitzy new centers of community life.

Affluent suburbs like Orange County, California, chose to renege on its debts rather than undertake a community-wide commitment, in the form of a slight increase in the sales tax, to discharge obligations. They'd all had a great time when gambling on derivatives was paying off, but the recriminations, chargings, jailings, and bankruptcy that followed wasn't accompanied by contrition, insight, or apologies.

Calls for a Marshall Plan for our cities ignore the core nature of the original, which was to help people help themselves. The simple acceptance of a metropolitan area government that combines suburban and urban forces to attack the entire area's problems would forge just such a partnership. We have the beginnings of regional, county, or metro governments in many parts of the country, but their powers are limited and their numbers few. Why doesn't it happen? For the same reason Americans don't want to abandon divorce—they're having too good a time. Ours has become a culture of instant gratification, where postponement of pleasure or long-range planning simply seem too onerous.

While the two main pillars of American society crumble palpably around us, the perspective of other institutions does not inspire confidence in the future, however many "the best is yet to come" reassurances our jingoists deliver to our receptive ears.

CULTURE

Our radio talk shows have become forums for bashing the underclass, promoting xenophobia, and encouraging divisiveness, appealing to and justifying hedonism and often hypocritically invoking puritanical slogans and posturings.

The deeply felt and usually unexpressed resentments, jealousies, and prejudices of an ignorant fringe receive voice and weight in the cuddly, chuckly, jolly heftiness of Rush Limbaugh's entertaining and cunning appeals.

Across the street, television's talk shows engage in public delectation by throwing freaks engaged in bizarre sexual or personal behaviors to a rabid studio audience only too ready to put thumbs up or down in this public theater of titillation. The spurious outrage voiced by those in the stands can hardly be likened to a call for morality. In between, brilliant commercials seduce us into taking drugs, buying toys, and satisfying every urge.

Television was replacing words with images, making us less literate, less discriminating in thought, more isolated and malleable, and more vulnerable to demagoguery as clever marketers devised new persuasions. It was also inviting us to materialism, consumerism, and hedonism as well as making us hungry for simple answers.

The intrusion of broad commercial ambitions and corporate interests led to the withholding of news accounts or to the issuance of apologies, not because the content was false but because it offended corporate interests that could dictate the material's suppression. Cautious corporate lawyers and executives not committed to journalism's indefatigable search for important truths were suddenly making news decisions at the networks. Nothing better illustrated the dilemma caused by the nexus of commercial, journalistic, and consumer interests than the tortured controversies attending the marketing and production practices of the tobacco industry.[9]

And, whether the cart of violence came before the horse of its depiction—or the other way round—it cannot be denied that repeated exposure to gore inures the viewer to its horror.

Our movies prove an accurate reflection of modern life as Capraesque virtues are derided as naive and irrelevant and toughness and force majeure are extolled as verities. We have, indeed, become a society in which the strong do what they can, and the weak suffer what they must. The profound nihilism of films in which evil triumphs, or in which death is the only sensible way out, contribute to the cheapening of such concepts of virtue as honor, patriotism, devotion to an idea, or selflessness and altruism.

In such tableaus, sex becomes the ultimate pleasure, rather than the expression of intimacy or the maturing of a relationship in which its fruit is sought and that is followed by a determination to nurture it.[10]

Literature reflects its views through obscene bidding wars for celebrity disclosures of scandals and huge advances. Payments are sometimes used as political payoffs for access or legislative edge and have little to do with literary merit or the book's prospects.

Shrinking newspaper markets accelerate consolidation and speed up the development of quick-read, multicolored papers that seek to emulate the superficial glare of the TV screen. In what might be labeled the titillation-of-weird-tastes-and-beliefs niche are the literally incredible accounts of the supermarket tabloids and their reports of alien sightings, after-death experiences, and other carnival aberrations.

In sports, fan rowdiness is increasingly expressed in street riots following a championship, assaults on visiting players, violence in the stands, objects thrown from the seats, or the search for celebrity on the field by interrupting contests.

We have become a nation that went from baseball to football as our sports-obsession-of-choice. That shift embodied our transformation from the aesthetic, passive, and cerebral to regimented violence, for which we recruited ever faster, bigger, stronger participants. By Super Bowl XXX, on January 28, 1996, advertisers were paying $1.2 million for each of 58 30-second TV commercials.[11]

And yet, it has to be admitted that American culture sweeps all before it in the world. Planet Earth eats our burgers, sees our movies, squeezes into our jeans, sings our songs, and reads our books. The power of American culture cannot be denied, nor can its variety or its breadth, which can encompass the lofty as well as the banal. The question is: What does it reveal, and what can we predict about our future from its content?

INSTITUTIONS

The view of other cherished institutions is hardly more edifying.

The military, among our most revered icons, is now rocked by disclosures worthy of Imperial Rome—with generals flying cats and servants at extravagant expense, while admirals get cashiered for sexually harassing or exploiting subordinates.

The pent-up energies of a hugely successful war led to their expression in the hallway gropings that were memorialized in the word "Tailhook." The final report on that disgrace said 140 Navy and Marine pilots assaulted 83 women. The case for formal penalties basically disintegrated under the protections of an old-boys' network. The Chief of Naval Operations finally took early retirement, but exacted an encomium from the Secretary of Defense as the price for his exit. His successor committed suicide in 1996. The Tailhook Association wound up paying hefty settlements to lawsuits arising from the scandal.

At Annapolis at least 125 midshipmen were suspected of having cheated on an electrical engineering test given in December 1992. At the end of the investigation 29 students were expelled, 42 others were given lesser punishment, and many others were suspected but not caught.

At West Point five members of the football team faced charges of groping female cadets at an October 20, 1994, pep rally.

In an Okinawa rape case, in which three Marines were accused and convicted of assaulting a 12-year-old girl, their commander was forced to retire for suggesting they should have been looking for prostitutes instead. The reaction trivialized the outrage and insulted the population.

In the fall of 1995 the Navy was conducting another inquiry in which it was believed five midshipmen had been selling LSD, marijuana, and other drugs and that as many as 19 others were thought to have been users.

And when the Marines were finally forced to move their headquarters into the Pentagon in 1995, their commandant insisted on having his own dining room built, despite having been offered the use of the Navy's top admiral's accommodations.

What might have more serious long-term consequences, however, is the general temptation to use the Armed Forces in law enforcement operations, in contravention of a long-standing policy and law. They would patrol our streets, interdict drug traffickers, and engage in police operations for which they have little training or experience. The military, anxious for a role in a world of diminished war opportunities, happily acquiesced in this dangerous initiative.

POLITICS

Too much is known about the state of American politics to require elaboration. The American people have developed a profound hostility toward a government that is too large and works too inefficiently, and they are disillusioned with smart, talented people corrupted by the political reality of having to raise obscene sums with which to attack opponents with expensive TV ads.

The dramatic decline in political discourse—reflected in the crazy actions of suggestible acolytes—reached new depths in the 1990s, with repeated comparisons of opponent's approaches to Adolf Hitler, Nazi tactics, and Holocaust images.

All bets were off and all bars were down.

Lobbyists have the money necessary to fuel political campaigns, and politicians can pass laws we have come to recognize as constituting corporate welfare. Politicians shamelessly offer personal access in exchange for contributions, while America waits on line and doesn't get either heard or served.

There is no area of political life free of taint. Somehow the message that everyone is getting theirs is flawlessly transmitted. The president is under investigation—as is the speaker of the House. We get solemn assurances of full cooperation in inquires, only to discover resistance and stonewalling. Senators are driven from office, and, probably even more disturbing, others seem to be leaving office in disgust and disillusionment in record numbers. If there is anything more alarming than the caliber of candidates seeking office, it is the exodus of the few respected leaders departing in thinly disguised disgust.

Others, though, fed the cynicism with enthusiasm. Congress, which was leading the attack on the frayed protections of the underclass, planned 25 trips abroad for its members over the three weeks ending January 16, 1996, in the face of their shutdown of the government as a result of a budget impasse. Participants in what were called "fact-finding missions" were going to ritzy locations and were actually lame ducks, due to exit with pensions at the end of 1996.

That Americans confront parking spaces reserved for these potentates, and other signs of imperial privileges, confirm their worst suspicions about what is not so visible.

Intense lobbying for B-2 bombers that were not even wanted by the Pentagon pushed Congress to add an appropriation that exceeded the Defense Department's request for funds. It was one of 54 examples of lobbying effectiveness of the 1995 Congress compiled by the Center for Responsive Politics.

Interestingly, artists contribute to this disillusionment, with highly suspect renderings of political life in movies like *JFK* and *Nixon*, which do nothing to inform and a very great deal to inspire suspicion, division, and prejudice.

How could even the best and the brightest fail to be influenced by a system that ensured defeat for those taking the high road? Wouldn't it be easy to justify expediency by accepting questionable help now, in order to do good things once in office? Morality and ethics could await more convenient moments, couldn't they? Faustian bargains, we've learned, are hard to break.

Party Politics

Our two-party system has served us well, as the outs work at keeping the ins honest. It's very much like having permanent inspector generals at work, and it supplements the inquiring media nicely. If humans have discovered any single thing, it is that one cannot have too many watchdogs.

Our system of self-selection limits the field to those who can raise money; who have the desire to devote over a year to the exhausting, often humiliating, and frequently embarrassing process of candidacy; and who have a point of view desperately seeking expression. Public financing of all campaigns would merely encourage armies of candidates. Some method of filtration has to come into play. Perhaps the only viable option is to continue requiring candidates to raise funds—a process so distasteful as to discourage all but the most elephant-hided—only doing so in ways that limit any single giver's influence.

The government's matching any contribution, up to $100 a year, is a good way of achieving voluntary limits, as is the ban on individual contributions over a certain amount, depending on whether the campaign is for local, statewide, or national office, but not exceeding $2000 a year, per person or organization.

Money is both the grease and the sand in political machines, but the costs of advertising demand it and the realities of opponent-bashing strongly suggest it as the logic of realpolitik. Even here, though, pledges might be made about the limits on negative approaches.

The parties themselves contribute seriously to the problems by moving to their margins. Party conventions to annoint standard-bearers have become conclaves of the most extreme elements within the tent.

Republican meetings have become the havens of the Religious Right, prolifers, National Rifle Association enthusiasts, ultraconservatives of all types, and others at the fringes. The Republican Party has, in state and local elections, frequently annointed champions who were so out of tune with the mainstream as to ensure their defeat, often in the primaries preceding general elections.

Democratic meetings have evolved into centers of union power (without much regard to low-level, exploited workers such as those in the fast-food industry), prochoice advocates, welfare state militants, and every fringe cause of the left-liberals, or even farther out. The 1972 presidential convention that nominated Senator George McGovern was a political quilt of splinter groups representing minority concerns that coalesced into a disastrous temporary majority.

Candidates have discovered that, to win, they have to sidle to the edges for the convention's blessing, then shuffle centerward in order to appeal to the general electorate.

Primary elections in presidential contests have tended to move the process to the center, but these are draining—monetarily and temporally to the candidate and to the electorate—and would, no doubt, in time be themselves corrupted to some nefarious purpose. This is the iron law of unintended consequences at work, sprinkled with the human experience that any process or institution can be corrupted and that introspection and renewal must be constantly pursued.

Besides evolving a system that imposes dependency on special interests, our leaders seem unable to summon the courage to show suburbanites that their safety and future lie in the cities and in preserving their families. The easier path is certainly to pander to the tireless search for pleasure. Our president could, in 1995, use the word "underclass" three times in his State of the Union address without sparking the slightest significant riposte. In the 1996 address, facing a tough re-election campaign, he eschewed any reference to such politically painful truths.

If suburbanites were being picked off one at a time, as in cases such as a kidnap or murder or carjacking from a suburban mall, who was going to attribute this to the policies of the victim and her friends and family, which perpetuate the underclass' hopelessness? And how could any constituency emerge from the ranks of unidentified and unknown potential victims? Still, Mothers Against Drunk Drivers (MADD) had shown how victims, actual and potential, might coalesce to attack a problem.

Our politicians' shrinking from the harsh truths surrounding domestic affairs abandoned the field to the fanatics, fantasists, lunatics, and demagogues at the political and religious fringes.

The United States had once been a country that welcomed the outcast and nurtured the exile. Now, especially in such debates as whether we should participate in stemming the rape, slaughter, and genocide in the Balkans or in our growing inhospitability to new arrivals, the strains of isolationism and xenophobia flow more strongly than ever.

Still, fairness demands that we acknowledge that our foreign policy is generally, except for the occasional pratfalls of over-enthusiastic intelligence services or the avarice of some business interests, both benign and reasonably successful. The pity lies in how far we've strayed from the inspiring words of Emma Lazarus at the base of the Statue of Liberty.

Despite the railings of Americans over their politicians, it should be clear that our leaders are not only our mirror images, but our echoes as well.

Royal France, Imperial Rome, Czarist Russia, Pharaonic Egypt, and every other such plutocracy was ultimately destroyed by the rifts of its people and the corruptions of its rulers. Dickensian England, by contrast, employed the genius and flexibility of democratic processes to cleanse itself, internally at least, of hideous social injustices and economic cruelties, and avoided bloodshed.

A glimpse of the horizon inspired the sort of foreboding that got expressed, in our commentaries, as a general sense of declining fortune. Everyone seemed to be expressing senses of disquiet as the century neared its end.

CORPORATE MORALITY—THE OXYMORON

Nowhere is the rapacious greed and Darwinian proclivity of our society more dramatically illustrated than in the halls of capitalism, where merciless efficiencies have proved the secret elixir for wealth-producing energies.[12]

A number of painful truths must be faced if we are to understand and cope with our economy. Capitalism is competitive, cruel, and enormously productive of wealth. Socialism is altruistic, but it doesn't work. It is a telling commentary that capitalism fits snugly with human nature. It needs a substantial pool of unemployed to use as leverage against unions, and it is kept vibrant by the grim realities of a hugely competitive global marketplace. The greatest current imbalance probably lies at the very top, where the executive corps is simply siphoning off too much of the brew. Corporate moguls are paid huge fortunes for creating wealth. Their perks—planes, homes, offices, expense accounts, and whatever else the human imagination might contrive—rival the opulent dreams of Arabian Nights princes.

In the drive for profit, consideration of workers' fates, ecological factors, or even—in such products as alcohol and tobacco—customers' health frequently give way to the inevitable cliché dubbed the "bottom line." And this is when ingenious capitalism is working within the law.

In an excess of irony the very same flinty-eyed, swashbuck-ling executives who boosted profits by cutting costs and eviscerat-ing unions and downsizings were perched atop a mountain of gold, perks, accoutrements, and princely baubles. Capitalism knows how to reward its gunslingers. A typical CEO of a large company was paid 35 times the wage of a manufacturing worker in 1974, and 120 times as much in 1995.

Corporate titans have, however, succumbed to the temptation to shave the law when their lobbyists were unable to change it. Just as citizens have foresworn loyalty to their city, American corporations have not hesitated to take American jobs elsewhere, nor have they declined to circumvent patriotic initiatives such as the Trading with the Enemy Act.

In countries where regulations are more lax, our companies have permitted the ingestion of toxic substances, like sniffing glue by Latin American youngsters, the despoliation of forests and resources, and the poisoning of workers—as fruit companies have done in such places as Ecuador—by using pesticides forbidden in America.[13] Do-mestically and abroad, corporations continued the exploitations through peculiar capitalist enterprises such as sweatshops.

Within the country, the struggle continues to weaken regula-tions, diminish the rights of citizens to seek redress from corporate wrongdoing, and push for the economic advantages of the busi-ness owners.

A review of tort cases in state courts in 1992 revealed that the majority involved damage caused by a motor vehicle and that complex cases like medical malpractice, product liability, or toxic substances, combined made up about 10% of the suits. Three-fourths were settled before trial or were voluntarily dismissed, and only 3% went to a trial verdict. In over one-fourth of the cases the defendant did not contest the case. Half were disposed of within 14 months, with auto cases taking less time. Most of the cases involved individuals suing other individuals and half in-volved three or more litigants.

All of it has more to do with human nature than with a human predilection for evil. The human is both malleable and morally neutral, but the instinct for advantage, greed, and gratification requires taming and directing.

In the areas of fraud we have seen how the amounts taken by white collar criminals dwarf the sums stolen by street criminals. And, although the carnage caused by the latter is certainly more dramatic, it is more than likely that the sum of human suffering caused by white collar criminals exceeds the misery occasioned by the mugger, rapist, and killer. It is a lot harder, though, to do a body count of the white collar criminal's victims.

MEDICINE

The American Medical Association sought and obtained concessions from the Speaker of the House before consenting to support his Medicare bill. The thrust of the agreement simply centered on giving doctors competitive economic advantages that promised to deepen and widen their incomes. And this in a nation that deprived its population of universal health coverage, persuading its citizens, through costly advertising, that this was for their own good and despite doing next to nothing to curb the wild growth of the national medical bill.

Democrats seemed as reluctant to attack the estimated $50–$100 billion in fraud in Medicaid and Medicare as Republicans seemed eager to eviscerate these programs and loosen the free market forces on the sick and dependent.

Our medical industry is enormously costly, wonderfully innovative and inventive, woefully inequitable, marvelously skilled, occasionally dishonest, sometimes devoted and altruistic, and always in need of control and oversight.

EDUCATION

Our learning plant is a precise reflection of medicine—in that it is, at once, the industrialized world's best and worst. There have been scandals involving huge salaries and perks, the presence and removal of asbestos, the admission of nonstudent athletes and the scandals in which they were frequently involved, cheating on tests and papers, academic plagiarism and worse, racism on both sides of the spectrum, diploma mills, sexual molestations, state take-overs of failed local systems, falsified applications for admission, school violence, kickbacks, huge drop-out rates in cities, and many other problems.

There have been attempts to subvert one of the adornments of our democracy—public education—with voucher systems. The privatization of public education has been an assault on crippling civil service regulations that won't allow attacking the unfit and on teacher's unions that have placed the members beyond the marketplace of competence or price.

The failure of many urban systems is reflected in the appallingly high levels of functional illiteracy in America found in a federal study in 1993. It showed that almost half of Americans possessed very limited proficiency in English and were unable to handle simple math problems.

Controversy raged over the immutability of intelligence, as expressed in measurements of IQ tests, and its racial implications. Were blacks not doing as well because of inherent flaws or because of life conditions imposed by the overclass? Racists embraced the idiotic notion of racial superiority, while determinists looked at the myriad facts surrounding the fate of blacks in America.

A college president in 1995 added fuel to the racist flame by speaking of disadvantaged students who lack the "genetic, hereditary background" to score well on college admission exams, thereby making recruitment of minorities even more difficult. If that wasn't a description of racial inferiority—cloaked in the genteel idioms of academe—what was?

Educational comparisons with other industrialized nations indicate that our averages aren't very prepossessing. Concealed within the figures, however, is a savage inequality. If a white American has 16 years of schooling and a black has 10, then the average is 13. Comforting.

It is precisely our unwillingness to confront the disparities—in income, education, health, or whatever other measures indicating well-being—that permits their perpetuation.

Over the past ten years, learned commissions and governmental agencies have thundered noisily about raising our educational standards—usually around a convenient target like the year 2000. As we approach that benchmark, however, the fervor for making our students better at math, science, reading, writing, and functioning in the labor market cools in the face of having to address the problems in the ghetto.

America is not only unwilling to educate its underclass, but, with such programs as vouchers and other supports for private and sometimes religious institutions, it is also actually moving in the opposite direction. The separation, hostility, and suspicion between the races weaves—like a malignant thread—through the fabric of America's life.

RACE

Nowhere is the national disease more pronounced than in our determined reluctance to face the issue of racial justice.[14]

Treatment of blacks doesn't just make for inequality, violence, injustice, and social dislocation; it also poisons the larger body in the way that oppressors are always corrupted and brutalized by their cruelties. Over the four centuries of the slave trade—the 16th through the 19th—12 million slaves were taken out of Africa. Ten percent died before reaching shore and millions perished in the cross-country trek to the boats. Of these, 427,000 came to North America, a number that swelled to 4,500,000 by 1865.

The United States abolished the African slave trade in 1808, forcing slave owners to the costly alternative of breeding and raising additional fieldhands and servants. The first slaves arrived in Jamestown, Virginia, in August 1619, and slavery was abolished with the Emancipation Proclamation on January 1, 1863. Thus ended almost two-and-a-half centuries of slavery in America. It was followed by segregationist laws and policies, known as Jim Crowism, for the next century.

Observers, scholars, philosophers, and writers have been warning us about the "Negro Problem" for all of that time, most notably in this century by Gunnar Myrdal in his *An American*

Dilemma (1944); the minister and preacher Reinhold Niebuhr (1882–1971); reports such as the Kerner Commission's,[15] which warned of "two societies, one black, one white, separate and unequal;" and hosts of literary works, most notably Richard Wright's *Native Son* in 1940.

We can't claim we haven't been warned.

And the data, wherever one looks, confirm the dangers.

Blacks constitute 12% of our population, so black males are about half that total, or only 6%.

Although infant mortality has declined, that of black babies remained more than twice as high as that of whites in 1990. The life expectancy of blacks is currently 69.2; that of whites is 75.6 years. The leading cause of death of black males in the prime of life is murder. More than half the killers and the killed are black. More than half our enormous prison population consists of black males. One in three black males is under one form or another of criminal justice system control. Almost half those on death row are black males, yet 84% of the victims in these cases were white. There can be no doubt that the importance of the victim is differential.

Of course, we can point to the superstrong salmon who have forged the raging stream of American racism. There were 246,000 black and white couples in 1992, four times the total of 1970. The number of college graduates among blacks jumped from 5.1% in 1970 to 11% in 1990—but a lot of these graduates were women, creating an educational and probably economic imbalance between the sexes that has serious implications for family formation. The rate for white college graduates went from 12.5% to 19%. The numbers of blacks in the ranks of bank tellers, cops, government workers, members of the armed forces, telephone operators, cashiers, and related fields grew under the impact of the civil rights legislation of the 1960s. Still, the jobless rate among blacks remains much higher than that of whites.

Race has been a roller-coaster ride, with apologists citing the wonderful legislation of the Great Society and the strides made since, while critics point to the dips characterizing the black experience.

As the disparities in the distribution of American wealth widen, the underclass receives less and less—and this spells trouble for blacks. The sweep and flow of legislative initiatives on health, housing, welfare, education, employment, and other social programs is determinedly against liberal leanings.

Wherever the studies go they show our rich getting richer, our poor poorer, the chasm widening. Of the 25 richest nations studied by the Economic Cooperation and Development Organization, America ranked as the one with the greatest distance between rich and poor in the 1980s. Another analysis—this one by the Luxembourg Income Study—revealed that our poor children were worse off economically in 1991 than those in all of the 18 western, industrialized nations studied, except for Israel and Ireland.

In another demonstration of the roller-coaster metaphor—this one economic but impinging on race nevertheless—the gap between the richest and the poorest, was, in the late 1970s, the narrowest it had been since the 1830s. Since then the rapidly yawning separation has widened to a distance not seen since 1929.

The current economic trends are, generally, that the rich are getting richer and the poor and middle are staying put, in our winner-take-all economy, which is becoming increasingly inhospitable to those who are young, without skills, or with little education. The top 1% of Americans now control more of the country's wealth than the bottom 90%.

And who was stalking the halls of power to pass laws benefitting the underclass?

And the historic duality among African Americans was itself contributing to the oppression, as it drained and divided energies that needed desperately to be focused.

Since the beginning of active expression, the black voice of integration has produced an echo of separatism.

Where Frederick Douglass (1817–1895), an escaped slave who was the son of a black mother and a white father, preached abolition and the use of political methods and Booker T. Washington (1856–1915) urged vocational training and economic independence, the scholarly W. E. B. DuBois (1868–1963), who had helped found the NAACP, joined the Communist Party in 1961 and departed for Africa.

A. Philip Randolph, born in 1889, fought for civil rights and organized the Pullman porters and the 1963 march on Washington, while Marcus Garvey (1887–1940) fought integration, preached racial pride, and organized an ill-fated "Back to Africa" movement that landed him in jail and resulted in his deportation to Jamaica for defrauding the investors in his shipping line, which would take blacks back to their origins.

In there, somewhere, came the heroic figure of Paul Robeson, born in 1898, a superb athlete, gifted actor, and moving concert singer who had the effrontery to believe—and act on—the notion that he was as good as whites. His chutzpah led to his voluntary, Chaplinesque exile to England after being awarded the Stalin Peace Prize in McCarthyist 1952.

Malcolm X (1925–1965)[16] and the Reverend Martin Luther King, Jr. (1929–1968), continued the *mano-a-mano* of separation versus integration until their violent deaths, with Malcolm experiencing what appears to be a genuine epiphany in the last months of his life. He had, as a leader in Elijah Muhammad's Nation of Islam, preached separatism and anti-Semitism until the historic break with his leader—mostly occasioned by the latter—in 1963. Malcolm had been recruited in prison and it was a disturbing truth that, for all their vitriol about separatism and white evil, the Nation of Islam had been the one organization that had shown it could get its male members sober, clean, out of jail, working, and looking after their families, while exhibiting formerly absent pride.[17,18] Today the debate is carried on by their spiritual heirs— Minister Louis Farrakhan and the Reverend Jesse Jackson.

The legacy of such duality is a split that prevents uniting behind the sort of one-vision leadership that has animated the struggles of other immigrant groups coming voluntarily to America and not suffering the disabilities of racism. Alienation is one result; divisions among blacks themselves is another. Dualism also keeps a lot of blacks from voting, a critical omission in any group's climb to a measure of power.

Politics in a democracy must strike a resonant chord in the body politic if leadership is to be reached. The would-be Moses lifted his divining rod in the air, seeking the liquid of widely held, even if not always clearly articulated, beliefs.

What are these beliefs? They are very different for blacks and whites. Blacks are much more inclined to think Farrakhan speaks the truth, that he is not a racist, and that he stands up to whites. Whites see the opposite images. It seems likely that blacks reflexively believe that it is logically inconsistent for a black to be a racist in a racist society aimed at them. Polled, blacks think things have gotten worse over the past ten years and that the biggest problems have been teen pregnancy, broken families, drug abuse, high crime rates, lack of black-owned businesses, poor education, AIDS, and unemployment—with significant percentages seeing a white racist conspiracy behind each problem.

The degrees of separation reveal not one, but two nations, and the reality of the separation confirms growing inequality and widening racial chasms.

The end result for blacks is a life condition that makes criminality a form of escape or rebellion from the intolerability of the daily experience of being black in contemporary America.[19] The end product of white myopia is that it blinds whites to their own interests—that of renewing themselves through dispensing racial justice, even as the criminals are punished for their misdeeds.

But even those fighting for these lofty goals—the NAACP, the United Way, and others—are succumbing to the temptations of the age. And the temptations, too, are spreading, like a devouring flame over the dry husk of American life.

ADDICTIONS

America believes in drugs.

Its pharmaceutical industry has provided a steady stream of miraculous cures for dreaded diseases or inconvenient symptoms. The pressures on the Food and Drug Administration to release nostrums such as those that might be used for AIDS places that agency in the crossfire between safety and the desperate search for relief.

The wonderfully effective, hugely educational, and marvelously expensive ads by the Partnership for a Drug-Free America are, at once, the expression of corporate responsibility and, perhaps, the residue of guilt over having persuaded the nation to see for itself the wonders of drugs—from which the flight from safe and useful substances to harmful, illegal, and addicting substances is merely a short hop.

Working in evil partnership with the power of drugs to enslave is the accompanying human conceit that disables us from envisioning our own addiction.[20-22] A nation distracted into taking patent medicines laced with opium until early in the twentieth century, which were generically described as "snake oil" and which signed into the association of glamour with booze and cigarettes on our silver screens in the 1930s and 1940s, learned to continue its costly search for anything that delivered a buzz without horrific consequences.

And, as if to prove our determination to surrender to pleasure without consequence, our chemists understood there were princely sums to be made from the invention of substances that enabled us to snack without taking in either calories or fat.[23]

Addiction became a swamp of ironies and unexpected results. The most "respectable" of the habits—smoking[24]—turned out to be the deadliest, as 400,000 Americans were estimated to have been killed by tobacco-related maladies in 1990. As the twentieth century was ending, the key question was just how calculating were the corporate efforts to enslave customers to nicotine. A series of potentially devastating lawsuits, brought by the survivors of smokers who had died from the habit, bid fair to reveal whether tobacco companies lied, deliberately altered the amounts of nicotine in their products, or engaged in practices that went beyond the mere provision of a substance that begged user caution. Even allowing for the total commercial integrity of the enterprise did not erase the effect of intense lobbying efforts, lavish campaign contributions, and tireless legislative initiatives by what might be called the "Vice Industry of Addictions." That tobacco is an entirely legal industry affords us a measure of experience with such dangerous freedom.

Alcohol,[25,26] estimated to have caused 150,000 deaths in 1990, was banned from 1919 to 1932, giving us a unique opportunity to assess the effects of decriminalizing an illegal drug. The result was a mixed bag, with hosts of crimes attributed to its consumption.

We are able to point to hosts of countries, in Europe especially but also Australia and Argentina and others, that consume more pure alcohol a year per capita than we do. Many European countries are at the level of well over ten quarts of pure alcohol consumed, while we, in 1993, were at 7.2 quarts. There were an estimated 18.5 million persons with alcohol problems in America in 1991, meaning that the substance was impacting their lives negatively and that they had lost the ability to control intake. When combined with other addictions or ingestions such as gambling, marijuana, and hard drugs, the harvest of violence becomes horrific. The popularity of alcohol has endured with minor variations, as binge drinking remained one of college's most alluring cultural expressions.

In recent years, the leading educational–legislative impetus for alerting the public to alcohol's dangers has come from Mothers Against Drunk Drivers (MADD), which focused on the bloodletting on the roads caused by drunks at the wheel. Alcoholics Anonymous remains the leading venue for counsel, support, and spiritual buttressing for addicts seeking to ditch their compulsion.

Just as tobacco was found to be something more than a glamorous expression of the inner workings of the haute monde, alcohol also turned out to be more that the accoutrement of the sophisticated habitué of Rick's Bar. But just as the tobacco industry had learned that the warning label they'd so stoutly resisted turned out to be, ultimately, a sort of caveat emptor that protected them from lawsuits, alcohol companies too learned that such a notice really was—at least legally—fair warning of the dangers in the contents.

Gambling

Life is a gamble.

Using gambling as a metaphor for human existence proves a serious mistake because, while life is full of risk, dangers can be reduced and the chances of success enhanced through planning, budgeting, working, saving, and postponing. The reality is that there do exist ways of getting the odds to favor the player in the game of life, but at the roulette wheel, its owner has insuperable advantages.

Gambling is, today, the fastest-growing American industry, with almost $500 billion wagered in 1994, producing revenues of $40 billion. The industry, with lavish contributions and intensive lobbying, has become a major player in the nation's political life.[27,28] It is a measure of the alacrity with which democracies attack social problems that it took over 30 years of ferocious growth to convince Congress that it should, perhaps, study gambling's direction, effect, and costs—both hidden and obvious.

Since 1964, casinos, slots, lotteries, riverboats evoking the Mississippi gamblers' romantic visions, horse and dog racing, Native American gaming, and every other form of wagering has spread, like a forest fire, over the nation's landscape.

Again, the addictive power of repeated exposure was either ignored, underestimated, or unknown. The recognition of compulsive gambling as a disease was not made until late in this century, joining alcoholism, but not smoking, as a recognized malady.

Government found the painless, voluntary taxation of gamblers irresistible and didn't worry much about the pigeons' ability to pay. It was another transfer of wealth, from the poor player to the rich watchers. The road was greased with pious assertions of the good causes helped—totally ignoring the truism that dedicated funds preclude the debate that is the hallmark of the democratic process in our legislative chambers.

Yes, the proceeds went to help the elderly or educational or environmental causes, but—since the money was transferred automatically and without analysis or discussion—the chances were good that there would be gross waste and inefficiency in the process. By justifying the vice through assertions that the proceeds went to good causes, its promoters precluded governmental examination or citizen inquiries that attend every allocation of public funds and that question the morality of public policies. Even politicians—occasionally and penuriously—dedicated proceeds for the treatment of the army of compulsive gamblers they worked so hard to create.

The ubiquitousness of gambling opportunities forced many of the tempted to wander city streets with figurative blinders. The price of a full tank of gas became crucial, because so many were taking whatever change came from a $20 bill and spending it on the counter-available lottery tickets within easy reach.

The anecdotes were horrific, as the limitless devastation of the uncontrolled bettor was loosed on his or her husbanded resources and then spilled over to those of family, friends, and whatever acquaintance could be persuaded to make a loan. Penologists estimated that about 13% of prisoners were there because of some gambling-related crime. Bad checks, defaulted loans, repossessed cars and homes, embezzlement of funds, and other crimes became the markers on the road to ruin. It was the rare compulsive gambler who hadn't broken the law.

While citizens wrung their hands over the possibility of organized crime involvement, the reality was that the mob was being driven from the field, as corporate America latched on to Las Vegas and Atlantic City and the government supplanted the local bookmaker with a dazzling array of products. The government would not brook competition and recognized the absolute necessity of keeping the games honest.

Crimes by hooked players spanned a variety of areas, from thefts, hold-ups, embezzlements, and betrayals of trust to forgeries, prostitution, and other desperate gambits. Suicide frequently accompanied the despair. The behavior of employees and those in positions of trust now included the added wrinkle of the danger of an unsuspected and invisible addiction that spelled trouble for any enterprise's cash. And manufacturers of the equipment had plenty of incentives to go beyond contributions and lobbying, oftentimes lapsing into outright bribery.

Patriotic organizations exploited veterans with pull tabs, while religious bodies seduced little old ladies with bingo. Corporations paved the way for scams among the gullible elderly with sweepstakes contests and highly publicized winners. In fact, "You may already be a winner" became the leitmotif of fraud.

The accumulated swelling of lottery prizes proved a windfall of free publicity and produced hysterias of ticket buying. Governors were photographed standing in line to buy their ticket. The shares of gambling stocks were hot items on Wall Street, and wasn't the stock market just another casino? This view reflected the apologists' inability to discern prudent, calculated saving and investment from the insanity of the roulette wheel.

Increasingly, kids were gambling. It was fast becoming a subset of the psychology of addictions. While no one knew the number of compulsive gamblers, everyone shared the certainty that the ranks were swelling.

Payoffs varied dramatically, from the more than 95 cents on the dollar returned as winnings by slot machines to the relatively confiscatory low pay-out of lotteries—about 50 cents on the dollar. Either way, however, no one got 100 cents. And perhaps the worst fate that could befall any starter would be a dazzling run of luck that sped the hooking of the player.

The industry would point to the jobs created, the taxes collected, and the prosperity wrought. Atlantic City was finally, after 20 years of broken promises and jailed mayors, having some gambling proceeds go to the town's improvement.

Some were still trying to guarantee the outcome of wagered-on sports events—an ever-present danger to the integrity of our latest passion.

Europe had, historically, placed its casinos in sequestered spas that required time, money, and effort to reach. Now gambling opportunities were everywhere—the one equal opportunity.

In New York State, Quick Draw became a way to play the numbers 158 times a day, with bets ranging from $1 to $10 and 20 games on each card. Using all the cards available enabled players to lose limitless amounts. The game, begun in September 1995, was everywhere and was proving a huge success.

Native American gaming—casinos on reservations—became the first vehicle to the economic independence of tribal members, ever. Native American became America's fastest-growing ethnic group, as applicants realized that membership in the Shakopee Mdewakanton Dakota—an exclusive list of 150—meant income of $400,000 per year in 1993 and $500,000 in 1994. Small wonder everyone searched their roots to see if they might qualify.

Native American casinos set up childcare centers for player convenience—and to avoid the embarrassment of kids in cars in the parking lot, especially in frozen tundra like Minnesota's. The prosperity of the tribe was directly related to the proximity of the tribe's hands to the operation. When outsiders built the casino, provided the equipment, staffed the operation, kept the books, and sent the tribe a monthly check, someone, in addition to the Native Americans was thriving—accounting, in large measure, for the attractiveness of gambling stocks.

In Connecticut, the governor convinced Native American casinos to pay the state a fixed percentage of the gross (about $160 to $180 million annually in the 1990s) in exchange for the monopoly. It developed that the only way to retain sequestration of casino gambling on the reservations was to threaten the Native Americans with a loss of the monopoly by surrendering to the pleas of the "hospitality industry" to allow slots and video gaming in every tavern, bar, and restaurant in the state.

Drugs

America, in its legislative tinkerings, garnered a wealth of experience with drugs, substances, and addictions as it criminalized and legalized their use and possession. Somehow, the logic never seemed to be extended to other areas, such as the possible legalization of hard drugs and what that might mean for the nation. The inescapable reality is that legalizing an action is tantamount to saying that the government feels that it's okay to do it, and it invariably results in widely expanding use and addictions.

A Martian might be excused for thinking that our war on drugs was an effort to return, Christian Scientist-like, to spirit and faith for a cure. It seemed something of a mantra. Others deride it as the failed promise of quick victory over addicting, harmful, illegal substances. Some see it as a costly, futile effort that has failed and that has an easy remedy in legalization.

Marijuana,[29] the smokable plant, appears to be a stepping-stone drug on the way to more serious addictions—like crack cocaine, heroin, amphetamines, or LSD. By the 1990s, marijuana had been effectively decriminalized in America, de facto if not de jure, as police departments ceased actively pursuing small-scale possession or use. Yes, they would arrest you if they stumbled across it and, yes, there were some folks in prison for large-scale transactions, but, while still on the books as illegal, marijuana, in the 1990s, was not a serious police priority anywhere in America.

Marijuana, as a result of successful interdiction and crop destruction efforts in Mexico especially, became America's biggest cash crop, at $32 billion in 1995. Its use by black males as young as 11 tripled from 1991 to 1995, and the percentage of teenagers who acknowledged smoking it at least four times a month went from 6% in 1990 to 12% in 1994.

While the only constant in drug use is the perennial search for the high without the hangover—which leads to radical popularity shifts among drugs—it seems clear that the cocaine/crack epidemic peaked in 1985. There were a total of 3618 deaths attributed to this drug in 1989, less than 1% of those attributed to tobacco.

The highly publicized use of hard drugs by revered rock groups did for contemporary youth what smoking and scotch-sipping on movie screens did for their parents. Just as the older generation's disillusionment grew with every reported death of once-worshipped heroes from alcoholism or lung cancer, the children were witnessing a parade of death, suicide, and self-destruction among current icons.

The devastation could be seen in its impact on the one stable factor in the black family culture—mothers—a percentage of whom became addicted. A survey showed that, in 1985, 37 million Americans had used marijuana, cocaine, or some other drug that year. By 1988 the number declined to 28 million, but no one was ready to declare the war won. One of the really alarming discoveries was the constant shifts in popularity and the time lag in discovering the movement to another drug. Alcohol and drugs remained the only cheap and available method of escaping the quotidian ghastliness of ghetto life.

The drug scourge, alcohol, and gambling are probably accounting for 90% of the street crime frightening America. While some protested the enormously high incidence of blacks among those arrested and locked-up for drugs, the fact was that any other enforcement action—aimed at any segment of street crime—would also have swept up disproportionate numbers of black males. A decoy operation would result in disproportionate collars of black males, as would a sting operation for burglars or a stake-out unit for robbers.

Agonizingly difficult issues surfaced, such as whether the government should distribute clean needles (clearly an evil in that it probably encourages even more drug use) or risk the spread of AIDS (a greater evil), the use of the military in interdiction efforts, drug-testing in schools and workplaces, and the possible adoption of policies such as those seen in Netherlands' coffee shops, where marijuana is sold in small quantities and smoked openly. There was also the burning question of legalizing hard drugs. There would be unquestioned benefits, such as ensured quality, possible tax receipts, reduction of cost, elimination of violence, ridding the industry of criminal control, possible treatment, and other likely positives. The enduring negative, however, is legalization's effect on the nation's moral fabric. Our experience with legalizing alcohol and gambling—and with the always-legal tobacco industry—hasn't been pretty.

Illegal drugs constitute a multibillion-dollar industry that attracts defectors from the ranks of prosecutors into the payrolls of smuggling cartels, corrupts bankers and lawyers, and addicts millions. The war on drugs—centering on single-minded, and mindless, enforcement efforts—is a failure.

In order for it to succeed, enforcement would have to be targeted at the executives transporting the drugs, laundering the money, and controlling the product's flow.[30] Every arrest or seizure should be used as a step to the next higher level, rather than as an end in itself. Resources must be poured into prevention, education, and treatment efforts. Addiction fuels the accelerating social disintegration and fans the flames of fear spreading over the nation. It is easy to hate the evildoers paraded before us every night.

THE NATURE OF MAN

Cops are the scientists in the great laboratory of human existence. They observe the animals at the extremes of behavior. Cops' cynicism results from their repeated exposure to the baleful view of the beast's underbelly.

So, is man's nature evil or good?

It is both, and failure to recognize this fact is loaded with consequence. For example, if we simply label someone who has committed an atrocious crime as evil, we preclude further analysis and thereby forfeit any chance of altering his behavior or creating the conditions that prevent others from following suit.

The criminal begs for understanding because the hope of human engineering to eliminate the conditions creating him rests on such explorations.

It is vital that it be grasped that understanding doesn't include excusing behavior or avoiding punishment. This is the common flaw in the argument—that understanding equates to exculpation. It doesn't, and it mustn't. Even as we punish the rapist, murderer, and burglar, however, we have got to figure out where he came from and what the forces were that shaped his actions.

COPS AND THE CRIMINAL JUSTICE SYSTEM

Paid to oversee all of this disintegration is the modern version of the Praetorian Guard—America's cops. It seems more than likely they will experience the same measure of success.

As an institution, American policing has come some distance toward professionalism—witness the tripling of the prison population even while cops had to observe the strictures so wisely imposed by the Earl Warren Supreme Court.

Assigned to control the underclass, cops are plagued by the problems of racism, brutality, and corruption and are worsened by their demure avoidance of raising educational and character standards or similar reforms.

The rest of the criminal justice system is arguably worse, as turf battles continue to divide the jealous fiefdoms. The appointment and monitoring of judges tends to remain a tawdry political pay-off gavotte. Judges resent and resist oversights like Court Watch and TV cameras and fight the computerization of the process that would link them to the other players in the criminal justice system but that might also expose back-scratching delays and other favors to lawyers and other colleagues.

That neither prosecutors nor judges ever report egregious examples of police brutality, perjury, or corruption—committed before their very eyes in their courtrooms—is the continuing, unmentioned scandal of inactivity that marks coziness in these relationships.

Other players tend to their fiefs and fight for the crumbs falling off the table after additional cops and bigger prisons are paid for. The notion of businesslike management is not just a stranger to the notions of governing the criminal justice system—and, indeed, all government—but it also actually engenders hostility because of its interruptions of time-honored practices involving taking care of cronies and other pay-offs.

The irony is that, judging from the promises of politicians anxious to please a frightened electorate, the people still retain faith in the bankrupt notion of concentrating all efforts at safety on punishments, while ignoring the societal corrections that might actually enhance safety.

The clouds gather and darken.

SEX

Another politically incorrect assertion is that a society's state of moral well-being is expressed by the degree of its control over the male libido. No on seems to be either able or willing to recognize the enormous and continuing power of this drive and the desperate need for its control. Libertine, licentious, morally decadent societies are characterized by the freeing of these animal energies upon women and, too often, children.

Where are we headed?

Movies, magazines, radio, CD-ROMS, computers, and tabloids are full of lurid scenes or descriptions, but the easiest place to find the expression of our current attitudes toward sex is to channel-surf among the offerings on cable, daytime TV talk shows, late night programming, and, more subtly but creeping to greater daring, prime time shows.

While no one really knows the numbers—because of the opprobrium still attached to a lot of sexual victimizations—what we do know is troubling.

Girls under 18 are the victims of over half the rapes reported to the police. The younger the victim, the likelier it is that the attacker is a relative or is known to the victim. When alcohol, other forms of sexual abuse of the young, and violence in the home are added, we discern the outline of the forces creating our population of street prostitutes. Certainly not all sexually abused girls take to the streets, but they are all scarred or injured.

Studies are showing that the nation's teenagers are more sexually active today, are more likely to be using contraceptives—as a result of fear of AIDS and other diseases—and are having fewer abortions and producing fewer pregnancies, but they are still experiencing much higher rates of pregnancy and childbirth than their counterparts in Western Europe, where extensive sex education and readily available contraceptives reduce pregnancies and childbirths.

After a leveling and slight decline in births to black, unmarried, 15- to 19-year-old females following *Roe v. Wade* in 1973, the number began to rise again in 1986, reaching 150,000 per year in 1991. Since this is the population producing "at-risk" males (impoverished, with low education and on welfare), the outlook for the future, starting in 2001, when the bulge cohort begins to reach age 15, is very bleak, however many cops are hired or prisons built. Had it not been for AIDS and *Roe v. Wade,* the future for street crime would look even bleaker.

Sex in America is as effectively studied anecdotally, impressionistically, or observationally as it is through amassing data because of the slipperiness of the figures. A change in information-gathering techniques drove the number of reported rapes from 155,000 in 1991–92 to 310,000 in 1992–93, with 80% perpetrated by a familiar.

Regarding homosexuality, a 1992 study revealed that 2.8% of the men polled described themselves as homosexual, yet 5.3% said they had had sex with a person of the same sex at least once since puberty; 7.7% reported a desire for same-sex experiences; and 10.1% indicated at least some wish for same-sex experiences. The percentages for women were generally substantially lower, except in the category of desiring same-sex experiences, in which they matched the men.

There can be no doubt that, like race or gender, homosexuality represents both a challenge and an opportunity for broadening human rights in our society, but our failure to acknowledge, discuss, or analyze the issue effectively preserves the status quo.

Anecdotally we have our icons, such as Michael Jackson and Madonna (whose very name connotes the shocking and confrontational approach embodied in the marketing of her image), rappers, rock stars, movie heroes, and sports idols, serving us a potpourri of escapades that, calculated or not, depict the lifestyles of the rich and celebrated. And isn't this the group we all seek to emulate? Even the Dionne quintuplets hadn't been spared, as was recently reported.

A 12-year-old girl is abducted from her bedroom and murdered, another child is held in a subterranean tomb to serve as a man's sex captive, a woman who claims to be battered and raped cuts off her husband's penis and launches both into what passes for stardom, two boys murder their parents and claim self-defense over a history of threats and sexual abuse, and a teenager shoots her lover's wife and launches another celebrity into our midst.

An entire new branch of medicine was begun by unlocking repressed childhood memories of sexual outrages and even murder. Some of these memories were discovered to have been the febrile imaginings of young minds or were perhaps even planted by the therapists rapidly achieving prosperity and fame. Ambitious or overzealous officials rocked communities with charges and arrests of sex-abuse rings of parents, teachers, ministers, day-care providers, and other trusted figures. The suggestibility, anxiety to please, and confusion of reality and imagination among the very young made it clear that enormous care had to go into pursuing such allegations—and that some were unable to resist the temptation of quick headlines.[31]

The confusions attending the broad question of sex in our lives surface in bizarre episodes.

The nation's sympathies extended to a mother who shot and killed her young son's molester as he sat in court on trial for the crime. She received ten years in January 1994.

Prostitutes risked rape, assault, or even murder as they plied their trade—and couldn't be persuaded to abandon a lucrative Florida highway on which five of their associates had been murdered by a serial killer. These murderous maniacs were often attracted to such women—although quite a few of the working prostitutes were actually transvestites offering oral or anal sex and rarely being discovered by their clients or johns. Patients testified to sexual abuse by doctors, dentists, or hospital orderlies; a group of Catholic bishops denounced the "media hype" in the press' reporting of sex abuse cases in 1993, but scandals continued surfacing; the Boy Scouts reported removing almost 2000 scoutmasters suspected of molesting boys from 1971 to 1991; cabbies raped passengers; and an interviewer attacked job applicants—and we'll never know how many went unreported. The brutal crime of gay-bashing continued to be reported, elliptically, as "Professor Is Found Fatally Beaten in His Home." At the paper's other end would be a litany of talented young males dead from AIDS, as "reported by their companion."

The arrest of a Hollywood madam sent ripples of titillation

across the continent. She no doubt had fascinating insights to offer on the darker side of the appetites of celebrities for sex and drugs. There were rumors of her selling the story for $1 million or of a hefty advance for her book. And there were the ever-present references to client lists that would embarrass the mighty. But how to distinguish the innocent entry in the date book from the guilty? Why couldn't one be a friend, another her dentist, and, in between, a client? And how much would she be able to prove—shielding herself from slander and libel suits—if she decided to tell all? There were good reasons for the suppression of such data; officialdom wasn't about to release a list of names that every reader would assume were johns.

There were the awful problems of rape—and the distinction between assaults by familiars or strangers. The issue of pornography and the clearly unconstitutional efforts to extend civil liability to a document that aroused a rapist to commit his atrocious assault launched a furious debate between feminists, who saw the material as inspiring rape, and civil libertarians, who saw it as a First Amendment exercise of free speech. Obscenity was another matter.

First Amendment issues of free speech clashed with society's legitimate concerns over spreading obscenity. The courts had held that pornography could be banned, providing it met narrow and specific legal definitions.

Treatment of sexual sociopaths seemed, at least in the 1990s, beyond medicine's scope—although that was no reason to stop the efforts to treat these compulsions to sexually assault. Arrested serial rapists often have records of prior sexual assaults and related crimes in their backgrounds. Even such procedures as voluntary castration, medication, or other surgical approaches were considered.[32] DNA was rapidly becoming to sex what fingerprints had long been to forensics. But errors in procedures such as in vitro fertilization, such as occurred in Amsterdam, when a mistake produced twin boys—one black and one white—reminded everyone of science's human fallibility.

New-sounding crimes, like stalking and sexual harassment, which were actually long-concealed practices, were being added to the lexicon in a long-overdue assault on hidden abuses. Efforts to identify menaces in the community—such as released sexual predators, who were required to register with the local police, who would advise neighborhoods of their presence—produced pariahs who became the targets of vigilantes. These were the modern donners of scarlet letters. The result of what was called Megan's Law, named in honor of a victim of just such a recidivist, reminded some of the Nazi's use of a pink triangle to identify homosexuals. Still, the children had to be protected. Dealing with the freed sexual abuser was proving a hideous legal dilemma. The question centers on whether this constitutes an unconstitutional additional punishment.[33]

CONCLUSION

Our leaders and our institutions are disappointing, failing or betraying us. The media is the enemy.

Politicians are corrupt.

"Those people" are evil and have to be locked-up.

A general unease sends Americans into the arms of charlatans, demagogues, and fringers, in a desperate search for truth.

The nation is beset by crime, violence, addictions, divorce, and racism. A fault line spreads between the overclass and the underclass.

Everywhere, Americans rail at the fraying dream, seeking scapegoats.

The search takes us everywhere but within.

The same people who spend a large chunk of their day in daily communion with their TV sets, who suck beer and become couch potatoes, who leave half a meal on their plate and order dessert, who won't rush to fight and die for their country, who abandon home and hearth at the first chill of dysfunction, who cheer the oppressors of the poor and weak, and who encourage attacks on "welfare queens" and spew similarly loaded labels now decry the slipping state of our common fortunes and search for targets on which to pin the blame.

How to undertake a moral renewal?

Such an act would have to fly in the face of the political correctness that exempts some subjects from discussion.

The war on poverty will have to be refought—this time bringing consequences and controls, measuring outcomes, and demanding accountability and performance from recipients. The national government has a role to play and its expansion appears inevitable, but management reforms and the correction of civil service regulations have to precede the effort. We have to bring effectiveness and efficiency to the bureaucracy, and this will require civil service and union reforms that will enable managers to make hiring, firing, promotion, and other personnel and administrative decisions on the basis of making things work better—and measuring the outcomes.

Social Security needs to be taxed as if it were ordinary income. Those earning up to $20,000 should pay no income taxes. And we are going to have to face the painful facts that simple, flat taxes screw the poor and that there is no currently visible way of fashioning an income tax that is both simple and just.

Social, economic, and racial justice should be pursued from the perspective of salvation. It is the redemption of white America that must be sought, through the moral renewal that the adoption of these policies would produce. A self-destructively hedonistic people are not likely to heed appeals to selflessness, but we should be able to recognize the self-interest connected to bridging the gaping chasms of economic and racial inequalities.

Winner-take-all economic systems, like lotteries, create too many losers. They are inherently unstable.

Racism produces violence—on both ends of the spectrum.

No justice, no peace.

What needs to be done is precisely the *opposite* of where we, as a people, are heading.

We need to keep the graduated income tax, tax the wealthy at a higher rate, and distribute more benefits—housing, health, education and welfare—to those on the lower rungs.

We need to confront racism—recognizing its corrosive effects on white America's soul—and work to stamp it out.

We need to generate a national debate on the need for renewal, introspection, and the self-examinations that lead us to question the moral imperatives surrounding environmental, economic, and political issues and how they connect to the "American Dream"—which must, itself, be defined.

Our dream ought to be a society that is both just and tough.

We need to examine many notions now seen as politically correct, such as that the war on poverty is lost, that government is unable to do anything right for anyone, and that unbridled capitalism is an unalloyed good.

America is being pulled to its margins, mostly rightward, by a growing paranoia produced by the ills and inequalities described in these pages. Scapegoatism is often the solution seized on by a desperate people—but rescue can be found in returning to hard, complex truths.

It is tragically easy to predict the future, since we know that unattended social problems do not cure themselves—they deteriorate when neglected. That is one of life's iron rules, and we are doing nothing to strengthen the family, to reinvigorate our cities, to ease the plight of the underclass, to attack the corrosive effects of racism, or to level the economic playing field.

When advised he was terminally ill, the writer Joseph W. Alsop reported that he hadn't been as depressed as he'd expected to be at the news, and, in 1992, wrote a final memoir, *I've Seen The Best of It*.[34] This should not and must not be our epitaph.

The ancient truths are still there—honor, duty, God, country, family, discipline, structure.

The Ten Commandments remain tablet-etched, but they are unread and unheeded.

Any hope for renewal lies not in having better leaders or more reliable institutions, but in seeking a return to being a better people.

Notes

Introduction

1. Galbraith, John Kenneth. *The Culture of Contentment*. Boston: Houghton Mifflin, 1992.
2. Galbraith, John Kenneth. *The Culture of Contentment*. Boston: Houghton Mifflin, 1984.
3. Lasch, Christopher. *The Culture of Narcissism*. New York: Norton, 1979.
4. Fukuyama, Francis. *The End of History and the Last Man*. New York: Free Press, 1992.
5. "At School in Chicago, a Scandal Grows Larger." *The New York Times*. April 12, 1995.
6. Kidder, Rushworth M. *How Good People Make Tough Choices*. New York: Morrow.
7. Bok, Sissela. *Secrets: On the Ethics of Concealment and Revelation*. New York: Pantheon, 1982.
8. Bok, Sissela. *Lying: Moral Choice in Public Life*. New York: Vintage Books, 1989.
9. From the film *Casablanca*, with Humphrey Bogart and Ingrid Bergman.
10. Rothenberg, Fred. "Glued to the Tube: Americans Set Record for Hours in Front of T.V. Set." *The Boston Globe*, January 25, 1984.

11. Garofalo, James. "Crime and the Mass Media—A Selective Review of Research," *Journal of Research in Crime and Delinquency* 18, July 1981, pp. 319–350.

12. Barbour, William, ed. *Mass Media: Opposing Viewpoints*. San Diego: Greenhaven Press, 1994.

13. Costello, Mark, and David Foster Wallace. *Signifying Rappers: Rap and Race in the Urban Present*. New York: Ecco Press, 1990.

14. Collier, Zena. *Seven for the People*. New York: Messner, 1979.

15. Geis, Gilbert. *White Collar Criminal*. New York: Atherton Press, 1968.

16. Pizzo, Stephen, Mary Fricker, and Paul Muolo. *Inside Job: The Looting of America's Savings and Loans*. New York: McGraw-Hill, 1989.

17. Noonan, Peggy. *What I Saw at the Revolution*. New York: Random House, 1990.

18. Phillips, Kevin P. *Arrogant Capital: Washington, Wall Street and the Frustration of American Politics*. Boston: Little, Brown, 1994.

19. *Choosing the President, 1992*. League of Women Voters of California, Sacramento.

20. Wayne, Stephen J. *The Road to the White House 1992*. New York: St. Martin's Press, 1992.

21. Scher, Patti, and Marion Koch. *The Untold Story About Breast Implants*. Charlotte, NC: 1993.

22. Carville, James, and Mary Matalin. *All's Fair: Love, War, and Running for President*. New York: Random House, 1994.

23. Drew, Elizabeth. *Politics and Money: The New Road to Corruption*. New York: Macmillan, 1983.

24. Shawcross, Tim. *The War against the Mafia*. New York: Harper Collins, 1994.

25. *The Figgie Report on Fear of Crime*. Willoughby, OH: Figgie International Corp., 1982.

26. Boyle, James J. *Killer Cults*. New York: St. Martin's Press, 1995.

27. Cosell, Howard, with Shelby Whitfield. *What's Wrong with Sports*. New York: Simon & Schuster, 1991.

28. McMillen, Tom. *Out of Bounds*. New York: Simon & Schuster, 1992.

29. Dudley, William, ed. *Sports in America: Opposing Viewpoints*. San Diego: Greenhaven Press, 1994.

CHAPTER 1. WHITE COLLAR CRIME

1. Sutherland, Edwin H. *White Collar Crime: The Uncut Version*. New Haven, CT: Yale University Press, 1983.

2. Galaway, Burt. "The Use of Restitution." *Crime and Delinquency* 23, January 1977, pp. 57–67.

3. Day, Kathleen. *S and L Hell*. New York: Norton, 1993.

4. Gordon, David M. "Capitalism, Class and Crime in America." *Crime and Delinquency* 19, April 1973, pp. 163–186.

5. Quinney, Richard. *Class, State, and Crime.* New York: Longman, 1977.

6. Potts, Mark. *Banking Scandals: The S & Ls and B.C.C.I.*

7. Long, Robert Emmet, ed. *Dirty Money.* Bethesda, MD: National Press Books, 1992.

8. The scandal sparked a number of books on both BCCI and the principals. One that centered on Clark Clifford was Douglas Frantz and David McKena, *Friends in High Places.* Boston: Little, Brown, 1995.

9. Meyer, Martin. *The Greatest Ever Bank Robbery.* New York: Scribner's, 1990.

10. Pilzer, Paul Zane. *Other People's Money.* New York: Simon & Schuster, 1989.

11. Wilmsen, Steven, K. *Silverado: Neil Bush and the S & L Scandal.* Bethesda, MD: National Press Books, 1991.

12. Binstein, Michael. *Trust Me: Charles Keating and the Missing Billions.* New York: Random House, 1993.

13. Simon, David R., and Stanley Eitzen. *Elite Deviance.* New York: Simon & Schuster, 1990.

14. Insurance Industry study by the Consumer Federation of America and Common Cause, August 31, 1995.

15. Cramer, James J., column in February 1995 issue of *Smart Money*, in which the author touts four of his favorite stocks without advising the reader that his brokerage company, Cramer & Co., had bought, and continued to buy, these stocks, which jumped on the news. It was perfectly legal, too.

16. Roth, Jeffrey, John T. Scholz, and Ann Dryden Witte, eds. *Taxpayer Compliance.* Philadelphia: University of Pennsylvania Press, 1989.

CHAPTER 2. CAPITALISM

1. Schillit, Howard M. *Financial Shenanigans.* New York: McGraw Hill, 1993.

2. This subject received extensive periodic coverage in *The Wall Street Journal*, *The New York Times*, and other publications from 1993 to 1996.

3. "S.E.C. Charges Former Trader for Kidder with Fraud." *The New York Times*, January 10, 1996.

4. Stewart, James B. *Den of Thieves: The Untold Story of the Men Who Plundered Wall Street and the Chase That Brought Them Down.* New York: Simon & Schuster, 1991.

5. Kornbluth, Jesse. *Highly Confidential: The True Story of the Crime and Punishment of Michael Milken.* New York: Morrow, 1993.

6. Zey, Mary. *Banking on Fraud.* Hawthorne, NY: Aldine de Gruyter, 1993.

7. Burrough, Bryan, and John Helyar. *Barbarians at the Gate*. New York: Harper & Row.

8. Reported in *The New York Times* and in other newspapers throughout 1995.

9. Mayer, Martin. *Nightmare on Wall Street*. New York: Simon & Schuster, 1993.

10. This issue is the subject of one of the biggest lawsuits in American history and is destined to play out well into the twenty-first century, with spates of disclosures and refutations. It is also the subject of a 1995 Food and Drug Administration report that sought to control tobacco as a drug.

11. Eichenwald, Kurt. *Serpent on the Rock*. New York: HarperCollins, 1995.

12. Sharp, Kathleen. *In Good Faith*. New York: St. Martin's Press, 1995.

13. Tuccille, Jerome. *Kingdom: The Story of the Hunt Family of Texas*. Ottawa, IL: Jameson Books, 1984.

14. The fraud, suits, settlements, and related developments were covered extensively in news stories in *The Wall Street Journal*, *The New York Times*, and other publications and inspired several books over a period spanning well over a decade from the mid-1980s to mid-1990s.

15. "Three Firms Discuss Pact with the S.E.C." *The Wall Street Journal*, January 26, 1996.

16. The case continued in litigation in 1996 and had also been covered widely in 1995.

17. "Accused of Stealing from Lindbergh Widow, Darien Woman Says Clients Back Her." *The New York Times*, August 20, 1995.

18. "Battling the Computer Pirates." *The New York Times*, January 5, 1983.

19. Parker, Donn B. *Fighting Computer Crime*. New York: Scribner's, 1983.

20. Ex-Honda Executives Guilty in Bribe Case. *The New York Times*, June 2, 1995.

21. Ermann, M. David, and Richard J. Lundman. *Corporate and Governmental Deviance*. New York: Oxford University Press, 1987.

22. "S.E.C. Said to Be Looking at Archer–Daniels." *The New York Times*, October 10, 1995.

23. "Cheers and Boos, at Archer–Daniels Meeting." *The New York Times*, October 20, 1995.

24. Clinard, M. B., and P. C. Yeager. *Corporate Crime*. New York: Free Press, 1980.

CHAPTER 3. WHOM CAN YOU TRUST?

1. The revelations, scandal, trial, and conviction of the CEO and associates played out over many months and was widely reported in the

nation's press, news magazines, and other periodicals. (See, e.g., "Ex-United Way Leader Gets 7 years for Embezzlement." *The New York Times*, June 23, 1995.)

2. The internal strife, scandals, settlements, removal of officers, and elections of the NAACP resulted in wide press coverage over many months in 1994–96. At the end the organization was badly shaken and trying to find its footing. (See, e.g., "N.A.A.C.P. Audit Shows Lavish Spending, Members Say," *The New York Times*, July 13, 1995, and "Fund Raiser Sues N.A.A.C.P. for $4 Million." *The New York Times*, June 22, 1995.)

3. It has been estimated that medical fraud may consume as much as 10% or more of the nation's health bill. Problems at our educational institutions have dotted both national and local press coverage. (See, e.g., "Bribes for Doctors." *The New York Times*, October 15, 1995, and "Rivals Call Out Troops in Different Drug War," *The New York Times*, November 11, 1995.)

4. "Najarian's Image Poses Tricky Legal Challenge." *Minneapolis Star-Tribune*, January 14, 1996.

5. Cited from various accounts in the *Minneapolis Star-Tribune* in 1995.

6. Reported in the *Minneapolis Star-Tribune* and other local papers in 1995.

7. The institution and its members were the subjects of investigations and commentary relating to academic dishonesty as well as internal problems of a threatening and criminal nature.

8. "In a Coma 10 Years, Woman, 29, Is Pregnant after Rape." *The New York Times*, January 25, 1996.

9. "Genentech and Caremark Executives Acquitted." *The New York Times*, October 4, 1995.

10. Genentech Ousts Chief Over a Loan Guarantee Bid. *The New York Times*, July 11, 1995.

11. "Caremark to Pay $161 Million in Fraud Settlement." *Minneapolis Star-Tribune*, June 17, 1995.

12. Halcion is a prime example, as was thalidomide, of the dangers involved in caving in to consumer demand before prudent trials and analyses are undertaken and documented. England banned Halcion, while the President of the United States was taking it and directing the fortunes of the world's most powerful nation.

13. "Phar-Mor Founder Gets Long Sentence." *The New York Times*. December 2, 1995.

14. The Empire Blue Cross scandal was the subject of extended hearings by the New York State legislature and was frequently mentioned in *New York Times* reports.

CHAPTER 4. POLITICS

1. "Dole's Campaign Drawing 'Investors'." *The Los Angeles Times*, July 29, 1995.
2. "In New York, a Partisan Makeover." *The New York Times*, January 10, 1995.
3. Wright, Martin, and William Imfeld. "Environmental Crimes: Investigative Basics." *F.B.I. Law Enforcement Bulletin* 60, April 1991.
4. It was James Watt who outraged the nation by asserting that one of his committees was perfectly balanced, with minorities, handicapped persons, and Jews. His plea of guilty was reported in *The New York Times* in January 1996.
5. Bernstein, Carl. *All the President's Men*. New York: Simon & Schuster, 1974.
6. McNamara, Robert S. *In Retrospect: The Tragedy and Lessons of Vietnam*. New York: Times Books, 1995.
7. Walsh, Lawrence E. *Final Report of the Independent Counsel for Iran/Contra Matters*. Washington, DC: U.S. Court of Appeals for the District of Columbia Circuit, 1993.
8. Whitewater was a national story in America's press from the inception of Clinton's candidacy through his first term, surfacing in congressional hearings, indictments by a special prosecutor, and repeatedly unfolding revelations.
9. The accounts following were reported in *The New York Times* and in the local papers serving the jurisdiction in question and were otherwise publicly revealed in radio or TV newscasts contemporaneous with the events.
10. "Mayor's Aide in Newark Indicted." *The New York Times*, January 26, 1996.
11. "Indicted Aide Is Reassigned in Newark." *The New York Times*, January 27, 1996.
12. "Ex-Members of Gang See Defeat at Polls in Chicago." *The New York Times*, April 6, 1995.
13. "Chicago Officials Complain of Too Many Sting Operations." *The New York Times*, January 18, 1996.
14. The default and bankruptcy of Orange County received wide mention in the national press, including *The New York Times* and *The Wall Street Journal*, throughout 1995 and continuing beyond, in a tangled web of lawsuits, recriminations, elections, guilty pleas, and such. (See, e.g., "Orange County Is Suing Former Auditor KPMG Peat Marwick," Associated Press, December 2, 1995.
15. "Orange County Settlement Sends a Signal from S.E.C." *The New York Times*, January 25, 1996.

16. "S.E.C. Accuses Orange County, Others, of Defrauding Investors." *The Wall Street Journal*, January 25, 1996.
17. "Packwood Diaries at Washington's Tangled Web." *The New York Times*, September 10, 1995, and other stories.
18. "N.Y. Faces Changes in How Judges Are Selected." *The New York Times*, December 7, 1994.
19. "High Stakes and Hot Competition." *Minneapolis Star-Tribune*, March 6, 1995 (an account of West Publishing's wooing of Supreme Court justices).

CHAPTER 5. ORGANIZED CRIME

1. Peterson, Virgil. *The Mob: 200 Years of Organized Crime in N.Y.C.* Ottawa: Green Hill, 1983.
2. "Hard Lesson in Gambling and the Law." *The New York Times*, December 5, 1995.
3. After eons of silence, the presses roared with new disclosures and fresh books. Among these were Ovid Demaris, *The Last Mafioso*. New York: Times Books, 1981; Gay Talese, *Honor Thy Father*. New York: World, 1971; and Vincent Teresa, *My Life in the Mafia*. New York: Doubleday, 1973.
4. Joe, Delbert, and Norman Robinson. "Chinatown's Immigrant Gangs: The New Young Warrior Class." *Criminology* 18, November 1980, pp. 337–345.
5. Lasky, Victor. *It Didn't Start with Watergate*. New York: Dial, 1977.
6. Powers, Richard Gid. *G Men: Hoover's F.B.I. in American Popular Culture*. Carbondale, IL: Southern Illinois University Press, 1983.
7. *The Challenge of Crime in a Free Society*. Washington, DC: U.S. Government Printing Office, February 1967.
8. See the Congressional Reports on these hearings for detailed exchanges and insights.
9. *An Introduction to Organized Crime in the United States* (FBI report). Washington: DC: 1993.
10. "Faces of Reputed Mobster: Very Sick or Very Clever." *The New York Times*, September 12, 1995.
11. "Jury Convicts Philadelphia's Mob Leader." *The New York Times*, November 22, 1995.
12. Cummings, John. *Goombata: The Improbable Rise and Fall of John Gotti and His Gang*. Boston: Little, Brown, 1990.
13. *The Edge: Organized Crime, Business and Labor Unions*. Washington, DC: President's Commission on Organized Crime, 1986.

14. "Labor Costs Still Sky-High at Shaken-Up Javits Center." *The New York Times*, October 29, 1995.
15. "U.S. Contends Major Festival Is Run by Mob." *The New York Times*, September 2, 1995.
16. "San Gennaro's Officials Outearn Charity." *The New York Times*, September 24, 1995.
17. "Government to Take Over Hotel Union." *The New York Times*, August 27, 1995.
18. "Witness Says Crime Figures Rule Disposal of Toxic Waste." *The New York Times*, September 20, 1984.

CHAPTER 6. TERRORISM

1. Friedlander, Robert. *Terrorism*. Dobbs Ferry, NY: Oceana Publishing, 1979.
2. For a criticism of this surveillance, see Gary Marx, *Under Cover*. Los Angeles: Twentieth-Century Fund, 1988.
3. Van Peebles, Mario. *Panther: A Pictorial History*. New York: Newmarket Press, 1995.
4. Theoharris, Athan G. *Spying on Americans*. Philadelphia: Temple University Press, 1978.
5. "Florida Bomb Kills Man and Raises Concern on Increase in Random Attacks." *The New York Times*, January 25, 1996.
6. The explosion and the ensuing trials extended from February 1993 into 1996 and were extensively covered in all aspects by *The New York Times* and other publications.
7. "To Church's Dismay, Priest Talks of 'Justifiable Homicide' of Abortion Doctors." *The New York Times*, August 24, 1994.
8. "Clinic Firebombed in Pennsylvania." *The New York Times*, September 30, 1993.
9. "Abortions, Bibles and Bullets, and the Making of a Militant." *The New York Times*, August 28, 1993.
10. "Gunman Kills Two at Abortion Clinics in Boston Suburb." *The New York Times*, December 31, 1994.
11. "Abortion Violence Stirs Debate among Church Leaders." *The New York Times*, January 9, 1995.
12. Rabbi Meir Kahane, leader of the Jewish Defense League, militant Zionist, and foe of Arabs in Israel.
13. This story was probably second to the O.J. Simpson trial as the biggest of 1995 and was extensively and widely reported by the national press. It will likely be a major event in 1996, as the suspects' trial unfolds.

14. For a critical analysis of the FBI's handling of this event, see the report of the Senate's hearings on this crisis, which were conducted by Senator Arlen Specter in 1995.

15. Tabor, James D., and Eugene V. Gallagher. *Why Waco?* Berkeley: University of California Press, 1995.

16. Reavis, Dick J. *The Ashes of Waco*. New York: Simon & Schuster, 1995.

17. "To Some, Soldier Is a Hero for Refusing to Obey an Order." *The Wall Street Journal*, January 24, 1996.

18. "Who Is He?" *Newsweek*, May 8, 1995.

19. "Death in the Mail: Clues and Theories but Still No Suspect." *The New York Times*, December 18, 1994.

20. "The Newest Christian Faction Injects a Thrill into Theology." *The New York Times*, October 30, 1995.

21. Hyde, Margaret O. *Terrorism: A Special Kind of Violence*. New York: Dodd, Mead, 1987.

22. Watson, Francis M. *Political Terrorism: The Threat and the Response*. New York: R.B. Luce, 1976.

CHAPTER 7. RELIGION, SECTS, CULTS, AND OTHER SEARCHES

1. Butteworth, John. *Cults and New Faiths: A Book of Beliefs*. Washington, DC: Cook Publishing, 1981.

2. See the *McNeil–Lehrer News Hour* report on the Promise Keepers, Fall 1995.

3. Martz, Larry. *Ministry of Greed*. New York: Weidenfeld and Nicholson, 1988.

4. Schultze, Quentin J. *Televangelism and American Culture*. Grand Rapids, MI: Baker Book House, 1991.

5. Sennott, Charles M. *Broken Covenant*. New York: Simon & Schuster, 1992.

6. Jenkins, Philip. *Pedophiles and Priests*. New York: Oxford University Press, 1995.

7. McCuen, Gary E. *The Religious Right*. G.E. McCuen Publications, 1989.

8. Kronenwetter, Michael. *United They Hate: White Supremacist Groups in America*. New York: Walter, 1992.

9. "A Cloud of Terror—and Suspicion." *Newsweek*, April 3, 1995.

10. "Sixteen Burned Bodies Found in France: Cult Tie Suspected." *The New York Times*, December 24, 1995.

11. Kemperman, Steve. *Lord of the Second Advent*. Ventura, CA: Regal Books, 1991.

12. Hassan, Steven. *Combatting Cult Mind Control*. New York: Park Street Press, 1990.

13. Underwood, Barbara. *Hostage to Heaven*. New York: Crown, 1979.
14. Hubbard, L. Ron. *Scientology: The Fundamentals of Thought*. Los Angeles, CA: Bridge Publications, 1988.

CHAPTER 8. THE CUSTODIANS

1. A great number of books have been written on the CIA, including memoirs by former directors. Among them are Evan Thomas, *The Very Best Men: Four Who Dared: The Early Years of the C.I.A.* New York: Simon & Schuster, 1995. and Victor Marchetti and John D. Marks, *The C.I.A. and the Cult of Intelligence*. New York: Knopf, 1974.
2. Blum, William. *Killing Hope: U.S. Military and C.I.A. Interventions Since World War II*. Monroe, ME: Common Courage Press, 1995.
3. Kessler, Ronald. *The F.B.I.: Inside the World's Most Powerful Law Enforcement Agency*. New York: Pocket Books, 1993.
4. Tully, Andrew. *Inside the F.B.I.: From the Files of the F.B.I. and Independent Sources*. New York: McGraw-Hill, 1980.
5. Gentry, Curt. *J. Edgar Hoover: The Man and His Secrets*. New York: Plume, 1992.
6. Haddad, William. *Hard Driving*.
7. Goddard, Donald. *Undercover: The Secret Lives of a Federal Agent*. New York: Times Books, 1988.
8. Reported in the national press in the fall of 1995 as a continuing story that had resulted in no arrests as of early 1996.

CHAPTER 9. STREET CRIME

1. One is the *F.B.I. Uniform Crime Report*, compiled since 1930 from statistics provided by the nation's police chiefs', the other is the *Bureau of Justice Statistics*, which cites annual surveys of the crimes experienced in American households over the past year.
2. The U.S. Justice Department compiles the country's statistics on street crime and violence. See "Crime Statistics: A Historical Perspective," *Crime and Delinquency* 23, January 1977, pp. 32–40.
3. Blumstein, Alfred, Jacqueline Cohen, Jeffery A. Roth, and Christy A. Visher, eds. *Criminal Careers and Career Criminals*. Washington, DC: National Academy Press, 1986.
4. Coffey, Thomas M. *The Long Thirst: Prohibition in America* 1920–1933. New York: Norton, 1975.

5. Both of these cases were exhaustively reported by the local and the national press, with the latter case arousing by far the greater national interest.

6. The biggest of 1994 and 1995, this story seemed destined to keep surfacing prominently for at least the rest of the century, inspiring books, movies, and the widest possible coverage in all other media.

7. The death of Elisa Izquierdo was seized on, by the system and the press, as a paradigm of the times. The tragedy sparked investigations, legislative initiatives, and deep analysis by *The New York Times* and others in late 1995 and early 1996.

8. Cook, Philip J. "The Influence of Gun Availability on Violent Crime Patterns." In *Crime and Justice: An Annual Review of Research*, Vol. 4. Chicago: University of Chicago Press, 1983, pp. 49–89.

9. Fox, J.A., and J. Levin. *Mass Murder: America's Growing Menace*. New York: Plenum Press, 1985.

10. Butterfield, Fox. *All God's Children: The Bosket Family and the American Tradition of Violence*. New York: Knopf, 1995.

11. Martin, John M., and Joseph P. Fitzpatrick. *Delinquent Behavior*. New York: Random House, 1964.

12. Canada, Geoffrey. *Fist Stick Knife Gun*. Boston: Beacon Press, 1995.

13. The Children's Defense Fund and its director, Marion Wright Edelman, have performed heroically in documenting the plight of our "underclass children."

14. Colson, Charles W. "The New Criminal Class." *The Wall Street Journal*, January 24, 1996.

15. Glueck, Sheldon, and Eleanor Glueck. *Family Environment and Delinquency*. Boston: Houghton Mifflin, 1962.

16. Carroll, Leo, and Pamela Irving Jackson. "Inequality, Opportunity and Crime Rates in Central Cities." *Criminology*, May 1983, pp. 178–194.

17. Conklin, John E. *Criminology*. New York: Macmillan, 1986.

18. Wilson, James Q., and George L. Kelling. "Broken Windows." *Atlantic Monthly* 249, March 1981, pp. 29–38.

CHAPTER 10. THE SYSTEM'S RESPONSE

1. Blumstein, Alfred. "Prisons: Population, Capacity and Alternatives." In *Crime and Public Policy*, San Francisco: ICS Press, 1983.

2. *Prisoners and Drugs*. Washington, DC: U.S. Justice Department, Bureau of Justice Statistics, March 1983.

3. Chaiken, Jan M., and Marcia R. Chaiken. "Crime Rates and the Active Criminal. In *Crime and Public Policy*, San Francisco: ICS Press, 1983.

4. "Morgenthau Says Data Link a Third of Crimes to the Career Criminal." *The New York Times*, April 9, 1981.
5. "Hartford Plans to End the Private Management of Its Public Schools." *The New York Times*, January 24, 1996.
6. Greenwood, Peter W. "Selective Incapacitation: A Method of Using Our Prisons More Effectively," *N.I.J. Reports*, January 1984.
7. van den Haag, Ernest, and John P. Conrad. *The Death Penalty: A Debate*. New York: Plenum Press, 1983.
8. Bedau, Hugo Adam, and Chester M. Pierce. *Capital Punishment in the U.S.* New York: AMS Press, 1975.
9. *Violent Crime by Strangers*. Washington, DC: U.S. Justice Department, Bureau of Justice Statistics, April 1982.
10. Joyce, Fay S. "Courts Study Link Between Victim's Race and Imposition of Death Penalty." *The New York Times*, January 5, 1984.
11. Poll says 72% of Americans favor death penalty for murder. *The New York Times*, February 3, 1985.
12. Fisher, Jim. *The Lindbergh Case*. New Brunswick, NJ: Rutgers University Press, 1987.
13. Farrington, David P. "Longitudinal Research on Crime and Delinquency." In *Crime and Justice: An Annual Review of Research, Vol. 1.* Chicago: University of Chicago Press, 1979.

CHAPTER 11. THE CULTURE

1. Voy, Robert, with Kirk B. Deeter. *Drugs, Sports and Politics*. New York: Leisure Press, 1991.
2. Nardo, Don. *Drugs and Sports*. San Diego, CA: Lucent Books, 1990.
3. Newfield, Jack. *Only in America: The Life and Crimes of Don King*. New York: Morrow, 1995.
4. Morris, Mercury. *Against the Grain*. New York: McGraw-Hill, 1994.
5. Cohen, Jeff. *Through the Media Looking Glass*. Monroe, ME: Common Courage Press, 1995.
6. Douglass, Carter, and Stephen Strickland. *T.V. Violence and the Child: The Evolution and Fate of the Surgeon General's Report*. New York: Russell Sage Foundation, 1975.
7. Lichter, Linda S., and S. Robert Lichter. *Prime Time Crime: Criminals and Law Enforcers in T.V. Entertainment*. Washington, DC: Media Institute, 1983.
8. King, Paul. *Sex, Drugs and Rock 'N Roll: Healing Our Troubled Youth in the '90s*. Redmond, WA: Professional Counselor Books, 1990.
9. Hutchinson, Earl Ofari. *The Assassination of the Black Male Image*. Los Angeles: Middle Passage Press, 1994.

10. Gray, Susan H. "Exposure to Pornography and Aggression Toward Women: The Case of the Angry Male." *Social Problems* 29, April 1982, pp. 387–398.
11. Sullivan, Walter. "Violent Pornography Elevates Aggression, Researchers Say." *The New York Times*, September 30, 1980.

CHAPTER 12. THE END?

1. Medved, Diane. *The Case Against Divorce*. New York: Donald I. Fine, 1989.
2. Doyle, Patricia. *The Child in Crisis*. New York: McGraw-Hill, 1986.
3. Magid, Ken. *High Risk*. New York: Bantam Books, 1987.
4. Fanning, Beverly J. *Workfare vs. Welfare*. G. E. McCuen Publications, 1989.
5. Netzer, Dick, ed. *Rebuilding Urban America*. New York: Institute for the Study of the City, 1976.
6. Hatt, Paul K., and Albert, J. Reiss, Jr., eds. *Cities and Society*. New York: The Free Press, 1965.
7. Harris, Chauncy D., and Edward L. Ullman. "The Nature of Cities." *Annals of the American Academy of Political and Social Sciences* 242, November 1945, pp. 7–17.
8. Jacobs, Jane. *The Death and Life of Great American Cities*. New York: Vintage Books, 1961.
9. "Cigarette Defector Says C.E.O. Lied to Congress about View of Nicotine." *The Wall Street Journal*, January 26, 1996.
10. Prus, Robert, and Styllianos Irini. *Hookers, Rounders and Desk Clerks*. Salem, WI: Sheffield Publishing Co., 1988.
11. "For More Than a Quarter of the Advertisers It'll Be a Super Bowl I." *The New York Times*, January 26, 1996.
12. Madsen, Peter, ed. *Essentials of Business Ethics*. Meridian Press, 1990.
13. Norris, Ruth. *Pills, Pesticides and Profits*. Cronton-on-Hudson, NY: North River Press, 1982.
14. Terkel, Studs. *Race*. New York: The New Press, 1992.
15. *Report of the National Advisory Commission on Civil Disorders*. New York: Bantam Books, 1968.
16. *Malcolm X Speaks*. New York: Merit Publishers, 1965.
17. Lincoln, C. Eric. *The Black Muslims in America*. Boston: Beacon Press, 1961.
18. Essien-Udom, E.U. *Black Nationalism*. New York: Dell, 1964.
19. Wolfgang, Marvin E., Robert M. Figlio, and Thorsten Sellin. *Delinquency in a Birth Cohort*. Chicago: University of Chicago Press, 1972.

20. Gropper, Bernard A. "Probing the Links Between Drugs and Crime." *N.I.J. Reports*, November 1984.

21. Hunt, Leon Gibson, and Carl D. Chambers. *The Heroin Epidemics: A Study of Heroin Use in the U.S. 1965–1975*. New York: Spectrum, 1976.

22. Joint Committee on N.Y. Drug Law Evaluating. *The Nation's Toughest Drug Laws: Evaluation the N.Y. Experience*. Washington, DC: U.S. Government Printing Office, 1978.

23. "U.S. Approves Fake Fat for Use in Snack Foods." *The New York Times*, January 25, 1996.

24. White, Larry C. *Merchants of Death*. Beech Tree Books, 1988.

25. Greenberg, Stephanie W. *Alcohol and Crime: A Methodological Critique of the Literature*. New York: Guilford Press, 1981.

26. Wilbanks, William. "Does Alcohol Cause Homicide?" *Journal of Criminal Justice* 4, 1981, pp. 149–170.

27. See the series in the *Minneapolis Star-Tribune*, December 3–5, 1995.

28. Riconda, Andrew. *Gambling*. New York: H. W. Wilson, 1995.

29. Tobias, Ann. *Pot—What It Is, What It Does*. New York: Morrow.

30. Powis, Robert E. *The Money Launderers*. Chicago, IL: Probus Publishing, 1992.

31. Groth, Nicholas A., Robert E. Longo, and J. Bradley McFadin. "Undetected Recidivism among Rapists and Child Molesters." *Crime and Delinquency* 28, July 1982, pp. 450–458.

32. "Sentence Giving Rapists Choice of Castration Creates Controversy." *The Boston Globe*, Dec. 11, 1983.

33. "Judge Delays Notification in Sex Case." *The New York Times*, January 24, 1996.

34. Alsop, Joseph W. *I've Seen the Best of It*. New York: Norton, 1992.

Index